THE COMPACT DICTIONARY OF DOCTRINAL WORDS

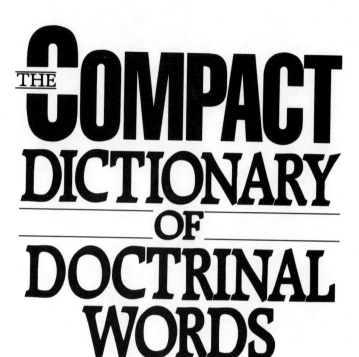

THE COMPACT DICTIONARY OF DOCTRINAL WORDS

TERRY L. MIETHE

BETHANY HOUSE PUBLISHERS
MINNEAPOLIS, MINNESOTA 55438
A Division of Bethany Fellowship, Inc.

Published by Bethany House Publishers
A Division of Bethany Fellowship, Inc.
6820 Auto Club Road, Minneapolis, Minnesota 55438

Printed in the United States of America

Library of Congress Cataloging-in-Publication Data

Miethe, Terry L., 1948–
    The compact dictionary of doctrinal words /Terry L. Miethe.
       p. cm.
    Includes bibliographical references.
    1. Theology—Dictionaries. I. Title.
BR95.M48   1988
230′.03′21—dc19   88–12161
ISBN 0–87123–678–8   CIP

Dedicated to my special students, that remnant of the faithful who long for a new reformation and have a burning desire to change the world toward the Christian ideal, with the challenge that they will live their lives, as Augustine said, learning as much about as many things as possible!

Deo adiuvante, Deo optimo maximo!

II Corinthians 10:3–5

Other Works by Terry L. Miethe

The Metaphysics of Leonard James Eslick: His Philosophy of God. Ann Arbor, Mich.: University Microfilms, Inc., 1976.

Reflections, Volume One, 1980, Volume Two, 1983.

Thomistic Bibliography, 1940–1978, with Vernon J. Bourke. Westport, Conn.: Greenwood Press, 1980.

"Atheism: Nietzsche," Chapter Six in *Biblical Errancy: An Analysis of its Philosophical Roots*, edited by Norman L. Geisler. Grand Rapids, Mich.: Zondervan Publishing House, 1981.

Augustinian Bibliography, 1970–1980: With Essays on the Fundamentals of Augustinian Scholarship. Westport, Conn.: Greenwood Press, 1982.

The New Christian's Guide to Following Jesus. Minneapolis, Minn.: Bethany House Publishers, 1984.

The Philosophy and Ethics of Alexander Campbell: From the Context of American Religious Thought. Ann Arbor, Mich.: University Microfilms, Inc., 1984.

Did Jesus Rise from the Dead? The Resurrection Debate, with Gary R. Habermas and Antony G.N. Flew. San Francisco, Calif.: Harper & Row Publishers, 1987.

A Christian's Guide to Faith and Reason. Minneapolis, Minn.: Bethany House Publishers, 1987.

"The Universal Power of the Atonement," Chapter in *The Grace of God/The Will of Man* edited by Clark H. Pinnock. Grand Rapids, Mich.: Zondervan Publishing House, 1989.

About the Author

TERRY L. MIETHE holds six earned degrees with honors, including a Ph.D. in philosophy from Saint Louis University and a second Ph.D. in theology and social ethics from the University of Southern California. He has taught at several schools, including Saint Louis University; Fuller Theological Seminary; Regent College, Vancouver, B.C.; and the University of Southern California, and has lectured in over twenty colleges and universities in the United States, Canada, and England. He is a member of eight scholastic honor societies in history, psychology, classical languages, English, and philosophy, including Phi Beta Kappa, Alpha Sigma Nu, and the National Jesuit Honor Society. Currently, he is the Dean of the Oxford Study Centre, Oxford, England.

Dr. Miethe has over forty articles in print in such journals as: *The Modern Schoolman, Faith & Reason, Journal of the Evangelical Theological Society, Christian Standard, The New Scholasticism, Augustinian Studies*, etc. He has authored eleven books, including books on Augustine, and Thomas Aquinas, *The New Christian's Guide to Following Jesus, The Christian's Guide to Faith and Reason, The Compact Dictionary of Doctrinal Words*, all with Bethany House Publishers; and has edited: *Did Jesus Rise from the Dead? The Resurrection Debate* with Gary R. Habermas and Antony G. N. Flew, published by Harper & Row. He is listed in eighteen editions of Who's Who, including *Who's Who in Religion, Personalities of America, International Who's Who of Intellectuals, Dictionary of International Biography,* and *Contemporary Authors.*

Foreword

There are some 206 bones in the human body. As a first-year medical school student could attest to, one of the first steps in understanding the human body is to identify and explain the function of these bones, which support the entire fleshly structure. Like a skilled physician, Dr. Terry Miethe has succinctly and successfully identified and briefly explained more than 550 "biblical bones," that is, theological concepts, upon which the Holy Scriptures are built.

If the very words in the Bible were revealed by God himself (and they were), then it becomes vital that we comprehend these words. Miethe's book can help us immensely in achieving this goal!

Harold Willmington
Author, *Willmington's Guide
to the Bible*
Director, International Bible
Center

Preface

You were sitting in church listening to a sermon, trying to sift through eloquent language and theoretical terms that meant nothing to you, which you did not understand, or which you were not sure you understood. You probably experienced considerable anxiety as you tried to understand the message, or finally "tuned out" the speaker. If only you'd had this book to provide clear, simple definitions of those words, you wouldn't have had to remain confused!

One of Satan's greatest victories has been allowing the church to have a high-sounding religious vocabulary the average member doesn't really understand.[1] Granted, we Christians have a rich theological vocabulary, developed over the centuries to communicate Christian truth and to teach important aspects of the faith, to provide shades of meaning, and to give insights into God and His revelation. But even though you often hear many of these words, do you understand the meaning these words really communicate?

This volume will help you, the Christian (though probably not a trained theologian), to understand these words so you can benefit from our rich theological vocabulary, because *The Compact Dictionary of Doctrinal Words* gives understandable meanings, references to biblical texts, and resources for further study where appropriate. The definitions in this dictionary should help you in at least four ways:

(1) *Increase your vocabulary,* and therefore your understanding. As a Christian, you need to communicate effectively and accurately what you mean to the unbeliever. You cannot explain what you do not understand.

---

[1]This is perhaps one of the most powerful reasons why we need very strong Christian education programs today, more than ever!

11

(2) *Eliminate ambiguity* in language and the meanings of words. The problem of ambiguity causes many errors in argumentation or logic. Once ambiguity is exposed, it is easy to show that confusing meanings lead to faulty logic. Ambiguity also may cause two individuals to unwittingly talk about different things and thus argue past each other.

(3) *Reduce vagueness.* Often you know the meaning of a word, but you may not be sure of the limits of its application. Clarification of the meaning of the word will help you think and communicate clearly.

(4) *Explain theoretical words.* (This is a very important purpose of the definitions in this dictionary.) Much of theological vocabulary was developed to give "theoretically adequate" meanings to theological concepts. These technical definitions embody and explain a very important part of the truth claims of the Christian Church, and are essential to help you understand the revelational claims of the Christian faith and to build an accurate body of biblical doctrine.[2]

I hope a better understanding of the terms explained in this book will motivate you to apply the concepts and truths more fully in your life, and to better understand and communicate your faith effectively to others. A fruitful Christian life involves worship, ministry, and witness. I pray that God will touch these areas of your life through this book.

I thank God for language, logic, and truth—three inseparable and essential elements in the ability He gives us to think His thoughts after Him and to communicate these thoughts to others.

Terry L. Miethe
December 25, 1987
On the day of celebration of
His birth

---

[2]See: Irving M. Copi, *Introduction to Logic*, 7th edition, (New York: Macmillan Publishing Company, 1986), pp. 130–136.

Abba ■ From the Aramaic language, the common language of Palestine in Jesus' day and probably His native tongue. Children used the word "Abba" to address their fathers; it is equivalent to the English words "papa" or "daddy." In the NT, "Abba" is always joined with the Greek for "father," and is always used in addressing God. The term is significant because it clearly shows that a Christian, through the Holy Spirit, has an intimate relationship with God—that of a son or daughter to their father. "Abba" is used three times in the NT: Jesus used it when He prayed in Gethsemane (Mark 14:36). Paul used it in Romans 8:15 and Galatians 4:6 (see also 2 Cor. 6:18).

Abomination of Desolation ■ The term appears twice in the NT: Matthew 24:15 and Mark 13:14 (see also Luke 21:20). In both instances the writers quote Jesus' prophetic statements concerning a transgression against the Temple at Jerusalem in which a pagan idol or personage is introduced into the sanctuary. Scholars disagree about the exact meaning of this reference, particularly regarding two points. The first involves the time at which this abomination will manifest itself. Because Jesus refers to the Book of Daniel (8:13; 9:27; 11:31; 12:11) when He speaks of the "Abomination of Desolation," some liberal scholars believe that Jesus was mistaken in His use of this term. They believe that the verses describe the desecration of the Temple in 168 B.C. by Antiochus Epiphanes, the pagan king of Syria, not some future event as Christ depicts.

Others hold this same view—that the verses in Daniel refer to Antiochus Epiphanes—but believe that Jesus used the references from Daniel to foreshadow the future. If this is the case, then the coming abomination to which Jesus refers is only similar, not identical, to what the passages in Daniel describe. Jesus' use of the term then becomes apocalyptic. Still other scholars believe that the destruction of the Temple in Jerusalem in A.D. 70 by the Romans was the coming abomination about which Jesus spoke.

The second area of disagreement lies in the nature or form of the coming abomination. Some believe that the abomination is an idol of some type that will be brought to the temple for all to worship. Others believe that the abomination is the Antichrist, who will come to the Temple to be worshiped at the end of the age.

Absolute ■ From the Latin *absolutus*, "separated," "free from" or "complete," "that which is totally free or independent of restrictions." The word can be used as an adjective or as a noun. As an adjective, *absolute* signifies perfection, completeness, universality, non-relativity, and exemption from limitation or restriction—as in "absolute truth," "absolute beauty," "absolute being," or "absolute time."

As a noun, *absolute* has two philosophical meanings. For philosophers such as Georg Wilhelm Friedrich Hegel (1770–1831), the absolute is reality seen as a self-aware whole (Pantheism). For Hegel and others, the absolute is an all-inclusive embodiment of reality.

The second meaning of absolute comes from a Christian philosophical/theological context, and is another name for the concept of a "Necessary Being." A Necessary Being depends on nothing else, while everything else depends on the Necessary Being for existence and activity. Such a Being is transcendent, infinite and independent of any other objects, yet imminent, continuously holding in existence all of reality. In the Judeo-Christian world view, such an absolute can only be called God. There can be only one absolute in a theistic system, God himself. See: **Pantheism, Theism.**

Absolution ■ This term is widely used in the Roman Catholic Church to refer to the setting free from the guilt a sinner merits when he sins after baptism.

This term involves the idea of excommunication, which is the exiling of sinning members from the church. The Catholic church believes that the Church, as the "Holy Church," is by nature incompatible with sin. A sinning member, therefore, needs reconciliation to the body of Christ, the Church, and may not be reinstated until he comes before the Church and God in repentance for his sin. The sinner goes before the Church to admit his guilt through the act of confession. A priest then grants forgiveness in the name of Christ to the repentant sinner after completion of confession and penance. Absolution is considered one of the seven Holy Sacraments of the Catholic church. Scripture passages used to justify absolution are 2 Corinthians 5:18; Matthew 6:12; 1 John 5:16; Matthew 18:15; 1 Timothy 5:20; and 1 Corinthians 5:5; 1 Timothy 1:20; John 20:19–23, which have to do with excommunication.

The early Church disagreed over the number of times a person could be absolved of sin. Until the sixth century in the Western Church (the Roman Catholic Church), the Sacrament of Penance was administered only once. Therefore, it became common practice to postpone absolution until the recipient was close to death, thus ensuring there was little possibility of committing further sin.

Absolution is used in a broader sense in much of the Christian church to mean a pastoral announcement of forgiveness for all who truly repent of their sins. Rather than being a *means* of forgiveness, in this wider view absolution is a *declaration* of God's judgment and forgiveness. See: **Excommunication, Penance.**

Abyss ■ From the Greek *abussos*, "bottomless," and connotes "depth" or "deepness." The term is used in Luke 8:31 and Revelation 9:1, 11; 11:7; 17:8; and 20:1 to symbolize the bottomless pit, the dwelling place of demons. The abyss is the kingdom of Satan and the place of his imprisonment during Christ's millennial reign on earth. It is synonymous with Sheol or Hell. It is also referred to in Genesis 1:2–10, where the Septuagint (LXX) translates the Hebrew word as "abyss." In this passage, abyss refers to the primeval watery void that God divided into "heaven" and "earth and seas." See: **Hell, Sheol.**

Accident, Fallacy of ■ This fallacy consists of applying a *general* rule to a *particular* case whose "accidental" circumstances make the rule inapplicable. An example: "I should pay my debts.

Suppose a friend of mine loaned me his rifle one day, then had a nervous breakdown where he became violent and threatened to kill someone. Should I then give him his rifle? Certainly not." The key here is that what is true generally may not be true universally—applicable in every case without qualification—because circumstances alter cases. See: **Logical Fallacies.**

Adoptionism ■ In church history, a heresy regarding the nature of Christ. It can be traced to Paul of Samosata (Bishop of Antioch from A.D. 260 to 272), but did not come into any official teaching until the eighth century under Elipandus, the Archbishop of Toledo, Spain, in the year A.D. 785. It is the belief that Christ maintained a double sonship to God the Father: Christ is the eternally begotten Son of God and is divine, God's son by nature; and Jesus, the human son born to Mary, was adopted by God because Christ (God's son) had supernaturally assumed the human Jesus. The son of Mary, then, was the Son of God only because he had been "assumed" by the eternal Son of God and adopted by God the Father.

The error lies in distinguishing between Jesus the man born of Mary and Jesus the divine Son of God. Christ is only one person with two distinct natures, both divine and human. There is, therefore, no need to attribute sonship separately to both natures, but only to Christ as a single entity or person. See: **Christology, Ebionite, Monarchianism, Hypostatic Union.**

Advent ■ From the Latin *adventus*, "coming." There are three uses of the word: (1) Its association with feasts, especially the feast of the Epiphany. Advent was the period prior to the actual feast, a time of preparation in which Christians fasted and prayed for about three weeks. The period was called "Advent" because it signaled the approach of the celebration. (2) Advent is also associated with the birth of Christ and His entrance into the world in the Incarnation. In the sixth century, the church in Rome began calling the season before Christmas Advent. Originally, Advent lasted for about six weeks, but was shortened by Gregory I to about four weeks. (3) Finally, Advent is used to refer to Christ's Second Coming, in which He will overcome His enemies. See: **Epiphany, Incarnation.**

Adventism ▪ Refers to the Second Coming of Jesus. In general, it refers to those who believe that the return of Christ is imminent and to a Christian group called the Seventh-Day Adventists. See: **Seventh-Day Adventists.**

Adversary ▪ From the Greek *antidikos*; in the NT the word is legal terminology for an opponent in a lawsuit (Matt. 5:25; Luke 12:58; 18:3). It is also used to refer to Satan, the enemy, or "adversary" of Christians, as in 1 Peter 5:8. See: **Beelzebub, Devil, Demons, Satan.**

Aesthetics ▪ From the Greek *aesthetikos*, "perceptive." In philosophy, the study of beauty or theories of art. Part of the area of philosophy known as axiology, it can be either normative or descriptive. See: **Axiology.**
See: V.C. Aldrich, *Philosophy of Art* (Prentice-Hall, 1963); A. Berleant, *The Aesthetic Field* (Charles C. Thomas, 1970); C.S. Kilby, *Christianity and Aesthetics* (InterVarsity Press, 1961); S.K. Langer, *Problems of Art* (Scribners, 1957); H.R. Rookmaaker, *Modern Art and the Death of a Culture* (InterVarsity Press, 1970); F.A. Schaeffer, *Art & the Bible* (InterVarsity Press, 1973).

Against the Man ▪ In Latin, *Argumentum ad Hominem*, often called an "ad hominem argument." This fallacy is an argument directed "against the man," and has two forms: (1) An "abusive ad hominem" is committed when someone attacks a person's character rather than his argument. The character of a person is logically irrelevant to the truth or falsehood of that person's argument. (2) A "circumstantial ad hominem" is committed when an opponent claims that one should assent to his argument, because, for example, both belong to the same political party. Ideally, one should defeat an opponent's argument, not appeal to his beliefs or affiliations. See: **Logical Fallacies.**

Agape ▪ From the Greek word that means "love." This is a distinctly Christian term and has no counterpart in the Hebrew OT. It is used various ways in the NT: (1) To describe God's relationship to both individuals and groups: in John 17:26 and 2 Peter 1:17 toward Jesus; in John 3:16 and Romans 5:8 toward the human race; in John 14:21 toward those who believe. (2) It is used to describe God's will concerning the attitude of His children: in John 13:34 their attitude toward one another; in 1 Thessalonians 3:12, 1 Corinthians 16:14 and 2 Peter 1:17, their attitude toward all people. (3) Finally, in 1 John 4:8 it is used to express God's essential nature.

The ultimate expression of *agape* is in the Lord Jesus Christ (2 Cor. 5:14; Eph. 2:4; 3:19; 5:2). It is through God's love and the gift of His Son (1 John 4:9–10) that people are able to understand *agape* and to return this gift of love by obedience and self-denial (John 14:15, 21, 23; 15:10; 1 John 2:5; 5:3; 2 John 6). Christian love means more than a love for the Giver of love. It is love in action among God's children, toward themselves as well as those who do not yet know such love. *Agape* is the standard that guides Christian ethics. *Agape* in the NT could be defined as "intelligently, intensely willing the best for another."

See: A. Nygren, *Agape and Eros* (S.P.C.K., 1953).

Agnosticism ■ From the Greek *agnostikos*, "unknowing," or "a profession of ignorance." The term was coined by Thomas H. Huxley (1825–1895) in 1869, who used it to show his opposition to those who claimed to have metaphysical explanations of all kinds of philosophical mysteries. It became a prominent banner in the nineteenth-century debate over religious beliefs, and was understood to mean one who held that knowledge of God is impossible because of the inherent limitations of the human mind.

Robert Flint refuted Huxley's use of the term in his book *Agnosticism* (Scribner and Sons, 1903), arguing that the ancient term "skepticism" more accurately describes what Huxley believed about God. Flint maintains that Huxley simply wanted to hide his negative religious views.

There have been two types of agnostics throughout history: (1) Those who deny that reason can know God and therefore suspend judgment on God's existence (Bertrand Russell, 1872–1970); and (2) Those who deny that reason can prove or disprove God, but nonetheless continue to believe in such a Being (Immanuel Kant, 1724–1804). The latter group could be called "religious agnostics." There are five philosophical systems in which agnosticism is considered a valid option: nominalism, empiricism, Kantianism, logical positivism, and existentialism. See: **Skepticism.**

Agony ■ The Greek word *agonia* refers to the struggle involved in the public games of ancient times. Metaphorically, it means a severe struggle or conflict accompanied by intense emotion, emotional strain and anguish. Luke uses this word when he describes Jesus' ordeal in the Garden of Gethsemane in Luke 22:44.

There are several theories about the source of Christ's agony: (1) Some argue that Jesus' agony was the result of contemplating the horror of the death He was about to suffer on the cross. This view sees Jesus struggling to decide whether to suffer the death the Father had appointed for Him. But this explanation is inadequate. Christ was familiar with the prospect of death, and saw it as the appointed end of His ministry (Matt. 16:21; 17:9–12; Mark 10:32–34; John 10:18).

(2) Other scholars feel that Christ's doubts about His ability to remain sinless in the extreme suffering He would endure—and His knowing that if He failed there would be no other Savior—accounts for the agony He felt.

(3) Still other scholars feel these two previous explanations are inadequate because (a) to say Christ feared death degrades His character and contradicts the actual account of His patient and fearless suffering of torture and death, and (b) to claim Christ feared He might sin disagrees with previous experiences and statements in which He perfectly fulfilled the will of God and displayed no possibility of doing otherwise.

(4) There must, therefore, be a further explanation: His agony grew from the realization that as He bore the sins of mankind, He would be separated from the Father for the first time. With this in mind, Jesus agonized over the cup set before Him. See: **Atonement.**

Agrapha ■ This word means "unwritten sayings," and refers to the sayings of Jesus that are missing from the canonical Gospels but known through tradition. They are also called the "unknown" or "lost sayings." Though some cite Acts 20:35 (" . . . remember the words of the Lord Jesus, that He Himself said, 'It is more blessed to give than to receive.' ") as an example of agrapha, this passage is part of the historically accepted canon of Scripture and is therefore inspired Scripture, not agrapha. Most biblical scholars feel it will never be possible to prove the authenticity of any of the agrapha. See: **Canon of the Old Testament, Canon of the New Testament, Inspiration.**

Alienation ▪ From the Greek *apallotrioo* and the Latin *alienare,* "to estrange," "to withdraw." In the NT, the alienation between God and man, and between man and man is called sin. Paul shows how the sin/alienation of humanity is healed through reconciliation/salvation in Christ in Colossians 1:21–22 when he says, "And although you were formerly alienated and hostile in mind, engaged in evil deeds, yet He has now reconciled you in His fleshly body through death, in order to present you before Him bold and blameless and beyond reproach. . . ." Christ came to restore, or reconcile, mankind to our loving and merciful Creator (John 3:16). See: **Atonement, Salvation.**

Allegorical Interpretation ▪ A method of interpreting biblical texts in which the interpreter looks beyond the literal meaning of the text to find a hidden allegorical meaning. This method of interpretation was common among the early Church fathers. Clement of Rome (?–c. A.D. 100), Irenaeus (c. 130–200), Tertullian (c. 155–220), Origen (c. 185–254), Ambrose (340–397), Jerome (c. 340–420) and Augustine (354–430) frequently used this method.

Modern theologians usually frown on allegorical interpretation because of the outrageous conclusions sometimes reached. But they say that a literal interpretation of the Bible can illuminate contemporary situations, allowing the Christian to draw practical applications from the text for everyday life. There are few allegorical interpretations in Scripture itself. One of the few is Galatians 4:21–25, where Paul says that Hagar and Sarah represent two covenants, bondage and freedom.

Allegory ▪ Found only once in the NT, in Galatians 4:24, the word is derived from the words that mean "other" and "to speak in a place of assembly." The word came to mean "a secondary or hidden meaning underlying a primary or obvious meaning."

It is also known as a "prolonged" or "extended metaphor." Allegory should be distinguished from a parable. A parable uses an everyday situation to express practical exhortations, while an allegory systematically presents an idea that expresses theoretical truths not obvious in the text but uncovered through personal interpretation.

Alleluia ▪ See: **Hallelujah.**

Alms, Almsgiving ▪ From the Greek *eleemosune,* "mercy" or "pity" (Matt. 6:1–4; Acts 10:2; 24:17). Derived from the Hebrew word for "justice," the word signified the redistribution of wealth to the less fortunate, a practice in keeping with God's original will of justice on earth. What an almsgiver gives to the poor he gives to God (Prov. 19:17). Giving alms is said to purify the heart of the believer: "But give that which is within as charity, and then all things are clean for you" (Luke 11:41). Almsgiving also promotes brotherly love between the giver and recipient (Rom. 15:25–26) and is a witness to the Lord Jesus Christ (2 Cor. 9:11–14). Jesus taught that alms should be given in secret, not in an obvious manner (Matt. 6:2–4). Giving alms should be done out of a heart of love, not from expectation of return or benefit (Luke 6:35). Thomas Aquinas believed that giving alms was the principle work of mercy.

Alpha and Omega ▪ The first and last letters of the Greek alphabet (A, α and Ω, ω). The probable origin of the phrase "Alpha and Omega" is the Jewish use of the first and last letters of the Hebrew language to signify the totality of a thing. In Revelation 22:13, it is a divine title of Jesus Christ showing that He is the Eternal One, the beginning and the end of all that exists. The title also signifies Christ's place in history as both the first ("In the beginning was the word . . ."—John 1:1) and the last (Christ's Second Coming). See: Revelation 1:8; 21:6; 22:13, also Isaiah 44:6.

Altar ▪ From the Greek *thusiasterion,* which is from *thusiazo,* "to sacrifice." An altar is a place on which sacrifices were made to God (Matt. 5:23–24; 23:18–20, 35; Luke 11:51). In Luke 1:11 the word is used to denote the altar of incense. This meaning contrasts with the Greek word *bomos*, which signifies a pagan altar or "high place" raised without divine permission. It was at these high places that Jews offered sacrifices and carried on heathen practices. For this reason, in 621 B.C. King Josiah attempted to confine all sacrifices to the temple in Jerusalem, but without success.

After the exile the Israelites voluntarily followed this rule. All sacrifices were offered at the altar located in the Priests' Court. People were admitted to this court because the Law required the laying on of hands upon the victim to be sacrificed (Lev. 1:4). The altar—*mizbeah* in Hebrew, "place of sacrifice"—was situated below the steps leading to the sanctuary and was furnished with altar horns projecting from each of four corners. See: **Sanctuary.**

Ambassador ■ From Hebrew words (2 Chron. 32:31; 35:21) meaning "messenger" or "sent for another." It usually refers to officials who represented a king or government. In the NT, two Greek words expressed a similar idea: *presbeuo* (2 Cor. 5:20; Eph. 6:20), and *presbeia* (Luke 14:32). Both words referred to the representative of Christ, the King of Kings. In 2 Corinthians 5:17–20, Paul writes that Christians are new creations, reconciled to God through Christ, and therefore given a ministry: "Therefore, we are ambassadors of Christ, as though God were entreating through us; we beg you on behalf of Christ, be reconciled to God." As Christians, we are to persuade people with the Gospel.

Amen ■ "Amen" is one of the few Hebrew words transliterated into the Greek NT as well as into modern translations of Scripture. In the NT it invariably appears as an adverb and has the meaning of "so be it"—a weak translation, because it expresses more of a wish than a certitude. The Hebrew root of this adverb actually implies a stronger meaning: firmness, solidity and sureness. Using this term indicated that the speaker adopted as his own what another had already expressed.

When Christ uses "amen" to introduce a statement—the word behind the phrase "Truly, Truly"—He makes a demand on His listeners' faith in His words and power (John 8:58). Paul uses the word "amen" in his epistles to conclude a prayer or doxology (Rom. 11:36). It is also sometimes used after expressing blessing

(Rom. 15:33). As a title of God, it expresses God's faithfulness to His promises (Isa. 65:15), the fulfillment of which has been expressed in Jesus Christ. See: Psalm 41:13; 72:19; 89:52; 106:48; 1 Chronicles 16:36; Nehemiah 8:6; Revelation 3:14.

Amillennialism ■ One view concerning the millennium spoken of in Revelation. Although the negative prefix *a –* appears to deny entirely the concept of a millennium, the doctrine actually expresses the opinion that there is no sufficient ground for belief in a millennium that will last for a thousand years. This position's advocates do not believe the NT teaches that a millennium will begin after Christ's Second Coming, but that His coming will usher in the final judgment and the eternal state.

This position rests on an interpretation of Revelation 20 in which the expression "thousand years" is understood to be a symbolic use of numbers, a common feature of apocalyptic language. According to this interpretation, numbers do not represent arithmetical values, but ideas. The figure 1000 is therefore regarded as a symbol of fullness and completeness. (See W. W. Millegan, *The Expositor's Bible: The Book of Revelation*.) Arguments against amillennialism all stem from the difficulty some expositors find in accepting a completely symbolic interpretation of Revelation 20. See: **Millennialism, Postmillennialism, Premillennialism.**

See: Herman N. Ridderbos, *The Coming of the Kingdom* (Presbyterian and Reformed, 1962).

Anabaptists ■ This term was first used in the fourth century to refer to a group that "rebaptized" persons who had been baptized in some unacceptable manner. Today the term more commonly refers to a movement that began during the Reformation. In the 1520s, a number of groups came into existence that rejected the view of the sacraments held at the time, particularly infant baptism. They held that public confession of sin and faith—sealed by adult baptism—was the only correct baptism. They also believed in studying the Bible directly, immersion as the only form of baptism, separation of church and state, and pacifism. Some were antitrinitarian. They also believed in the resurrection of humans after a sleep of their soul at death. Known as the Radical Reformation, the Anabaptists developed

into groups that include the Mennonites and various Brethren groups. See: **Immersion, Mennonites, Soul Sleep.**

See: George H. Williams, *The Radical Reformation* (Westminster Press, 1962); William R. Estep, *The Anabaptist Story* (Broadman Press, 1963).

Analogy ■ From the Greek *analogos,* "proportionate." The word is applied to two or more things because of the likeness, relation or order between them. For example, when Scripture refers to God as our Father, there are only three possibilities of what this religious language means: (1) It is obvious Scripture cannot mean that God is our Father in exactly the same way our earthly father is our father. This is "univocal language," language with only one meaning.

(2) Neither can it mean that there is no meaning of the concept "father" relevant to both our Heavenly Father and our earthly father—"equivocal," or ambiguous language.

(3) There must be some sense in which the label "father" fits both God the Father and our earthly father, showing that they are partly the same and partly different at one and the same time. Otherwise, our religious language or statements in Scripture would be meaningless. This is the function of analogical language, or "analogy." Analogies are like parables, metaphors from human experience that help us understand God. Thomas Aquinas (1224/5–1274) was the first to develop a systematic doctrine of analogy to solve the paradox of how limited human minds can have knowledge about an infinite God. Because of the limitations of human nature, knowledge and perceptions, man knows the nature and perfections of God only through analogy. See: **Thomism.**

See: Norman L. Geisler, "God and Language," *Philosophy of Religion,* Part III (Zondervan, 1974), pp. 229–289; Battista Mondin, *The Principle of Analogy in Protestant and Catholic Theology* (The Hague, 1963); Thomas Aquinas, *Summa Theologica* I, 13, and *Summa Contra Gentiles* I, pp. 29–34.

Anathema ■ From the Greek for "that which is devoted to evil," "accursed." It is derived from the Hebrew word *herem,* "to set aside." In the NT, anathema refers to the calling down of the wrath of God on the faithless (Gal. 1:8; 1 Cor. 16:22); a curse (Luke 21:5); and a curse against oneself in the event of committing perjury (Mark 14:71). Since the fourth century, this word has referred to the excluding from the church of those considered heretics. In the Roman Catholic Church, the pronouncement of an anathema is synonymous with excommunication, although pronouncing an anathema is often regarded as a stronger measure than excommunication; in Catholic canon (church) law, anathema is the name given to excommunication inflicted with the full ceremony of the pope. Roman Catholics think Paul's use of the term in 1 Corinthians 16:22 is the severest form of excommunication, a "double curse."

Angel ■ From the Greek *angelos*, literally a "messenger." The word can refer to a human or to a created spiritual, or supernatural, being whose purpose is to serve God as His messenger or ambassador. The supernatural beings we call "angels" were present at creation (Job 38:7). They seem to be ranked in a hierarchy, for some are called "archangels" (1 Thess. 4:16; Jude 9). They were present at both the birth of Jesus (Matt. 1:20; Luke 1 and 2) and the resurrection (Matt. 28:2). Some scholars feel Jude 6 suggests that there has been a fall of angels. Irenaeus (c. 130–200), in his *Against Heresies* (4,37,1), and many other Church fathers held this view. The first fully developed work on the topic of angels was that of Pseudo-Dionysius, *On the Celestial Hierarchy* (A.D. 500). An elaborate system of degrees and ranks of angelic powers was developed in this work. See: Matthew 25:41; Ephesians 6:12; Colossians 2:15; Revelation 12:7. See also: Matthew 4:11; Luke 1:13, 26, 28, 2:9; Acts 5:19ff.; Ephesians 3:10.
    See: Arno C. Gaebelein, *The Angels of God* (Zondervan, 1969); Herbert Lockyer, *The Mystery and Ministry of Angels* (Eerdmans, 1958).

Angelic Doctor ■ A title given to St. Thomas Aquinas (1224/5–1274). See: **Thomism.**

Angelology ■ The study, or doctrine, of angels. Angelology is the area of Christian theology that deals with clarifying and systematizing belief about the existence, nature and function of angels.

Anger ■ To be angry in moderation and for a just cause is often praiseworthy. Certainly the NT indicates that one can be angry and yet not sin (Eph. 4:26); but it just as certainly warns Christians about undue anger (Matt. 5:22; Titus 1:7). Anger becomes a sin when one gives way to an anger that is out of proportion to the offense. In Roman Catholic theology, anger is one of the Seven Deadly Sins. It is a venial sin, but may lead to the mortal sins of blasphemy, scandal, etc. See: **Sins, Seven Deadly; Sins, Mortal and Venial; Blasphemy.**

Anglicans ■ Also known as the Church of England. A branch of the sixteenth-century Reformation, Anglicanism is a worldwide fellowship of churches that looks to the Archbishop of Canterbury (England) as its head. The group began in 1534 when King Henry VIII declared himself the head of the Church of England in a separation from the Roman Catholic Church.

The *Book of Common Prayer* contains the church's liturgy as well as important doctrinal standards. Scripture is said to be the Word of God and to contain all that is necessary for salvation; the Nicene and Apostles' creeds are accepted as correct NT teaching. Also found in the *Book of Common Prayer* are the "Thirty-nine Articles," which affirm such teachings as justification by faith, the Trinity, the dual nature of Christ, and unlimited atonement. See: **Episcopalian, Reformation.**

See: *The Book of Common Prayer* (Oxford University Press, 1969); S.C. Carpenter, *The Church of England: 1597–1688* (London: John Murray, 1954); H.M. Smith, *Henry VIII and the Reformation* (Russell and Russell, 1962).

Anglo-Catholicism ■ Sometimes called "High-Church Anglicanism" or "The Oxford Movement." This term refers to a group within the Church of England that accepted many of the doctrinal tenets and ritualistic forms of the Eastern Orthodox Church and Roman Catholicism. While most adherents remained in the Church of England, Oxford scholar John Henry Newman (1801–1890), an early leader of the movement, converted to Roman Catholicism in 1845 and later became a Roman Catholic cardinal. Other prominent Anglo-Catholics were Edward Bouverie Pusey and John Keble. For works emphasizing this tradition see: *Lux Mundi* (1889) and *Essays Catholic and Critical* (1926).

Anhypostasis ■ Derived from the Greek word *anhypostasis*, which means "impersonality" or "non-self-subsistence." The term asserts that the human nature of Christ has no subsistence of itself, but subsists in the person of the Word for the sake of the Incarnation. In other words, Christ's human nature was an abstract, generic human nature, rather than that of a specific individual. Christ was thus not incarnate as a real, individual man. This position was held by Cyril of Alexandria (c. 376–444). Modern approximations can be found in the works of Leonard Hodgson and Emil Brunner.

Animism ■ In its simplest form, animism is the widespread belief that material objects such as trees and stones are possessed by spirits or have a life of their own. A similar idea is expressed in the philosophical theory of Panpsychism, which holds that all objects in the universe, animate as well as inanimate, have an "inner" or "psychological" being. This position has been held by many prominent thinkers throughout history, even though it generally has been ridiculed as a philosophical position. Some prominent thinkers to hold such a view in some form are: Thales, Anaximenes, Empedocles, Leibniz, Schopenhauer, Royce, C. S. Peirce, A. N. Whitehead, P. Teilhard de Chardin, and Charles Hartshorne.

Annihilationism ■ From the Latin *nihil*, "nothing." In theology this term refers to the position held by some that some (possibly all) human souls will cease to exist at death. This teaching has three forms: (1) Materialism: the material and mental elements of human beings will cease to exist at death. (2) Conditional immortality: God imparts immortality to the redeemed while everyone else sinks into nothingness. This option may include a period of punishment for sins or evil in this life before annihilation. (3) Annihilationism proper: God annihilates non-believers at their deaths, while the redeemed retain their original immortality. The orthodox view maintains that the human souls of both Christians and non-Christians will endure through eternity and that one's destiny—heaven or hell—is irrevocably sealed at death. Annihilationism was condemned by the Fifth Lateran Council in 1513.

Annunciation ▪ The angel Gabriel's visitation to Mary to reveal that she would be the mother of the Messiah is known as the "annunciation" (Luke 1:26–38): "And the angel said to her, 'Do not be afraid, Mary; for you have found favor with God. And behold, you will conceive in your womb, and bear a son, and you shall name Him Jesus. He will be great, and will be called the Son of the Most High; and the Lord God will give Him the throne of His father David; and He will reign over the house of Jacob forever; and His kingdom will have no end' " (vv. 30–33). The angel discloses that conception would take place without a human father through the power of the Holy Spirit and that the baby would be the Son of God (v. 35).

Matthew contains no record of the annunciation to Mary. We learn only that an angel told Joseph in a dream what would happen. The feast associated with this event is called the Feast of Annunciation (also known as "Lady Day"). It is held on March 25, nine months before the traditional date for the birth of Jesus. See: **Virgin Birth.**

Anoint, Anointing ▪ "Anointing" is the practice of applying oil to persons or things. The word can be traced to the Hebrew roots *masiah* and *suk*; the Greek equivalents, *aleipho* (a general term used for anointing of any kind) and *chrio* (a derivative of the name "Christ," confined to sacred and symbolic anointings); and the Latin *inungere*, "to anoint." In the OT, references to this practice usually concern the anointing of kings or priests. Anointing with oil set a person or object apart, symbolizing dedication to divine service. In Genesis 28:18, Jacob anointed a pillar to commemorate the sight of his dream, the first mention of anointing in Scripture. Exodus, Leviticus and Numbers give detailed instructions for anointing the tabernacle, Aaron, and his sons. Anointing can symbolize the coming of the Holy Spirit of God upon His chosen priest, king, or prophet (1 Kings 19:16). In Samuel, the Spirit of the Lord came on Saul as he was anointed; and when Samuel anointed David, the Spirit of the Lord departed from Saul and came on David. Isaiah 61:1 says that the Messiah shall be anointed by the Holy Spirit; the word "Messiah" itself means "Anointed One."

In the NT, Christ is called the "Anointed of God" (*chrio*) in Luke 4:18; Acts 4:27; 10:38; and Hebrews 1:9. The word "Christos" means "His Anointed" (Acts 4:26). Anointing is used as a means of healing (James 5:14), although some scholars dispute this claim and credit healing to prayer.

In post-biblical history, anointing is still used in the coronation of kings and queens. In a ritual traced back to the coronation of King Edgar in 973, the English monarch was anointed on the head, breast and palms with oil from a twelfth-century spoon, the oldest item used in the ceremony. See: **Unction, Extreme.**

Anthropology ■ Popularly used to denote the scientific study of the life and environment of mankind both past and present, the field consists of physical anthropology, which studies human evolutionary biology, racial variation, and classification; and cultural anthropology, which studies behavior patterns, arts, beliefs, and institutions characteristic of a given people.

In a theological context, anthropology is the study of human origins, nature, and destiny from a theistic or biblical perspective (sometimes referred to as the "doctrine of man"). See: **Man.**

Anthropomorphism ■ From the Greek words *anthropos* (man) and *morphe* (form); literally meaning "in the form of man," the term means "to attribute human characteristics to God." There are two basic types of anthropomorphism. The first is the tendency to attribute to God human form or physical characteristics—hands, feet, face—a common trait of many primitive religions. Critics often accuse Judaism of this practice because of such verses as Exodus 15:3 (where God is given human form), Genesis 3:8 (feet), and Exodus 24:11 (hands). Looking more closely, however, one can clearly see that the charge is unjust. These terms are only figurative or metaphorical, and the Israelites understood that God has no form (Deut. 4:12–19).

The second type of anthropomorphism is attributing to God human nonphysical traits such as emotion, personality and will. Some say Christianity makes God little more than a glorified human being, reasoning that if God is infinitely greater than human beings, then God cannot be thought of as having humanlike characteristics. God is indeed infinitely greater, but this does not imply that He is infinitely different. Obviously there is a likeness between God and the human beings He has created. This link is one justification for the biblical practice of using anthropomorphic language to describe God. See: **Analogy.**

See: Terry L. Miethe, "God's Image Shines in Us," in *A Christian's Guide to Faith and Reason* (Bethany House Publishers, 1987), pp. 42–53.

Antichrist ■ First used in the Johannine Epistles (1 John 2:18, 22; 4:3; 2 John 7), the term signifies those who deny Christ's Incarnation (see: **Docetism**).

It has also been used to signify the prince of the enemies of Christ. In the Gospels, Christ warns of one who would come and try to deceive the elect in His name (Matt. 24:24; Mark 13:22). Paul warns of the "man of lawlessness" (2 Thess. 2:3, 8, 9) who will come and do miracles (2 Thess. 2:9–10) and deceive many. The Antichrist is described in Revelation as "the Beast," and his appearance is the prelude to the parousia (Second Coming) of the Lord Jesus. At this time the Antichrist will be defeated by the Lord.

Speculation about the identity of the Antichrist has been common throughout church history. The early Church believed the Antichrist was a person such as Caligula, Simon Magus, or Nero. Others felt that the Antichrist was the Arian heresy popular in the early Church. During the Reformation (and to this day in some less-educated Protestant circles) the Antichrist has been identified as the pope of the Roman Catholic Church. See: **Satan.**

Antinomianism ■ Derived from the Greek words *anti*, "against," and *nomos*, "law," antinomianism is the belief that being saved by grace rather than works frees Christians from all moral obligations and principles. The term was first used by Martin Luther in his controversy with Johann Agricola during the Reformation, but it is rooted in the NT, where Paul refutes the misconception that justification by faith allows the Christian to persist in sin (Rom. 6).

There are two basic forms of antinomianism. The first holds that the moral law plays no necessary part in bringing a sinner to repentance. Paul clearly rejects this view in Romans 7:7 and Galatians 3:24. The second form holds that though the moral law can and does lead one to repentance, it has no relevance to the life of the repentant believer afterward; the believer can then live as he chooses because he has been forgiven by God. This view is a rejection of God's command to believers to live holy lives (1 Pet. 1:16), and is the form of antinomianism Paul rejects in Romans 6.

Antinomy ■ A philosophical term for a pair of contradictory assertions (a "thesis" and an "antithesis"), each of which possesses equal validity. Immanuel Kant (1724–1804) used antinomies in his *Critique of Pure Reason* (1781) to show that reason is limited to dealing with sense experience, making metaphysical speculation impossible. This is so, according to Kant, because reason is able to defend both sides of an antinomy and is therefore self-contradictory, functioning beyond its limits. Metaphysics becomes impossible because the antinomies are beyond reason's ability to resolve. See: **Metaphysics.**

Apocalypse ■ From the Greek *apokalypsis*, "to uncover," meaning "revelation." When capitalized, it refers to the Book of Revelation; when not, it refers to other prophetic revelations.

Apocalyptic Literature ■ A style or type (genre) of literature containing real or alleged revelations about the events regarding the end of the world, including the inauguration of the kingdom of God. In the Bible see particularly the books of Daniel and Revelation.

Apocatastasis ■ Also known as universalism, the doctrine that in the end all free moral creatures will be saved by God's grace rather than damned. This doctrine was espoused by the early teachers Clement (c. 150–215) and Origen of Alexandria (c. 185–254), who emphasized God's love and therefore could not believe that the wrath of God could be God's final manifestation of His love, His most loving solution to the problem of evil and sin. These views were condemned as heretical at the Council of Constantinople in 543. In modern times this position has been held by some Anabaptists and Moravians and also by such theologians as Schleiermacher. See: **Anabaptists, Universalism.**

Apocrypha ■ From the Greek *ta apokrypha*, "the hidden things." In regard to the OT, this refers to thirteen books dating from the period between the Old and New Testaments: 1 and 2 Esdras, Tobit, Judith, additions to Esther, the Wisdom of Solomon, Ecclesiasticus (Ben Sirach), Baruch, the Letter of Jeremiah, additions to Daniel, the Prayer of Manasses, and 1 and 2 Maccabees. The books were included after the canonical OT books in the Septuagint (LXX), a third-century B.C. Greek translation of the OT. The Jews, however, did not regard the books as canonical (inspired, authoritative Scripture) and so did not include them in the Hebrew Bible, nor did the early Church accept them.

The Roman Catholic Church recognized the Apocrypha as an unquestioned part of the canon or text of the Bible (excluding 1 and 2 Esdras and the Prayer of Manasses) at the Council of Trent in 1548. The Reformers rejected the Apocrypha, though Luther said that they were "profitable and good to read." As noncanonical literature, the Apocrypha has no more authority than any other human writing. Among Protestant churches today, only the Anglican Church uses the Apocrypha.

In regard to the NT, the term refers to books dating from the second century and later (including *Protevangelium of James*, *Gospel of Pseudo-Matthew*, *Gospel of the Nativity of Mary*, *History of Joseph the Carpenter*, *Gospel of Thomas*, *Gospel of the Infancy*, *Gospel of Nicodemus*, *Gospel of Philip*, *Gospel of the Egyptians*) which were not accepted into the NT canon. See: **Pseudepigrapha.**

See: H.T. Andrews, *An Introduction to Apocryphal Books of the Old and New Testament* (Baker, 1964); R.H. Charles, *The Apocrypha and Pseudepigrapha*, 2 vols. (Oxford: Clarendon Press, 1963); E. Hennecke, *New Testament Apocrypha*, 2 vols. (Westminster, 1963–65), B.M. Metzger, *An Introduction to the Apocrypha* (Oxford University Press, 1975).

Apologetics ■ From the Greek *apologia* or *apologetikos*, "to speak in defense of." The word is used eight times in the NT: Acts 22:1; 25:16; 1 Corinthians 9:3; 2 Corinthians 7:11; Philippians 1:7; 16; 2 Timothy 4:16; and 1 Peter 3:15—the classic text—which reads: "But sanctify Christ as Lord in your hearts, always being ready to make a defense to every one who asks you to give an account for the hope that is in you, yet with gentleness and reverence."

Apologetics is the area of Christian theology, or philosophy, that aims to intelligently defend the Christian faith in areas such as: the relationship of faith and reason, proofs for the existence of God, miracles, the problem of evil, evidence for the resurrection of Christ, the inspiration of Scripture, prophecy, and the defense of creation. It includes both positive arguments for the truth of Christianity and rebuttals of criticisms leveled against it.

See: W.L. Graig, *Apologetics: An Introduction* (Moody Press, 1984);

N.L. Geisler, *Christian Apologetics* (Baker, 1976); S.C. Hackett, *The Resurrection of Theism* (Baker, 1982); J.P. Moreland, *Scaling the Secular City: A Defense of Christianity* (Baker, 1987); and T.L. Miethe, *The Christian's Guide to Faith and Reason* (Bethany House Publishers, 1987).

Apollinarianism
■ A heretical teaching in the early Church that stated Christ in His Incarnation did not take on a complete human nature, but only a body. Appollinarius (born about 310), bishop of Laodicea, argued that the divine Logos (or Word) replaced Jesus' human spirit, thus limiting Jesus' humanity to His having a physical body. The view was condemned by the Council of Constantinople in 381. The importance of the orthodox view—that Christ possessed all elements of human nature, including body, soul, and mind—is that only a Christ who had all the elements of human nature could redeem mankind. Only a fully human Christ could rightly be said to be sinless, a fit sacrifice for our sins. See: **Constantinople, Council of.**

Apostasy
■ From the Greek *apostasia*, "defection." Apostasy is a "falling away," a deliberate and complete abandonment of the Christian faith (Heb. 3:12). In the NT, Judas Iscariot and his betrayal of Jesus and later death (Matt. 26:14–25, 47–57; 27:3–10) is an example. The apostles warned of the danger of apostasy in the NT (Heb. 6:5–8; 10:26).

Apostle
■ From the Greek *apostolos*, "one sent forth," the title of one chosen by Jesus and sent out in His power. In the NT there are the original chosen twelve, as well as others: Simon, called Peter; Andrew his brother; James, the son of Zebedee; John his brother; Philip; Bartholomew; Thomas; Matthew the publican; James, the son of Alphaeus; Thaddaeus; Simon the Zealot, Judas Iscariot (Matt. 10:1–4; Luke 6:13–16). After Judas' death the remaining eleven apostles chose Matthias by lot to replace Judas (Acts 1:23–26). Barnabas, who was sent out after Jesus' death, is called an apostle, though probably in a limited sense (Acts 13:2; 14:4, 14). Paul was directly appointed an apostle by Christ (Gal. 1:1) to the Gentiles (Rom. 1:5; Gal. 1:16; 2:8) and claimed the title of "apostle" because he had seen the risen Christ (Acts 26:16–18; 1 Cor. 9:1). James, Jesus' brother, is called an

apostle (Gal. 1:19; 1 Cor. 15:5–8). Others were also referred to as apostles (see: Rom. 16:7; 1 Thess. 2:6; 1 Cor. 9:5, 15:7).

Apostolic Succession ▪ Apostolic succession is one of three developments in the early Church that arose to guard against threats such as gnosticism, Montanism, and Marcionism. Along with the concentration of power in the office of the bishop and the collecting of the books of the New Testament, apostolic succession attempted to guarantee the teaching of pure doctrine. Irenaeus, bishop of Lyons, argued in the late second century that the apostles had faithfully relayed the teachings of Christ, and, moreover, appointed as successors bishops entrusted to pass on correct doctrine. Irenaeus implies that all true churches could list this succession of bishops, and lists the twelve bishops who had ruled Rome in succession until his time.

Today, the doctrine of apostolic succession largely concerns the Roman Catholic Church, which teaches that apostolic succession is "the authoritative and unbroken transmission of the mission and powers conferred by Jesus Christ on St. Peter and the Apostles from them to the present pope and bishops." Matthew 16:18–19 is used to support the idea that Jesus appointed Peter as the head of the twelve apostles. The Catholic claim is that Peter is the rock upon which Jesus will build His church (v. 16); Protestants argue that the rock is Peter's confession that Jesus was "the Son of the living God" (v. 16). Roman Catholics also contend that Jesus gave to Peter "the keys of the kingdom of heaven," power to set policy for the church. But as an apostle, Peter only had power to teach what God had already ordained. (See also 2 Tim. 2:2.) Most Protestants see apostolic succession as a faithful passing down of the doctrines taught by the apostles, not as an unbroken chain of office.

Apostles' Creed ▪ A brief summary of the Christian faith, believed by some—though practically all scholars think this only legend—to have been constructed by the twelve apostles. In its present form, the creed probably dates from about A.D. 700:

I believe in God the Father Almighty, Maker of heaven and earth: And in Jesus Christ his only Son our Lord, who was conceived by the Holy Ghost, born of the Virgin Mary, suffered under Pontius Pilate, was crucified, dead, and buried, he descended into Hell; the third day he rose again from the dead, he ascended into heaven, and sitteth on the right hand of God the Father Almighty; from thence he shall come to judge the quick and the dead. I believe in the Holy Ghost; the holy Christian Church; the Communion of Saints; the Forgiveness of sins; the Resurrection of the body; and the life everlasting. Amen.

See: **Nicene Creed.**

See: J.N.D. Kelly, *Early Christian Creeds* (Harper & Row, 1960); P. Schaff, *The Creeds of Christendom* 6th ed., 3 vols. (Baker Book House).

Aramaic ■ A Semitic language and cognate (related by descent from the same ancestral language) of Hebrew. Parts of Daniel (2:4—7:28) and Ezra (4:8–6:18; 7:12–26) were written in Aramaic. Aramaic was probably the language spoken by Jesus. See: **Greek, Hebrew.**

Arianism ■ The idea based on the teaching of Arius (c. 250–c. 336) that Christ is the highest of the created beings—god, but not God. Arius held that Jesus is not eternal, as is the Father, but that Jesus was created (begotten) by God the Father. Jesus is the "Logos," the Word, who mediates between God and humanity, but is not of the same substance as the Father, and therefore not God. The Council of Nicea, which was called by Emperor Constantine, condemned Arianism as heretical. In A.D. 325 Arius was banished, but in 335 he was readmitted to communion as he was dying.

The orthodox view holds that while the Father "begot" Christ, He did not "make" Christ, and that like the Father, Christ has existed from eternity and is fully God. The deity of Christ separates Him from the ranks of great teachers and makes Him God, deserving of worship. Thus in the Nicene Creed, "true God from true God . . . of one substance (*homoousia*) with the Father" was written against the teachings of Arius.

Today, the Jehovah's Witnesses cult exalts Arius as a central teacher. See: **Nicea, Council of; Nicene Creed; Homoousion.**

See: J.W.C. Wand, *The Four Great Heresies* (London: A.R. Mowbray, 1955).

Aristotelianism ■ A system of thought begun by Aristotle (384–322 B.C.), a Greek philosopher and student of Plato (427–347 B.C.). Aristotle developed an empirical philosophy, which asserts that all knowledge is gained through sense perception. This contrasts with Plato's rationalism, which saw a realm of ideals as true reality, and the world the senses perceive as merely a passing reflection of that eternal realm. Among his major works are: *Ethics*; *Physics*; *Metaphysics*; the *Organon* (on logic); *On the Heavens*; *On the Soul*; *On Politics*, *Rhetoric*, *Poetics*. Aristotle's thought was important to Thomas Aquinas (1224/5–1274). See: **Thomism, Platonism.**

See: F. Copleston, *A History of Philosophy*, Vol. I, Part Four "Aristotle" (Doubleday, 1962); J. Owens, *The Doctrine of Being in the Aristotelian Metaphysics* (Pontifical Institute of Mediaeval Studies, 1951); W.D. Ross, *The Works of Aristotle Translated Into English*, 12 vols. (Oxford, 1928).

Armageddon ▪ In Greek, *harmagedon*, the final battle between the forces of God and those of Satan. Revelation 16:16 is the only mention in the Bible. Some scholars do not think the name refers to a place, but rather to an event, the final great battle. See: **Eschatology, Millennialism, Tribulation.**

Arminianism ▪ A theological system with roots in the thought of James Arminius (1560–1609), a Dutch Reformed minister. Arminius was a student at Geneva of Theodore Beza, John Calvin's son-in-law. He argued against two versions of predestination, Beza's supralapsarianism and Augustine and Luther's sublapsarianism.

Arminianism teaches that God decides to give salvation to certain persons and not to others based on His foreknowledge of who will believe, not on a choice "before the foundations of the world" of some to be saved and some to be damned, as in Calvinism. Some call this position "conditional predestination." Arminius was not Pelagian—he believed in original sin and that the human will was entirely unable to do any good thing apart from the prior grace of God. Arminius taught that Christ died for all people, that saving grace is not irresistible and that believers can lose their salvation. See: **Calvinism; Dort, Synod of; Pelagianism; Infralapsarianism; Sublapsarianism; Supralapsarianism.**

See: *The Works of James Arminius*, 3 vols. (Baker, 1986); I.H. Marshall, *Kept by the Power of God: A Study of Perseverance and Falling Away* (Bethany House Publishers, 1969); T.L. Miethe's "The Universal Power of the Atonement" in *Grace Abounding*, edited by C.H. Pinnock (Zondervan, 1988); C.H. Pinnock, editor, *Grace Unlimited* (Bethany House Publishers,

1975); R. Shank, *Elect in the Son: A Study of the Doctrine of Election* (Westcott Publishers, 1970).

Ascension ■ Christ's bodily departure from the earth and return to heaven on the fortieth day after His resurrection (Mark 16:19; Luke 24:50–53; John 20:17; Eph. 4:10). Acts 1:9 reads: "And after He had said these things, He was lifted up while they were looking on, and a cloud received Him out of their sight" (see also vv. 10–11).

Assumption ■ The taking of a person into heaven. In the Roman Catholic Church, assumption particularly refers to the teaching that Mary the Mother of Jesus was taken up body and spirit unto heaven. The assumption of Mary is known to have been celebrated in the fifth century in Palestine. However, it was not until November 1, 1950, that Pope Pius XII codified the belief in the Assumption of the Blessed Virgin Mary in the papal bull *Manificientissimus Deus*. The Feast of the Assumption is celebrated on August 15.

Assurance ■ The idea that a believer can know that he or she is truly saved. Some believe this assurance is divinely given, while others contend that assurance comes from taking God at His Word, "that whoever believes in Him should not perish, but have eternal life" (John 3:16). It is certain that assurance must be based not on an emotional experience but on the saving work of Christ and the believer's acceptance of this truth in Scripture. If this truth is understood and accepted, then there certainly should be a deep personal conviction or assurance. An individual can and should have an assurance of salvation. See: John 5:24; Romans 8:15–17, 29–30, 38–39; Galatians 4:6; Colossians 2:2; 1 Thessalonians 1:5; Hebrews 6:11; 10:22; 1 John 3:18–19; 4:13; 5:10; 5:13. See: **Calvinism, Five Points of; Salvation.**

Atheism ■ From the Greek *atheos*, "godless," a word found only once in the NT, in Ephesians 2:12—the belief that there is no God. In the twentieth century, atheism has grown with the advance of Communism—an atheistic religion—and the establishment of atheist organizations such as the American Association for the Advancement of Atheism (1925), the League of Militant Atheists (1929), and with documents like the "Humanist Manifesto I" (1933), the "Humanist Manifesto II" (1973), and "A Secular Humanist Declaration" (1980).

See: A. Flew, *God and Philosophy* (Harcourt Brace and World, 1967) and *The Presumption of Atheism* (Barnes and Noble, 1976); N.L. Geisler, "The Collapse of Modern Atheism" in *The Intellectuals Speak Out About God*, ed. by R.A. Varghese (Regnery Gatway, 1984); *False Gods of Our Time* (Harvest House, 1985); *Is Man the Measure?: An Evaluation of Contemporary Humanism* (Baker, 1983); T.L. Miethe, *The Christian's Guide to Faith and Reason* (Bethany House Publishers, 1987), pp. 72–75.

Atonement ■ That aspect of the work of Christ, particularly His death, that makes possible the restoration of fellowship between God and man. The need for reconciliation between God and mankind is clear from the fact that people are sinners separated from God (Rom. 3:9–23). The doctrine of the atonement states that Christ died, or "atoned," for our sins, making reconciliation with God the Father possible. Atonement is effective because Christ bore the punishment justly due all sinners. Christ's dying on behalf of sinners is known as "vicarious" or "substitutionary" atonement.

In the late sixteenth and early seventeenth century, two theories of the atonement were pitted against each other: (1) the Calvinist interpretation, which says that Christ died only for the elect, and (2) the Arminian doctrine that Christ died for all persons, whether elect or not.

See: N.F. Douty, *The Death of Christ*, a treatise that considers the question: "Did Christ Die Only for the Elect?" (Williams and Watrous Publishing Co., 1978); R.P. Lightner, *The Death Christ Died: A Case for Unlimited Atonement* (Regular Baptist Press, 1967); T.L. Miethe, "The Universal Power of the Atonement" in *The Grace of God/The Will of Man*, ed. by C.H. Pinnock (Zondervan, 1989).

Attributes of God ■ The characteristics of God that make Him God. They are not something we merely attribute to Him, but qualities inseparable from His very Being. In every way that God exists, He exists without limit, that is, in perfection. God is eternal, without beginning or end (self-existent); all-powerful (see: **Omnipotence**); all-knowing (see: **Omniscience**); all-loving; long-suffering; present everywhere at all times (see: **Omnipresence**); unlimited in creative power (see: **Omnificence**). God is limited only by His own nature or character. He cannot do any-thing that would contradict His very Nature or Being; this does not mean, however, that God is limited or imperfect, but only that God is God and cannot be other than himself.

See: H. Bavinck, *The Doctrine of God* (Baker, 1977); W.N. Clarke, *The Christian Doctrine of God* (T. and T. Clark, 1912); S.T. Davis, *Logic and the Nature of God* (Eerdmans, 1983); E.J. Fortman, *The Triune God* (Baker, 1982); R.H. Nash, *The Concept of God* (Zondervan, 1983); J.I. Packer, *Knowing God* (InterVarsity Press, 1973).

Attrition
■ From the Latin *atterere*, meaning "to rub against." The sorrow for one's sins that arises from a motive other than love for God, such as fear of hell or fear of punishment. Roman Catholic theology states that attrition alone is not enough to re-ceive forgiveness for one's sin. See: **Contrition.**

Augustinianism
■ Theology based on the writings of St. Au-gustine of Hippo (A.D. 354–430), one of history's foremost de-fenders of the Christian faith. Augustine was the black bishop of Hippo born in Tagaste in North Africa. He studied and taught rhetoric in Carthage and Rome. As a young man, he was at-tracted philosophically to Manichaeism, skepticism, and neopla-tonism. He became a Christian at age 34 and a priest seven years later. In his many works one finds the nuclei of most of the ethical thought from his time to our own. He had forty years of literary productivity.

Augustine lived in an interesting, turbulent time. In 410, Rome, the invincible "Eternal City," was captured and sacked by the barbarians. During this crisis—an event tantamount to the end of the world for people of that time—Augustine re-sponded with an answer for all time. He said the true cause of the calamity was the moral decay of Roman society. Much to his credit, Augustine was not satisfied with criticizing the evils of his surroundings, but rather attempted to construct a Christian world view (*Weltanschauung*), in hope of reconstructing the very fabric of the civilized world.

Thus his book *City of God* was born. Man's city was ruled by passion and pride, lacking true foundation. He echoed the sen-timents of the writer of Hebrews, "For here we do not have an enduring city, but we are looking for the city that is to come" (Heb. 13:14). In contrast, the city of God and Christ was marked by purity, love, and true life. It shall never pass away because it has a sure foundation, "whose architect and builder is God" (Heb. 11:10). The heavenly city would grow as the earthly city faded away.

Some of the more important aspects of Augustine's thought were: (1) God is pure Being—immaterial, eternal, immutable—and a unity. In this view, he was influenced by Plato (427–347 B.C.) and Plotinus (A.D. 205–270). (2) The soul rules the body and its spiritual condition causes good and evil. (3) Humans have free will, and evil exists because they choose it. Evil is a lack of good, with no existence, so God could not have produced it. (4) The human soul can take part in the divine ideas of God and His will. (5) God can illuminate the soul. (6) Humans are corrupted by sin and cannot reach God or salvation by themselves. (7) Faith is a gift of God. (9) The Gospel must be preached so humans can come to faith. (10) The Trinity is one and the same without distinction. See: **Pelagianism.**

See: V.J. Bourke, *Augustine's Quest of Wisdom: Life and Philosophy of the Bishop of Hippo* (Bruce, 1945) and *The Essential Augustine* (Hackett Publishing Co., 1974); T.L. Miethe, *Augustine Bibliography, 1970–1980: With Essays on the Fundamentals of Augustinian Scholarship* (Greenwood Press, 1982).

Authority, Appeal to ■ In Latin, *Argumentum ad Verecundiam*. If a layman is disputing a question of physical science and he appeals to the testimony of Einstein on the matter, his testimony is relevant, although it does not prove the point. It certainly tends to support it. But when someone appeals to an authority for testimony outside the area of that authority's expertise, then the person commits the fallacy of Appealing to Authority. See: **Logical Fallacies.**

Axiology ■ From the Greek *axios*, "of like value," and *logos*, "theory." That branch of philosophy that studies the theory of values, as in ethics, aesthetics and religion. The problems of axiology fall into four groups: (1) the nature of value, (2) the types of value, (3) the criterion of value, and (4) the metaphysical status of value. See: **Philosophy, Synderesis Rule.**

Baal ▪ A Hebrew word, "Baal" means "master, owner." When the Israelites entered Canaan, they found that every area had its own god. The deity of each place had a surname from the area, such as Baal-berith in Judges 8:33; 9:4. Later, "Baal" became the proper name of the great fertility god of the people of Canaan. Baal worship involved sexual acts in fertility rituals and even child sacrifice (Jer. 19:5). See also: 1 Kings 18; 19:18.

Baha'i ▪ Two nineteenth-century Persian prophets began the Baha'i religion as an offshoot of Islam. One of them—Baha'u'llah—wrote 100 volumes. Followers of Baha'i advocate "the fostering of the unfettered search for truth, world concord as the fruit of world religion, abolition of prejudice and superstition, harmonious cooperation between science and religion, the equality of men and women, universal compulsory education, elimination of the extremes of poverty and wealth, adoption of an auxiliary universal language, an international tribunal to settle disputes, and the reduction of armaments and attainment of world peace." Baha'i teaches that every few hundred years God "manifests" himself through a prophet—Adam, Abraham, Moses, Krishna, Buddha, Zoroaster, Jesus, and Mohammed. Each prophet reveals as much divine truth as the people of that time can accept. Religious truth is relative rather than absolute, and divine revelation is a continuous and progressive process.

In 1844, Ali-Muhammed, a Persian, took the name "the Bab" (Gate) and wrote the *Bayan*, which presented the prescriptions of the Babi religion. In July of 1850, the Persian government executed the thirty-year-old Bab. Before his death, the Bab had appointed Mirza Yahya Subh-i-Ezel to succeed him. Mirza and his half brother, Mirza Husayn-'Ali, fled to Baghdad. The half brother changed his name to Baha'u'llah, which means "the Glory of God." He spent forty years in a Turkish penal colony, during which time he wrote the books that have become the basic scriptures of Baha'ism, including "The Most Holy Book," the *Al-Kitab Al-Aqdas*. He died in 1892. Baha'i gained its first American converts in 1894, and by 1895 there were small groups in Chicago and Kenosha, Wisconsin. The religion maintains a beautiful temple on the shoreline of Lake Michigan in Wilmette, Illinois, and exists in over 271 countries around the world.

See: J.R. Richards, *Baha'ism* (London, S.P.C.K., 1965).

Baptism ■ From the Greek word *baptizien*, "to immerse." Baptism is, at the least, the act of Christian initiation. We know that: (1) Jesus commanded baptism (Matt. 28:19–20), and in order to serve as an example for us, He allowed John to immerse Him in the river Jordan (Matt. 3:13–17). (2) Baptism is an open demonstration and declaration to the world of our acceptance of Christ as Lord, and of our entry into His Church (Mark 16:16; 1 Peter 3:21). (3) It represents our burial with Christ, whereby His atonement for sin becomes atonement for our own sins (Rom. 6:1–11).

In the history of the Church, three modes of baptism have been practiced: immersion (*baptizo*), sprinkling (*rantizo*), and pouring (*cheo*). Christians who practice immersion—usually baptizing only those old enough to confess belief in Christ—do not believe the last two forms have any scriptural basis. Those holding to sprinkling or pouring often argue that the outward form of baptism is unimportant, or that their practices picture different aspects of baptism: sprinkling portrays sprinkling with the blood of Christ, and pouring, the washing of the Holy Spirit in regeneration.

Since the Reformation, Church history has been filled with disagreement about baptizing infants. Those who practice adult (or believer's) baptism point to biblical passages such as Acts 2 that show a clear sequence: belief, *then* baptism. At the end of Peter's sermon on Pentecost, the people were "pierced to the heart" (Acts 2:37) because they realized they had crucified Jesus, who was Lord and Christ (v. 36). They asked Peter and the other apostles, "Brethren, what shall we do?" (v. 37). Peter answered their question: "Repent, and let each of you be baptized in the name of Jesus Christ for the forgiveness of your sins; and you shall receive the gift of the Holy Spirit" (Acts 2:38). Those who practice infant baptism (paedobaptists) generally do so for one of two reasons: (1) Some believe it removes original sin; and (2) others see it as a sign of the covenant of grace God makes with His people, into which a child of Christian parents may enter. Views on the efficacy of baptism range from baptismal regeneration (that baptism causes the recipient to be regenerated by the Holy Spirit) to belief that baptism is simply a sign of a change that has already taken place in the believer. See: Mark 1:5, 9; John 3:23; Acts 2:41; 8:32–39; 9:18; 10:45–48; 16:14–15; 16:33–34; 22:12–16.

See: K. Barth, *The Teaching of the Church Regarding Baptism* (London: SCM Press, 1948); G.R. Beasley-Murray, *Baptism in the New Testament* (Eerdmans, 1962); P.K. Jewett, *Infant Baptism and the Covenant of Grace* (Eerdmans, 1978); T.L. Watson, *Should Infants Be Baptized?* (Guardian Press, 1976).

Baptists ■ Baptists represent a great range of beliefs: There are Freewill Baptists, Calvinistic Baptists, Independent Baptists, Landmark Baptists (who teach that they can trace their origins not just to Jesus but back to John the Baptist), "open communion" Baptists (who admit non-Baptists to the Lord's Supper), "closed communion" Baptists (who may only admit members of their particular Baptist group), and even churches that use the name "First Baptist Church," yet bill themselves as "nondenominational," meaning that they accept all Christians.

Baptists are the largest Protestant group in America, claiming some 30 million members in 34 major denominational groups, in addition to many smaller or independent groups. The largest group, the Southern Baptist Convention, claims 14 million members in 35,000 churches.

The Baptists originated in the early 1600s. John Smyth (1554–1612), an Anglican minister, led a small group of Separatists who moved to Holland in 1606 and formed a Baptist church in 1610. Thomas Helwys (1550–1616) left Amsterdam in 1611 and formed the first Baptist group in England. The heirs of this group were called "General Baptists," because they believed everyone could be saved. In 1638 the "Particular Baptists," a group influenced by Calvinistic ideas of predestination and election, was formed. In 1639 Roger Williams (1604–1684), a Puritan minister expelled from the Massachusetts Bay Colony, founded the first Baptist church in America, in Providence, Rhode Island.

Although Baptists have varied beliefs, they generally hold to a few common tenets, claiming to draw their distinctive emphases from the NT: (1) The Bible is the supreme source of inspiration and direction. Some do, however, emphasize creedal statements as a test of fellowship. (2) Church and state should be separate. (3) Individual conscience has the right to interpret the teachings of the Bible. (4) Immersion is the true form of baptism. (5) Baptism and communion are ordinances, not sacraments. (6) Salvation comes by the grace of God through faith alone. (7) Congregationalism is the proper biblical form of church government.

See: C.J. Allen, *Encyclopedia of Southern Baptists* (Broadman Press, 1958); W. Carthcart, *The Baptist Encyclopedia* (Louis H. Everts, 1881); H.H. Hobbs, *The Baptist Faith and Message* (Convention Press, 1971); L. McBeth, *The Baptist Heritage* (Broadman, 1987); F. Stagg, *New Testament Theology* (Broadman Press, 1962); A. Wardin, *Baptist Atlas* (Broadman, 1980).

Beatification ▪ The first step in the Roman Catholic Church toward sainthood. Beatification is a legal process whereby a dead believer is judged worthy of public veneration. Once beatified, the person is called "Blessed," and worship of the beatified is permitted in a particular place or within a Catholic order. See: **Sainthood.**

Beatific Vision ▪ From the Latin *beatificare*, "to make happy." A term more common in Catholic than Protestant theology, beatific vision is direct or immediate knowledge (*visio Dei*) of God by a believer: "The souls of the blessed see God directly and face to face, unveiled, clearly, openly, as he is in himself; and in this vision they equally enjoy God." It is a supernatural vision, not proper to human nature. "The primary object of the Vision is God himself as he is, in all his perfections and in the three persons of the Trinity." Protestants use the term to refer primarily to a heavenly experience, while Roman Catholic theology teaches that it can be attained for brief periods in this life. This idea is based on scriptures such as Matthew 5:8; 1 Corinthians 13:12; 1 Timothy 6:16; Hebrews 12:14; 1 John 3:2, 6; and Revelation 22:4. Many early Church fathers, notably Augustine (354–430), interpreted Scripture in this way. The great Augustinian scholar Vernon J. Bourke says of the beatific vision: "No pagan philosopher . . . has risen to the concept of the beatific vision.

It is the vision which Augustine describes as the essential feature of the life of the saints in heaven." See: **Augustinianism.**

See: V.J. Bourke, *Augustine's Quest of Wisdom* (Bruce, 1945), p. 284, and *The Essential Augustine* (Hackett, 1974), p. 196.

Beatitude ■ From the Latin *beatitudo*, "blessing" or "blessed-ness." The term "beatitude" refers to Christ's Sermon on the Mount (Matt. 5:3–12), which lists eight blessings: "Blessed are the poor in spirit, for theirs is the kingdom of heaven. Blessed are they that mourn, for they shall be comforted. Blessed are the gentle, for they shall inherit the earth. Blessed are they which do hunger and thirst after righteousness, for they shall be sat-isfied. Blessed are the merciful, for they shall receive mercy. Blessed are the pure in heart, for they shall see God. Blessed are the peacemakers, for they shall be called the sons of God. Blessed are they which are persecuted for the sake of righteousness, for theirs is the kingdom of heaven. Blessed are you when men shall revile you, and persecute you, and shall say all kinds of evil against you falsely, on account of Me." Jesus goes on to say in verse 12: "Rejoice, and be glad, for your reward in heaven is great, for so they persecuted the prophets who were before you."

See: W. Fitch, *The Beatitudes of Jesus* (Eerdmans, 1961); A. McLaren, *A Garland of Gladness* (Eerdmans, 1945); T. Watson, *The Beatitudes: An Exposition of Matthew 5:1–12* (London: Banner of Truth Trust, 1971).

Beelzebub ■ Probably derived from the name of a god of the Philistines, the name "Baal-zebub" means "lord of the fly" (2 Kings 1:2–16). Some scholars believe the Philistines may have worshiped the fly. In the NT Jews used this name to refer to the prince of demons (Matt. 12:24; cf. Matt. 9:34; Luke 11:15) and accused Jesus of casting out demons by the power of Beelzebub. See: **Antichrist, Satan.**

Begging the Question ■ In Latin, *Petitio Principii*. When a person uses as a premise for his argument the conclusion he intends to prove, then he commits the fallacy of "begging the question." Example: "Shakespeare is a greater writer than Miethe because people with good taste in literature prefer Shake-speare. How can I tell who has good taste? Anyone who prefers Shakespeare." The conclusion states only what has already been asserted and does not establish the truth of its conclusion. See: **Logical Fallacies.**

Being ■ From the Latin, *ens*. The quality or state of having existence, that which is or exists; the real. God tells us in Exodus 3:13–14 that He is the one whose Nature is existence as such, the one who is existence: ". . . Now they may say to me, 'What is His name?' What shall I say to them? And God said to Moses, 'I AM WHO I AM'; and He said, 'Thus you shall say to the sons of Israel, I AM has sent me to you.' " Metaphysics studies being qua (as) being—of existence as such—the most foundational area of philosophy. See: **Philosophy, Metaphysics, Thomism.**

See: E. Gilson, *Being and Some Philosophers* (Pontifical Institute of Mediaeval Studies, 1949); J. Owens, *The Doctrine of Being in the Aristotelian Metaphysics: A study in the Greek Background of Mediaeval Thought* (Pontifical Institute of Mediaeval Studies, 1951).

Bible, Inerrancy and Infallibility of the ■ The position that the Bible is completely truthful in what it teaches. Evangelicals hold differing views regarding inerrancy, that (1) it relates only to biblical teaching on matters of faith and practice, or that (2) it extends to all the teaching of Scripture, including matters of scientific and historical detail. Both views agree that correct biblical interpretation takes into account such things as authorial intent, literary types and colloquial expressions.

Inerrancy and infallibility are often used interchangeably. Inerrancy has been more strictly defined as ". . . the view that when all the facts become known, they will demonstrate that the Bible in its original autographs and correctly interpreted is entirely true and never false in all it affirms, whether that relates to doctrine or ethics or to the social, physical, or life sciences." The statement drawn up by the International Conference on Biblical Inerrancy (ICBI) in October 1978, in Chicago is the best statement of what inerrancy means. Infallibility asserts a slightly different view, that the Bible is "unfailing in its purpose." See: **Inerrancy, Word of God.**

See: D.A. Carson and John D. Woodbridge, *Scripture and Truth* (Zondervan, 1983); N.L. Geisler, *Biblical Errancy: An Analysis of its Philosophical Roots* (Zondervan, 1981) and *Inerrancy* (Zondervan, 1979); Gordon Lewis and Bruce Demarest, *Challenges to Inerrancy: A Theological Response* (Moody Press, 1984); J.W. Montgomery, *God's Inerrant Word* (Bethany House Publishers, 1974).

Biblical Criticism ■ In theology, study that attempts to determine the true meaning of the Bible regarding its original wording, manner and date of composition, sources, and authorship by using techniques applied to other written documents and other kinds of literature. (1) Textual or "lower" criticism attempts to restore the original wording of a text altered in copying and recopying. (2) Literary or "higher" criticism attempts to examine the structure of a book, including source criticism, a study of the sources used by its author and the way these were used or combined. (3) Form criticism is concerned with classifying and examining the life-settings of the literary forms used in biblical texts. See: **Form Criticism, Higher Criticism, Lower Criticism, Redaction Criticism.**

See: N.L. Geisler and W.E. Nix, *General Introduction to the Bible* (Moody, 1968); T.H. Horne, *An Introduction to the Critical Study and Knowledge of the Holy Scriptures*, 5 vols., 8th ed. (Baker, 1970).

Biblicism ■ Adhering to the letter of the Bible, viewing it with a strong, unquestioning commitment to its authority in an excessively literalistic way. Those who take this view of the Bible frequently "proof-text," taking verses out of context to prove a point. Far from respect for God's Word, Biblicism is ultimately the greatest abuse of His Word: using it to justify a particular prejudice. If taken to extremes, it can become "bibliolatry," worship of the Bible, making it an idol.

Bibliology ■ A comprehensive analysis of the doctrine of Scripture as the foundation of all theological truth. Usually included is an examination of the distinctives and alleged problems in concepts such as authority, revelation, inspiration, illumination and inerrancy of the Bible.

Binitarianism ■ The tendency to view the Trinity in a two-fold rather than a three-fold relationship, a belief especially common in pre-Nicenian times. See: **Arianism; Monarchianism; Nicea, Council of.**

Bishop ■ From the Greek word *episkopos*, meaning "one who has oversight of others." In the NT the title seems interchangeable with "elder" or "presbyter," both translations of *presbyteros*.

A bishop's qualifications and duties are thus found in 1 Timothy 3:1–7 and Titus 1:5–7. Early in Church history—by the second century—the functions of elders and bishops were separated into two offices, with elders in local congregations and bishops ruling over them. During the Protestant Reformation, some churches abandoned the office of bishop, claiming they were returning to the apparent NT practice of not distinguishing between that office and eldership.

Present-day bishops, such as in the Lutheran or Methodist churches, exercise at least limited authority over a group of local congregations. In the Roman Catholic Church, a bishop holds an office established by Jesus through Peter. He has divine rights, governs a local diocese, and is forbidden to marry. The Bishop of Rome is the Pope of the Roman Church. See: Acts 20:17–36; Philippians 1:1; 1 Thessalonians 5:12; 1 Timothy 3:2ff.; Titus 1:5–7. See: **Apostolic Succession, Elder, Presbyter.**

Blasphemy ■ From the Greek *blasphemia*, "a curse." Blasphemy is using the name of God in an irreverent or slanderous way, taking the name of God in vain. It breaks the fourth of the Ten Commandments: "You shall not take the name of the Lord your God in vain, for the Lord will not leave him unpunished who takes His name in vain" (Ex. 20:7). (See also: Num. 15:30; Deut. 5:11; Isa. 65:7; Ezek. 20:27.) Blasphemy was punishable by stoning (Lev. 24:11–14; 1 Kings 21:9–10).

Jesus talks about the sin of blasphemy against the Holy Spirit in Matthew 12:31; Mark 3:28, 29; and Luke 12:10. While blasphemy is forgivable (Mark 3:28–29; Matt. 12:32), this particular form of blasphemy cannot be forgiven. There is some disagreement about what this sin entails. A common view is that it is not just a single act, but a continual, willful, conscious rejection of God by attributing the workings of the Holy Spirit to Satan. See: 1 John 5:16; Hebrews 6:4–6. See: **Sin Against the Holy Spirit.**

Born Again ■ Used to refer to a Christian, someone who is twice born—once of human parents and once of the Holy Spirit when he or she accepted Jesus as Lord and Savior. See: **Regeneration.**

Brahmanism ■ Orthodox Hinduism that adheres to the pantheism of the Vedas (any of four canonical collections of hymns, prayers, and liturgical formulas that compose the earliest Hindu sacred writings) and to the ancient sacrifices and family ceremonies. See: **Hinduism.**

Breaking of Bread ■ See: **Lord's Supper.**

British Israelism ■ A group that teaches that the Anglo-Saxon people are the true Israel. The idea can be found in John Sadler, *The Rights of the Kingdom* (1649), and in John Wilson, *Our Israelitish Origin* (1814). Beginning with OT promises that Israel would have a continuous existence from the time of Abraham, they argue that Zedekiah's daughters (Jer. 41:10) went to Egypt (Jer. 44:12–14) and then took refuge (Isa. 37:32) on one of the "isles of the sea" (Jer. 31:10), which they interpret as Ireland. Their descendants then went to England and became the royal family. The British royal family thus is directly related to the house of David.

Buddhism ■ A religion of eastern and central Asia that grew out of the teaching of Gautama Buddha (5th century B.C.), originally Siddhartha Gautama. It teaches that suffering is inherent in life and that one can be liberated from it by mental and moral self-purification. It is ambiguous about the existence of a personal God.

Apologists for Buddhism describe it as the richest, most lasting of Aryan religions. In the *Dharma*, or teaching, the master did not discard primitive Hinduism. There is a belief in gods and of evil spirits. It espouses a great concern for "deliverance," breaking through the chain of repeated birth and rebirth. To obtain this liberation, the disciple must discover and practice what the Buddha considered four basic or "noble" truths: (1) Existence involves suffering. (2) The cause of suffering is desire and the clinging to existence. (3) The way to escape from suffering and existence is to be rid of these desires. (4) To be delivered one must follow the eightfold path mapped out by "the enlightened one."

Each person must do the work by himself, though community

life is useful. In the final analysis, however, everyone saves himself. Buddha made monasticism an inseparable part of his creed. Men, normally admitted to the order after the age of twenty if they are healthy and otherwise suitable, must shave their heads and agree to keep the 220 Rules of the Order, known as the Patimikkha. Begging is a common custom.

Branches of Buddhism vary greatly. At one extreme is Zen Buddhism (meditation), a pure subjectivism or pantheism. In Zen, there is no dualism of heaven and earth, natural and supernatural, man and God, matter and spirit, mortal and immortal. Present existence (Samsara) and future destiny (Nirvana) are all the same. At the other extreme, many monks in the Mahayana tradition address a deity so compassionate that simple faith in Amitabha (Amida) may even dispense with the necessity of good works. So great is this Buddha's power and mercy, that uttering the name "Buddha Amitayus" at death expiates sins which would otherwise keep a person in a cycle of births and rebirths for eight million Kalpas (a period of cosmic time). See: **Hinduism, Pantheism.**

See: J.N.D. Anderson, *The World's Religions* (Eerdmans, 1950), and *Christianity and Comparative Religions* (InterVarsity Press, 1970).

Call, Calling ■ The Bible has many words and forms for "call" or "calling," words that appear some 800 times in an English Bible. The word frequently means God's invitation of a person to salvation or to a specific service. It is used to call or summon someone (Matt. 20:8); of God's call to redemption (Rom. 8:30; 1 Cor. 1:9); of the call in entrusting men with preaching the Gospel (Acts 13:2; 16:10); "His calling" (Eph. 1:18); the "high calling" (Phil. 3:14); "your calling" (2 Thess. 1:11); "holy calling" (2 Tim. 1:9); the call for fellowship (1 Cor. 1:9); and for service (Gal. 1:15). Christians in general are the "called" in 1 Corinthians 1:24. God's call is now "in Christ Jesus" (Phil. 3:14). And in 1 John 3:1 we are told ". . . that we should be called children of God; and such we are." See: Hebrews 3:1; 9:15; 1 Peter 2:21, etc. See also: **Ministry, Vocation, Will of God.**

See: T.L. Miethe, "Ministry and the Christian" and "God and the Day's Work," in *The New Christian's Guide to Following Jesus* (Bethany House Publishers, 1981), pp. 103–110, 117–122; Paul E. Little, *Affirming the Will of God* (InterVarsity Press, 1971); Garry Friesen, *Decision Making and the Will of God* (Multnomah Press, 1980).

Calling, Effectual ■ See: **Perseverance.**

Calvinism ■ A theological system associated with John Calvin (1509–1564) and later followers.

Calvin first published his *Institutes of the Christian Religion* in 1536. The formal principle of Calvin's theological system is embodied in the Latin phrase *sola Scriptura* (Scripture only), the common call of most of the sixteenth-century Reformation. Especially important to Calvinistic thought are the doctrines of the sovereignty of God and predestination. God rules all things in such a way that nothing happens "without His counsel." This includes God's destining some for salvation before the foundations of the world, not because of any merit or even foreseen faith, but simply by His free will and the unmerited grace which He extends. See: **Calvinism, Five Points of.**

See: J. Calvin, *Institutes of the Christian Religion* (Eerdmans, 1953); D. Engelsma, *Hyper-Calvinism and the Call of the Gospel* (Reformed Free Publishing Assoc., 1980); F. Wendel, *Calvin: The Origins and Development of His Religious Thought* (Collins, 1963); C. Van Til, *The Case for Calvinism* (Presbyterian and Reformed, 1964).

Calvinism, Five Points of ■ What is now referred to as

the "Five-Points of Calvinism," or "TULIP," was formulated at the Synod of Dort (1618–1619) in response to the Remonstrance of 1610, in which followers of James Arminius (1560–1609) rejected the major points of Calvinistic dogma. The Synod of Dort (1618–1619) affirmed the five points commonly held to be the key tenets of Calvinism. In his introductory essay to John Owen's book, *The Death of Death in the Death of Christ*, J. I. Packer summarizes the five points as follows: (1) *T*otal depravity: Fallen man in his natural state lacks all power to believe the gospel, just as he lacks all power to believe the Law, despite all external inducements extended to him. (2) *U*nconditional election: God's election is a free, sovereign, unconditional choice of sinners to be redeemed by Christ, given faith and brought to glory. (3) *L*imited atonement: The redeeming work of Christ had as its end and goal the salvation of the elect. (4) *I*rresistible grace: The work of the Holy Spirit in bringing men to faith never fails to achieve its object. (5) *P*erseverance of the saints: Believers are kept in faith and grace by the unconquerable power of God till they come to glory.

A "High Calvinist" is one who accepts all five points. Other Calvinists accept or reject various points, although High Calvinists would argue that all five points are logically and scripturally necessary. For example, some Calvinists do not subscribe to a limited atonement, that Christ died only for the elect. See, for instance, Norman F. Douty, *The Death of Christ* (Williams and Watrous, 1978), who accepts four of the five points, but strongly believes that the Bible does not teach limited atonement. Some have argued that even John Calvin did not hold to limited atonement. Calvinists Moise Amyraut, Richard Baxter, John Bunyan, John Newton, John Brown, and many others accept a generalism called "hypothetical universalism," the idea that Christ died for the sins of all and that all are capable of believing. (See: T. L. Miethe, "The Universal Power of the Atonement" in *The Grace of God/The Will of Man*, C. Pinnock, editor [Zondervan, 1989].) See: **TULIP.**

See: H. Hanko, H.C. Hoeksema, and G.J. Van Baren, *The Five Points of Calvinism* (Reformed Free Publishing Assoc., 1976).

Campbellite ▪ A follower of the thought of Alexander Campbell (1788–1866), founder of a Christian group known as the "Restoration Movement." Today his followers are divided into three groups.

Campbell grew up in Ireland. When he came to America in 1809, he found his father, a Presbyterian pastor, had withdrawn from the Presbyterians after disagreements over Calvinist doctrine. For a time, the church led by the Campbells joined the Redstone Baptist Association. The two groups agreed on many issues: the Bible as the final authority in religious matters, autonomy of local congregations, repudiation of sprinkling and acceptance of immersion of believers, the divinity of Christ and His atonement. They disagreed, however, on the use of creedal statements, the purpose of baptism, frequency of the Lord's Supper, operation of the Holy Spirit in conversion, and requirements for church membership. The Redstone Association excluded the Campbells' church in 1825. Though the movement led by Alexander Campbell existed to "restore simple evangelical Christianity" and unite Christians, it managed only one union; in 1831/32 Campbell's followers united with Barton W. Stone's group, who were known only as "the Christians."

Campbell was an important indigenous American theologian. He held a high view of the ordinances of baptism and communion, taught the unity of the church based on loyalty to Christ more than creeds, synthesized Christian revelation with the best thinking of his day, and practically applied his theology. He was an important champion of education. See: **Christian Church/ Church of Christ (Independent); Church of Christ (Non-Instrumental); Disciples of Christ, Christian.**

See: A. Campbell, *The Christian System* (Gospel Advocate Company, 1956), *Christian Baptism* (Standard Publishing Company, 1887), the *Christian Baptist* (published monthly from 1823–1830), and *The Millennial Harbinger* (published monthly from 1830–63), 34 vols.; R. Richardson, *Memoirs of Alexander Campbell* (Gospel Advocate Company, 1956); T.L. Miethe, *The Philosophy and Ethics of Alexander Campbell: From the Context of American Religious Thought: 1800–1866* (University Microfilms, 1984).

Canon of the New Testament
■ From the Greek *kanon*, "rule," the 27 books that are accepted as inspired by and intended by God for inclusion in the NT, the collection of books regarded as genuine, authoritative, and inspired.

The canon of the NT was completed with the writing of the last books—John's epistles and the Book of Revelation—in about A.D. 95, although it took about three hundred years for the Church to decide which books were true, inspired Scripture. Books whose divine authority was questioned during this period were Revelation, Hebrews, James, 2 Peter, 2 John, 3 John and Jude. At the Council of Carthage of A.D. 397, however, representatives unanimously recognized the 27 books of our NT as Scripture.

See: F.F. Bruce, *The New Testament Documents: Are They Reliable?* (InterVarsity Press, 1966); J. Martin, *Origin and History of the New Testament* (London: Hodder and Stoughton, 1884); B.F. Westcott, *A General Survey of the History of the Canon of the New Testament* (Macmillan, 1896).

Canon of the Old Testament
■ The genuine, authoritative, and inspired books of the OT. Protestants accept 39 books. The Roman Catholic Church, at the Council of Trent (1545–1563), officially accepted the books of the Apocrypha as authored by God and included in the canon. See: **Apocrypha; Pseudopigrapha; Trent, Council of.**

See: R.D. Wilson, *A Scientific Investigation of the Old Testament* (Moody Press, 1959).

Canonization
■ The second step to sainthood in the Roman Catholic Church. Canonization officially and publicly declares a person's heroic virtue and includes his or her name in the canon of saints. It must be proven that the candidate worked two miracles. Upon canonization by the pope, a feast day is appointed in the saint's honor, his relics are publicly venerated, churches and altars are dedicated in his honor, statues or pictures displayed, and public prayers made to him. Judgment in this process is infallible, according to Catholic theology. The first solemn canonization was of St. Ulrich of Augsburg by Pope John XV in 993. See: **Sainthood.**

Cardinal Virtues, the Seven
■ From the Latin *virtus* meaning "strength," "courage," the seven basic virtues espoused by the medieval church upon which all other Christian

virtues hinge: faith, hope, love, justice, prudence, temperance, and fortitude. The first three are considered "theological." (See: 1 Cor. 13:13; also, 1 Thess. 1:3; Gal. 5:5–6; Col. 1:4–5.) The last four are considered "natural" or "moral." Some scholars trace these to the Greek philosopher Plato. See: **Platonism; Sins, Seven Deadly; Virtues, Cardinal.**

See: J. Stalker, *Seven Cardinal Virtues* (Kregel, 1961).

Catechism ■ From the Greek word *katechizein*, "to impress or instruct by word of mouth." Catechism is a manual or systematic summary of Christian beliefs often used to teach people new in the faith— either children or new converts. The method of teaching is generally by asking questions and receiving prescribed (from a manual) answers. The teacher is called the "catechist"; the candidate is the "catechumen." Catechism can also refer to a set of formal questions asked of candidates of a religion, who must respond by reciting the correct answers. Catechism is most common in the Roman Catholic and Lutheran churches.

Catholic ■ From the Greek word *katholikos* meaning "general" or "the whole." The word means "universal" or "orthodox," or more generally, "pertaining to all humanity." The word is most often used to refer to a member of the Roman Catholic or Western Church after its separation from the Eastern Church, which took the title of "Orthodox." See: **Roman Catholicism.**

Chalcedon, Council of ■ A church council convened in A.D. 451 primarily because of the teachings of Eutyches (c. 375–454), a monk from Constantinople. Eutychianism, reacting to Nestorianism, declared that the incarnate Christ had only one nature, the divine—in other words, that Christ was not fully human. The Eastern emperor, Marcion, called the council, which brought together earlier statements of orthodoxy such as those made at the Council of Nicea (325), and issued a definitive statement of orthodox Christology: Christ is "perfect in Godhead and perfect in manhood, truly God and truly man." The council condemned monophysitism and reaffirmed the condemnation of Nestorianism. Roman Catholicism considers this to be the fourth ecumenical council. See: **Christology; Nicea, Council of; Nestorianism; Monophysitism.**

Charisma ■ From the Greek word for "gift." It is used to refer to a unique, special divine gift of spiritual significance to be used for the benefit of the faith. The term also refers to the gifts of the Holy Spirit as stated by Paul in 1 Corinthians 12:1–31; Galatians 5:22, 23.

Christ ■ From the Greek word *christos*, "the anointed one." The title designates Jesus as the Messiah. It translates the Hebrew word rendered "Messiah." In the OT, the term applied particularly to the High Priest (Lev. 4:3, 5, 16). The prophets were called *hoi christoi theou* "the anointed of God" (Ps. 105:15). In the NT, Jesus himself accepted the title three times (Matt. 16:16; Mark 14:61–62; John 4:26). The title was used by Jesus to speak of himself in John 17:3. See also: Matthew 1:17; 2:2, 4; Acts 2:31; Romans 7:4; 9:5; 15:19; 1 Corinthians 1:6. See: **Jesus, Messiah, Septuagint.**
See: J.A. Buell and O.Q. Hyder, *Jesus: God, Ghost or Guru?* (Zondervan, 1978); N. Geisler, *Christ: The Theme of the Bible* (Moody Press, 1968).

Christian ■ From the Greek words *Christos*, "the anointed one," "Christ," and *ian*, "like," "similar to." The word refers to one who lives a life like Jesus, and is the name by which followers of Jesus, the Christ, are generally known. It refers to one who believes in Jesus as the Christ, accepts Him as Savior and Lord, and seeks to live according to His teachings in the NT.

The name was first used in Antioch, according to Acts 11:26. The Christian is referred to by many names: disciple, a student of Jesus (Acts 9:1; 14:21); brother (Matt. 28:10; John 20:17; Acts 18:27; Rom. 8:29; 12:10; Heb. 2:11–12, 17; 1 Peter 3:8); saint (Eph. 2:19–22; Rom. 1:7; Phil. 1:1); believer (John 20:31; Acts 5:14; Rom. 3:22); follower of the Way (Acts 9:2; 19:9, 23; 22:4; 24:14, 22); Nazarene (Acts 24:5). See: **Disciple, Saint.**

Christian Churches/Churches of Christ (Independent) ■ Part of the Restoration Movement. Four men are generally considered founding fathers: Thomas and Alexander Campbell, Barton W. Stone, and Walter Scott.

The Christian Church/Churches of Christ (Independent) traces its roots to reform movements of the early 1800s. In 1831 Barton W. Stone's "Christians only" and the Campbell's "Reformers," or "Restorers," merged to form the "Restoration Movement," or the Christian Church (Disciples of Christ). Today one part—after two splits—is known as the Christian Church/ Churches of Christ. This group is in the midstream of evangelicalism, and holds to the following distinctives: immersion for the remission of sins as a condition for church membership, observance of the Lord's Supper each Sunday, no ecclesiastical structure above the elders of a local congregation, and a plurality of elders in each congregation. They accept the Bible as divinely inspired, alone and all-sufficient as the revelation of God for salvation and Christian living. They believe that contained in the NT is a basic pattern for the church, which is the duty of every faithful follower of Christ to restore and maintain. Some take a view close to baptismal regeneration; others are closer to Campbell's high view of baptism, but stop well short of making water baptism regenerative. In 1986 they had 5,671 congregations and a total membership of 1,074,834. See: **Church of Christ (Non-Instrumental); Disciples of Christ, Christian Church; Campbellite.**

See: L. Garrett, *The Stone-Campbell Movement: An Anecdotal History of Three Churches* (College Press, 1981); J.D. Murch, *Christians Only: A History of the Restoration Movement* (Standard Publishing, 1961); and M.W. Randall, *The Great Awakenings and the Restoration Movement* (College Press, 1983).

Christian Education ■ The discipline that provides a balance between the theories and the practices of Christian learning. In general, this discipline includes: (1) the nature of C.E. (definitions and the range of formal to informal instruction); (2) the foundations of C.E. (rudimentary truths from theology, to philosophy, educational psychology, and social science); (3) the process of C.E. (the dynamics of interpersonal relationships and the ministry of the Holy Spirit); and (4) the program of C.E. (recruitment/training, curriculum, and methodology). Christian education also supports the overarching goals of the Christian life, such as maturing in Christ while setting goals according to age-level appropriateness, holistic growth, and cross-cultural distinctiveness.

Specifically, Christian education should assist the individual learner in his faith pilgrimage: (1) to know the "what and why" of his belief in truth; (2) to utilize that truth to choose (among alternatives) a personal value system; and (3) to appropriate his value system to life in such a way that it will produce the "fruit" of godly character.

See: R.T. Habermas, "Gray Matters," in *Christianity Today* (August 7, 1987), pp. 23–25; G.R. Knight, *Philosophy and Education* (Andrews University Press, 1980); D.E. Miller, *Story and Context* (Abingdon, 1987); L.O. Richards, *A Theology of Christian Education* (Zondervan, 1975); A.E. Sanner and A.F. Harper, *Exploring Christian Education* (Beacon Hill Press, 1978); J.M. Stubblefield, *A Church Ministering to Adults* (Broadman, 1986); J. Wilhoit, *Christian Education and the Search for Meaning* (Baker, 1986); N. Wolterstorff, *Educating for Responsible Action* (Eerdmans, 1980).

Christian Evidences ▪ Apologetics and Christian evidences are often viewed as the same discipline. Occasionally, however, a distinction is made between apologetics as a philosophical discipline concerned with refuting non-Christian world views, and Christian evidences as historical and biblical evidences in favor of Christianity. Cornelius Van Til in *Apologetics* (Presbyterian and Reformed Publishing Co., 1980, p. 1) makes this distinction. See: **Apologetics.**

Christocentric ▪ A system of thought or practice in which Christ has the central or dominant place; centering theologically on Christ.

Christology ▪ From the Greek words *Christos*, "Christ" and *logos*, "the rational study of." In theology, the study of the doctrine of Christ centering on His life, person, works, faith, significance, and divinity.

Christology studies Jesus revealed in Messianic prophecy, the Incarnation, and His ministry as Prophet, Priest, and King. It attempts to show that God is present and active in Jesus, the mediator between humanity and the Father. The aim of Christology is to evoke a personal relationship with the divine reality of Jesus as the Christ. See: Acts 2:36; 5:42; 9:22; 18:5, 28. See: **Jesus, Lord, Messiah, Son of Man.**

See: G.C. Berkouwer, *The Person of Christ* (Eerdmans, 1954); H.E. Brunner, *The Mediator* (Westminster Press, 1934); L. Cerfaux, *Christ in the Theology of St. Paul* (Herder and Herder, 1959); R.N. Longenecker, *The Christology of Early Jewish Christianity* (London: SCM Press, 1970); H.R. Mackintosh, *The Doctrine of the Person of Christ* (Edinburgh: T. and T. Clark, 1914).

Church ■ From the Greek *kyriakon*, which means "the Lord's house." In the NT, the Greek word *ekklesia* is translated "church." The Church is called out of the world, but not in any radical sense of separation. The Church is to be holy, set apart to serve God (2 Thess. 2:13; Col. 3:12) and to be a holy priesthood (1 Peter 2:5). The Church is to be one body (John 17). The Church is to witness to Christ, who called us out of darkness and made us the light of the world (1 Peter 2:9). As individual Christians and as the Body of Christ we must be in the world—as salt, light, and leaven—but not of the world, not participants in the evil found there.

In Matthew 18:17; Acts 15:41; Romans 16:16; 1 Corinthians 4:17; 7:17; 14:33; and Colossians 4:15, the word refers to a local body of believers in Christ. In Matthew 16:18; Acts 20:28; 1 Corinthians 12:28; 15:9; and Ephesians 1:22, it refers to the Body of Christ, the Church in the larger sense. The Church was intended to be the instrument for establishing the kingdom of God on earth, a kingdom "whose architect and builder is God" (Heb. 11:10).

The Church of Jesus Christ was born at Pentecost, as recorded in Acts (see all of Acts 2). The Church has three grand tasks that are never complete and embody its very reason for existing: worship, praising God in all aspects of life; making disciples, teaching its own to mature in Christ; and evangelism, teaching others the good news of God's love. See: **Ecclesiology.**

See: F.J.A. Hort, *Christian Ecclesia* (Macmillan, 1900); H. Kung, *The Church* (Sheed and Ward, 1967); P.H. Miller, *The New Testament Church: Its Teaching and Its Scriptures* (Westminster, 1932); W. Robinson, *The Biblical Doctrine of the Church* (The Bethany Press, 1960); R.L. Saucy, *The Church in God's Program* (Moody, 1972).

Church of Christ (Non-Instrumental) ■ Part of the Restoration Movement. Four men are generally considered founding fathers: Thomas and Alexander Campbell, Barton W. Stone, and Walter Scott. The main emphases in this group are a strong emphasis on the eldership as the leaders of a local congregation and no instrumental music in worship, a stance much further to the right than either of the other two groups descended from the Restoration Movement. See: **Christian Churches/Churches of Christ (Independent); Disciples of Christ, Christian Church.**

See: L. Garrett, *The Stone-Campbell Movement: An Anecdotal History of Three Churches* (College Press, 1981).

Church of Christ, Scientist ■ Also known as Christian Science. A group founded by Mary Baker (Glover Patterson) Eddy in 1879. Her books, particularly *Science and Health with Key to the Scriptures*, are the authoritative interpretation of the Bible for members of this group. For Christian Scientists, the *Key to the Scriptures* is above the Bible in authority; it tells them how to properly interpret the Bible.

For the Church of Christ, Scientist, God is an eternal principle, not a Personal Being. Of Jesus it is said: "If there had never existed such a person as the Galilean Prophet, it would make no difference to me." (*The First Church of Christ, Scientist, and Miscellany*, pp. 318–319). The group holds to a type of idealism that believes sin and death are unreal. They also believe humans can avoid sickness and do not need atonement.

See: W.E. Biederwolf, *The Unvarnished Facts About Christian Science* (Eerdmans); W.R. Martin, *The Kingdom of the Cults* (Bethany House Publishers, 1985); W.R. Martin and N.H. Klann, *The Christian Science Myth* (Zondervan, 1955); G. Milmine, *The Life of Mary Baker G. Eddy and the History of Christian Science* (Baker, 1971).

Clergy ■ From the Greek *kleros*, meaning "one's portion," "one's lot," having to do with how a person was selected for a position. In Acts 1:26, the disciples "drew lots for them, and the lot fell to Matthias; and he was numbered with the eleven apostles." In early Church history "clergy" referred to all the members of a Christian community. By Tertullian's day (c. 155–220) it was used of ordained bishops, priests and deacons. Today it refers to ordained ministers of the church, in contrast to the laity. The modern strict distinction between clergy and laity is not supported in the NT, though there is support for a paid ministry (Luke 10:7). See: **Laity; Ministry; Priest; Priesthood of All Believers; Rabbi, Rabboni.**

See: C.S. Calian, *Today's Pastor in Tomorrow's World* (Hawthorn Books, 1977); L. Peabody, *Secular Work Is Full-time Service* (Christian Literature Crusade, 1974); T.L. Miethe, "Ministry and the Christian," in *The New Christian's Guide to Following Jesus* (Bethany House Publishers, 1984), pp. 103–110.

Communion ▪ From the Latin *communis*, "common." It refers to a meal shared because of common faith and discipline. It is a Christian ordinance in which bread and wine are partaken of as a commemoration of the death, burial and resurrection of Christ (Acts 2:42). Patterned after Jesus' example in Luke 22:14–20. See: **Lord's Supper, Eucharist.**

See: E.F. Kevan, *The Lord's Supper* (London: Evangelical Press, 1955); A. Murray, *The Lord's Table* (Christian Literature Crusade, 1962).

Communion of the Saints ▪ The term "the communion of the saints," part of the Apostles' Creed, signifies the common bond shared by all believers through the Holy Spirit. It implies not only a common faith but a common purpose and goal: becoming Christlike. The phrase also reflects the Greek word *koinonia*, which means communion, fellowship and sharing in common (1 Cor. 10:16). *Koinonia* is an intimate fellowship made possible by the Holy Spirit.

Roman Catholic and Anglican interpreters have used this article of the creed to develop the doctrine of saying prayers for the dead, though in no way does Scripture support this interpretation. See: **Apostles' Creed.**

Complex Question, Fallacy of ▪ "Have you stopped cheating at cards?" Obviously something is funny about this question: it does not allow a simple yes or no reply. Instead, it consists of several questions rolled into a single question. Such questions presuppose that a definite answer has already been given to a prior question that was not even asked. The first question might have been, "Do you cheat at cards?" and if the person said, "No," there would have been no need to ask the second part of the question. See: **Logical Fallacies.**

Concupiscence ▪ From the Greek *epithumia*, "a desire, craving, longing"; and the Latin, *concupiscere*, "to desire." It is used in the NT three times: Romans 7:8; Colossians 3:5; and 1 Thessalonians 4:5. The word refers to a deep longing for something, and is often used in a negative way with a meaning similar to "covet," or "lust," although it can be interpreted otherwise. In Roman Catholic theology, following Augustine (354–430), concupiscence was viewed as a part of the necessarily sinful human nature and its tendencies toward vice rather than virtue—a result of original sin.

See: T.L. Miethe, "Augustine and Concupiscence" in *Augustinian Bibliography, 1970–1980: With Essays on the Fundamentals of Augustinian Scholarship* (Greenwood Press, 1982), pp. 195–209.

Congregationalism ■ From the Latin *congregare*, "to congregate," "to collect into a flock or group." A form of church government that recognizes no authority or structure above that of the leadership of a local congregation of believers. A church of this type is usually overseen by elders. Groups following this type of church government say this is the only form in the NT. See: **Bishop, Church, Elders, Polity, Presbyterians.**

See: D.L. Norbie, *New Testament Church Organization* (Chicago: Interest, 1955); W. Robinson, *The Biblical Doctrine of the Church* (The Bethany Press, 1960).

Constantinople, Councils of ■ The first council at Constantinople was held in A.D. 381. It is considered the second ecumenical council of the Church, and helped to further establish orthodox Christology. It condemned Arianism and Apollinarianism and the heresy of Macedonius, who denied the perfect Godhead of the Holy Spirit. This council added to the Nicene Creed the words, "and in the Holy Ghost, the Lord and Giver of Life, who proceeds from the Father, who together with the Father and the Son is worshiped and glorified, who spoke by the prophets."

The second council held at Constantinople (553) is considered the fifth ecumenical council. The third council—considered the sixth ecumenical council—was held in 680–681. It condemned monotheletism ("one-will-ism") by stating that there were two wills in Christ, the human being subject to the divine. It condemned Pope Honorius I. The fourth council (the eighth ecumenical council) was held in 869. It excommunicated Photius, the patriarch of Constantinople, and also confirmed the Formula of Hormisdas. This was the last general council to be held in the East. See: **Arianism, Apollinarianism, Nicene Creed.**

Consubstantiation ■ From the Latin *consubstantialis* meaning "with or of the same nature and kind." This is the view that in communion the bread and wine are not transformed into the

actual body and blood of Christ, but that the flesh and blood coexist with and are present "in, with, and under" the bread and wine. This is a doctrine developed by Martin Luther (1483–1546) in The Augsburg Confession (1530) and The Articles of Smalkald (1539). It occupies middle ground between the Roman Catholic doctrine of transubstantiation, the belief that the bread and wine become the actual body and blood of Christ, and the teaching of Swiss Reformer Ulrich Zwingli, which emphasized that communion was a memorial and that Christ was not present at communion in any unique way. The Roman Catholic Council of Trent (1543–1547) officially rejected consubstantiation. See: **Communion, Eucharist, Lord's Supper, Lutheranism, Transubstantiation.**

Contingent ■ An object or being which is "contingent" is dependent (supported on all sides) on something or someone outside itself for its very being, that is, in every way it exists. In theology, contingency is used in the arguments for the existence of God. See: **Cosmological Argument, Philosophy.**

Contrition ■ One's sense of sorrow or remorse for one's sin. Not just sorrow "for sorrow's sake," contrition comes from a deep love for God and an understanding of the gravity of one's sin. Contrition is seen in David's prayer for forgiveness (Ps. 51) and the parable of the Prodigal Son (Luke 15:11–32).

Corban ■ From the Greek *korban*, "an offering," which is used in two ways. It was a Hebrew term related to the sacrifices, whether blood offering or not. It is also used to signify a gift given to God (Mark 7:11). The term was basically used to mean any offering given to the Temple.

Cosmological Argument ■ One of the philosophical arguments used as a proof for the existence of God. The argument moves from the effect to the cause of the universe. Early forms of the argument are found in the writings of Plato (427–347 B.C.) and Aristotle (384–322 B.C.), who concluded that the universe has a Prime Mover causing everything else to be. Thomas Aquinas (1224/5–1274) developed the argument in his *Summa Theologica*, perhaps the best known form of the argument. The argument is based on the principle that every effect must have a cause.

A summary of the cosmological argument can be stated as follows: (1) Limited, changing being(s)—people, animals, the world—exist. (2) The present existence of these limited, changing beings is caused by another. (3) There cannot be an infinite chain of causes of being; (4) therefore, there is a first Cause of the present existence of these beings. (5) The first Cause must be infinite, necessary, eternal, simple, unchangeable and one. (6) This first uncaused Cause is identical with the God of the Judeo-Christian tradition.

This is by no means a complete discussion of the argument. It still is debated by philosophers and theologians. See: **God, Arguments for the Existence of; Moral Argument; Ontological Argument; Teleological Argument.**

See: D.R. Burrill, *The Cosmological Argument: A Spectrum of Opinion* (Doubleday, 1967); N.L. Geisler, "Cosmological Arguments" and "The Cosmological Argument Reevaluated," in *Philosophy of Religion* (Zondervan, 1974), pp. 163–226; B.R. Reichenbach, *The Cosmological Argument: A Reassessment* (Charles C. Thomas, 1972).

Cosmology ■ In the discipline of philosophy, cosmology is a branch of metaphysics that studies the origin and nature of the universe as an orderly system. Its main concerns are contingency, necessity, eternity, limitations and formal laws of the world, and the nature and relationship of space and time. Though a more specific discipline, it cannot be sharply distinguished from the fields of metaphysics, ontology, or natural science. After Immanuel Kant (1724–1804) there has been a tendency to merge the topics treated in cosmology with those of metaphysics. See: **Metaphysics, Ontology, Philosophy.**

Covenant ■ A contract or pact made between two people or parties. Specifically in theology, it is an agreement between God and man in which God promises to bless those who accept and commit themselves to Him and express this by living according to the contract. In the OT God made covenants with His chosen person or people—Adam, Abraham, Jacob, or his descendants, the Israelites. In the NT God made a covenant (in Greek, *diatheke*) with the Church through His Son Jesus. The NT is often referred to as "The New Covenant."

Covenant Theology ■ A type of theology that sees the relationship between God and man as governed by agreements. Based on the understanding of covenants in the Bible, this concept was developed during the Reformation by such theologians as Ulrich Zwingli (1484–1531), John Calvin (1509–1564), and Olevianus (1536–1587). Though prominent in the Reformed tradition, covenant theology is not exclusive to that viewpoint. According to covenant theology, Adam failed to keep the first covenant, in which God had promised eternal life if Adam kept the divine commands. Because of this failure God made a second covenant, promising forgiveness and eternal life to all who accept the sacrifice of Jesus.

See: L. Berkhof, *Systematic Theology* (Eerdmans, 1941); C. Hodge, *Systematic Theology*, 3 vols. (Eerdmans, 1960).

Covetousness ■ A strong desire for an object that usually belongs to someone else, a serious sin in Scripture (see: Luke 12:15; Rom. 1:29; 1 Tim. 6:10; 2 Peter 2:14). In Roman Catholic theology, one of the Seven Deadly Sins. See: **Sins, Seven Deadly.**

Creation ■ Creation is the Christian teaching based on Genesis 1–2 that God formed the universe and everything in it by a direct act: "In the beginning, God created the heavens and the earth" (Gen. 1:1). Many interpret this creation to be "ex nihilo," which means that God spoke the world into existence "out of nothing." The Fourth Lateran Council (1215) made the term "ex nihilo" an official part of the teaching of the Church. See: **Teleological Argument.**

Creationism ■ In theology, creationism is the idea that the human spirit is separately created and presented by God at conception (or birth). Today the term is frequently used in reference to the ongoing creation/evolution debate. Creationists are a group of Christian theologians, philosophers, and scientists (Henry Morris, Duane Gish, Dean Kenyon and others) as well as some scientists from other religions (N. C. Wickramasinghe, for example) who defend creationism—that God created the universe by definite action, rather than by a naturalistic evolutionary process. They also hold that this view is a viable scientific alternative to evolution. See: **Evolution.**

See: N.L. Geisler, *The Creator in the Courtroom: "Scopes II"* (Mott Media, 1982); N. Macbeth, *Darwin Retried: An Appeal to Reason* (Gambit, 1971); H.M. Morris and G.E. Parker, *What Is Creation Science?* (Creation-Life Publishers, Inc., 1982); C.B. Thaxton, W.L. Bradley and R.L. Olsen, *The Mystery of Life's Origin: Reassessing Current Theories* (Philosophical Library, 1984); A.E. Wilder Smith, *Man's Origin, Man's Destiny* (Bethany House Publishers, 1968).

Cross ▪ From the Greek *stauros* and the Latin *crux*. Primarily a pointed, upright beam or stake with a second lateral stake, the cross was an instrument of punishment. There were basically four types of crosses: (1) "Crux simplex," a single pale or stake to which the victim was tied or impaled. (2) "Crux commissa," which was shaped like the capital letter "T." Some believe this to be derived from the mystic symbol Tau, the initial of the Chaidena god Tammuz. (3) "Crux decussata," shaped like the letter "X." It is also known as the St. Andrew's cross, because it is believed he was killed on this type of cross. (4) "Crux immissa," the traditional shape, believed to be the cross on which Jesus was crucified.

Crucifixion ▪ The most cruel, degrading punishment possible at the time of Jesus. First used by the Phoenicians and Carthaginians, crucifixion was later adopted and used extensively by the Romans. This punishment was reserved for slaves, provincials, and the most vile criminals in the Roman Empire.

Before being impaled, the victim was stripped naked and scourged with a flagellum, a whip with rock and bone bound to leather thongs, an act which tore the skin and muscle down to the bone. Often, victims to be crucified were disemboweled during the scourging process, yet their bodies were still publicly displayed on the cross. After being scourged, the victim was forced to carry the cross-beam (the "patibulum") of his cross outside the city to the place of crucifixion. During the process, the victim was led by a herald with the "title," the written accusation against the victim. Upon reaching the place of execution, the victim was laid on the ground, the beam placed under his shoulders, and his arms or hands tied and/or nailed to it. This cross-beam was then attached to an upright beam just high enough so the victim's feet could not touch the ground. The victim's feet were then tied and/or nailed to the upright beam; the main weight of the body was supported by a peg projecting from the upright beam called a "sedile."

The victim was usually left to die of starvation or exhaustion, though sometimes the death process was hastened by *crurifragium*, breaking the victim's legs. This hastened the death process; during scourging the diaphragm was usually damaged, forcing the victim to physically lift himself in order to breathe. Breaking the victim's legs prevented this, so *crurifragium*, in effect, caused suffocation.

See: L. Morris, *The Story of the Cross* (Eerdmans, 1957); J.M. Stalker, *The Trial and Death of Jesus Christ* (Zondervan, 1966); W.R. Wilson, *The Execution of Jesus: A Judicial, Literary and Historical Investigation* (Scribner's Sons, 1970).

Deacon ■ From the Greek *diakonos*, "servant," and *diakoneo*, "to serve." The record of the first deacons in the early Church is found in Acts 6:1–6, though they are not called by that name. The seven were chosen "in order to serve tables" so the twelve Apostles would not have "to neglect the word of God" (v. 2). These were to be "men of good reputation, full of the Spirit and of wisdom" (v. 3).

The qualifications for the office are found in 1 Timothy 3:8–13. "Deacons likewise must be men of dignity, not double-tongued, or addicted to much wine or fond of sordid gain, but holding to the mystery of the faith with a clear conscience" (v. 8). They are to "first be tested" before they can serve to see "if they are beyond reproach" (v. 9). They are to be "husbands of only one wife, and good managers of their children and their own households" (v. 12).

Deacons were to help with the administration of the social needs of the church, looking after the needs of the widows and orphans by ensuring that they were treated fairly in the distribution of resources. Certainly their role was much more involved than just serving communion, which is their sole duty in some denominations today.

Deaconess ■ A female deacon. In Romans 16:1, the word *diakoneo* describes the deaconess Phoebe. Many simply avoid the fact that a woman is given the title of a deacon. The text 1 Timothy 3:11 ("Women must likewise be dignified, not malicious gossips, but temperate, faithful in all things") may also refer to deacons, although some have interpreted this as referring to the wives of male deacons. In the early Church, deaconesses were intermediaries between clergy and the women of the congregation. The office died out or was suppressed in the eleventh century, but has been revived in modern times.

See: J.N.D. Kelly, *The Pastoral Epistles* (Harper & Row, 1963), pp. 83–84; R.A. Tucker and W. Liefeld, *Daughters of the Church: Women and Ministry from New Testament Times to the Present* (Zondervan, 1987).

Dead Sea Scrolls

Dead Sea Scrolls ■ The popular name of the manuscripts found in 1947 and later in caves west of the Dead Sea. These scrolls are divided into four basic groups: (1) The Qumran library, discovered in and around Wadi Qumran, northwest of the Dead Sea, is a collection of more than four hundred books, about one hundred of which are biblical. All the books of the OT are represented, except Esther. The biblical manuscripts, written in the centuries just before Christ or in the first century after Christ, attest to at least three distinct text-types: the Masoretic text, probably of Babylonian origin; the text underlying the Greek language OT (LXX), probably of Egyptian origin; and a text closely related to the Samarian Pentateuch, probably of Palestinian origin.

(2) The texts of the Bar-Kokhba war were discovered in 1952 in caves in the Wadi Murabba'at, about 18 km south of Qumran. The most important of these manuscripts belong to the era when Murabba'at was occupied by a garrison of Mimeon Ben Kosebah, known also as Bar-Kokhba, the leader of the second Jewish revolt against Rome. The find includes two letters written by the leader himself. Also found in these caves were fragments of Hebrew Scripture and a fragmentary copy of a Greek version of the Minor Prophets, using a text similar to that of Justin Martyr.

(3) The texts found north of the Kidron Valley at Khirbet Mird, formerly a Christian monastery, were unearthed by members of the Ta'amire tribe of Bedouin. This collection dates between the fifth and eighth centuries A.D., and contains several biblical texts in Greek, including fragments of uncial codices of Wisdom, Mark, John and Acts. There were also fragments of Joshua, Luke, John, Acts and Colossians written in Palestinian Syriac.

(4) The texts found at Masada during excavations between 1963–1965 had been placed there before Masada was stormed by the Romans in early A.D. 74. They included portions of Psalms, Leviticus, Ecclesiasticus, and Jubilees. All were written in Hebrew.

See: F.F. Bruce, *Biblical Exegesis in the Qumran Texts* (Tyndale, 1960), and *Second Thoughts on the Dead Sea Scrolls* (Eerdmans, 1961); F.M. Cross,

Ancient Library of Qumran and Modern Biblical Studies (London: Duckworth, 1958); J.T. Milik, *Ten Years of Discovery in the Wilderness of Judea* (London: SCM Press, 1959).

Death ▪ A permanent cessation of all vital functions, the end of life. Today, because of modern technology, death is usually defined as a cessation of all brain functions without the possibility of resuscitation. In theology, there are two deaths: (1) physical death, and (2) spiritual death, the final state of the wicked, an "eternal death" or eternal punishment in hell (Rev. 2:11; 20:6, 14; 21:8). Christians are also mortal. They die the first or physical death. But because they die "in Christ" (1 Thess. 4:16), they inherit "eternal life" (Rom. 6:22–23; 1 Cor. 15:20; Col. 1:12). Hebrews 2:14 says that it is Satan "who has the power of death." See: **Eternal Life, Eternity, Hell.**

See: D.T. Holden, *Death Shall Have No Dominion* (St. Louis: Bethany Press, 1971); J.A. Motyer, *After Death: A Sure and Certain Hope?* (Westminster Press, 1966).

Decrees, Eternal ▪ A theological term for the comprehensive plans of God that were made in eternity (1 Cor. 2:7; Eph. 1:4, 11; 2 Tim. 1:9; Heb. 4:3; 1 Peter 1:20). The Westminster Shorter Catechism says: "The decrees of God are his eternal purpose, according to the counsel of his will, whereby, for his own glory, he hath foreordained whatsoever comes to pass." The doctrine of God's eternal decree is a concern primarily in Reformed theology, and is related to predestination and God's sovereignty, though some theologians not of the Reformed tradition speak of the "Scheme of Redemption." God decreed, or planned, before the foundations of the world, but in a way that allows for both God's sovereignty and a more Arminian understanding of human free will. See: **Predestination, Election, Reformed Theology, Sovereignty of God.**

See: L. Berkhof, *Systematic Theology* (Eerdmans, 1941); R. Milligan, *Exposition and Defense of the Scheme of Redemption As It Is Revealed and Taught in the Holy Scriptures* (Gospel Advocate Co.).

Deism ▪ From the Greek *theos*, "God," which is transliterated into Latin as "Deus." The earliest known use of the term "Deism" was in 1564. Generally, it is belief in a God who created the world out of nothing but now is uninvolved with the world or its events. He governs through unchangeable, eternal laws, and is in no way imminent in creation. This religious philosophy developed in England in the early part of the seventeenth century and is associated with the Enlightenment or Age of Reason.

Deists were strong in America in the 1700s and taught the superiority of human reason over faith, revelation and miracles. They opposed any established church and believed in religious freedom and the separation of church and state, as did many Christians of that day. Several of the founding fathers of America were deists, among them, Thomas Jefferson (1743–1826), Thomas Paine (1737–1809), Ethan Allen (1738–1789), Benjamin Franklin (1706–1790) and George Washington (1732–1799).

See: J. Collins, *God in Modern Philosophy* (Henry Regnery, 1959); C. Leslie, *A Short and Easie Method with the Deists, Wherein the Certainty of the Christian Religion Is Demonstrated by Infallible Proof from Four Rules* (London: Strahan, 1711); J. Orr, *English Deism: Its Roots and Fruits* (Eerdmans, 1934).

Demons ▪ From the Greek *daimon*, "a divinity," and the Latin *daemon*, "evil spirit." Demons are evil supernatural beings who are servants of Satan. Some consider them to be fallen angels (Matt. 25:41; 2 Peter 2:4; Rev. 12:7–9). Others consider them the offspring of angels and antediluvian women (Gen. 6:2; Jude 6). In the NT they are often referred to as "unclean spirits" (Mark 1:24–27; 5:2–3; 7:26; 9:25; Acts 5:16; 8:7; Rev. 16:13). Demons acknowledged Christ; in the Gospel of Mark demons say: "What do we have to do with You, Jesus of Nazareth? Have You come to destroy us? I know who You are—the Holy One of God!" (1:24). See: Matthew 8:31; 12:28; Mark 1:23ff.; 3:11, 22; 5:1ff.; 9:17ff.; 1 Corinthians 10:20ff.

See: Wm. M. Alexander, *Demonology in the New Testament* (Edinburgh: T. and T. Clark, 1902); J.W. Montgomery, *Demon Possession: A Medical, Historical, Anthropological and Theological Symposium* (Bethany House Publishers, 1976); M.F. Unger, *Demons in the World Today: A Study of Occultism in the Light of God's Word* (Tyndale, 1971); J. St. Wright, *Christianity and the Occult* (Moody, 1972) and *Mind, Man and Spirits* (Zondervan, 1972).

Demythologizing ▪ To reinterpret mythological forms (forms lacking factual basis or historical validity) in order to uncover the meaning underlying them. Rudolf Bultmann (1884–1976), a German NT scholar at the University of Marburg, is famous for labeling the supernatural elements of Scripture—the virgin birth, Christ's deity, the resurrection, the Trinity, the Second Coming—as myths. Bultmann believed that the modern man who reads by Edison's light bulb can no longer accept a scientifically outdated world view, that is, the world view of the Bible. He accepted the Newtonian scientific world view as definitive.

See: M. Ashcraft, *Rudolf Bultmann* (Word, 1972); R. Bultmann, "New Testament and Mythology" in *Kerygma and Myth* (Harper & Row, 1961); G.E. Ladd, *Rudolf Bultmann* (InterVarsity Press, 1964).

Depravity, Total ■ From the Latin *depravare*, "to be wicked"; the theological discussion of the state of human beings after the Fall and the teaching that human sinfulness affects the whole of one's nature, every human faculty or function.

Views differ regarding exactly how "total" total depravity is. Some theologians say that it does *not* mean "that depraved people cannot or do not perform actions that are good in either man's or God's sight." (See: C. C. Ryrie "Depravity, Total" in W. A. Elwell's *Evangelical Dictionary of Theology*, Baker, 1984, p. 312.) It is crucial to stress, however, that such good actions cannot gain favor with God for salvation. Others teach a "double death," as in High Calvinism, a view much less optimistic about human ability to do real good in any situation, not just regarding salvation. (See: J. Owen's *The Death of Death in the Death of Christ*, London: Banner of Truth Trust, 1959.) Note that neither side believes human beings can save themselves.

In the Catholic tradition, following Augustine (354–430), depravity is thought to be inherited through the parents, passed on by sexual union and childbirth. See: Mark 7:20–23; Romans 1:28; Ephesians 4:18; Hebrews 9:14. See: **Calvinism; Calvinism, Five Points of; TULIP.**

Determinism ■ From the Latin *de* plus *terminus*, "end." In philosophy, the idea that all that happens is causally fixed and cannot happen any other way; the belief that all events in the universe, including human actions, are controlled by previous conditions. Many forms of Calvinism are variations of theological determinism. See: **Calvinism, Freedom of the Will.**

Devil ■ From the Greek *diabolos*, meaning "slanderer," "liar." See: **Satan.**

Disciple ■ From the Greek *mathetes* and the Latin *discipulus*, literally "a learner." Often used to refer to the twelve Apostles (Matt. 10:1; Luke 22:11), it is also one of the names given to Christians in the NT; the meaning is that Christians are learners or followers of Jesus.

In the Bible the word "disciple" implies a personal adherence, a living out of, the teachings of the Master Teacher. In the NT one is known as Jesus' disciple by abiding in His Word (John 8:31; 13:35; 15:8). In Acts, those who have believed upon Him and confessed Him are called disciples (6:1–2, 7; 14:20–22, 28; 15:10; 19:1).

Disciples of Christ, Christian Church ■ The Disciples of Christ traces its roots to the Restoration Movement, and to four men generally considered founding fathers: Thomas and Alexander Campbell, Barton W. Stone, and Walter Scott. The denomination sprang from two main groups: (1) The "Christians only" group of Stone, which came into existence during the Cane Ridge Kentucky Revival of 1801–1803; (2) The "Reformers" or "Disciples" of the Campbells. The Campbell movement began in 1809 in Pennsylvania. The groups led by Stone and the Campbells merged in 1831 to become the "Restoration Movement," and today one part—two splits later—is still known as The Christian Church (Disciples of Christ).

Until surpassed by the Mormons, this denomination was the largest indigenous American religious body well into this century. Originally the group had two strong emphases: (a) restoring "simple evangelical Christianity" and (b) attempting to unite various denominations under the Lordship of Jesus as the Christ, the Son of God, and the inspiration of the Bible. Campbell attempted to avoid both unity-at-all-costs and a rigid exclusivism that would prevent all unity.

For much of the Disciples' history, the following were almost universal practices: communion every Sunday, immersion for the remission of sins as a condition for church membership, congregational local autonomy, and a plurality of elders. Today, most congregations practice open membership and accept nonimmersed believers into fellowship as full members. As a denomination, they are found in the center of mainline liberal American Protestantism and place almost no emphasis on restoration. During the last twenty-five years, the Disciples have experienced sharp numerical decline; in 1986 the Disciples had 4,227 congregations, with a total membership in North America of 1,111,357, a drop of more than one hundred thousand since 1980. See: **Campbellite, Christian Church/Church of Christ (Independent), Church of Christ (Non-Instrumental).**

See: H. Adams, *Why I Am a Disciple of Christ* (Beacon Press, 1957); W.E. Garrison and A.T. DeGroot, *The Disciples of Christ: A History* (The Bethany Press, 1958); L.G. McAllister and W.E. Tucker, *Journey in Faith: A History of the Christian Church (Disciples of Christ)* (The Bethany Press, 1975); and K.L. Teegarden, *We Call Ourselves Disciples* (The Bethany Press, 1975).

Dispensationalism ■ From the Greek *oikonomia*, the management of a household or of household affairs (Luke 16:1–2). In theology, a system of interpreting the Bible that divides how God works into different periods He administers (Eph. 1:10; 3:2, 9; Col. 1:25) on different bases. It involves a literal interpretation of Scripture where every figure has a strict, literal meaning; a distinction between Israel and the Church; and a premillennial, pretribulational eschatology.

Dispensationalists commonly understand Paul to have mentioned three such periods: (1) what was then past (Col. 1:25–26), (2) his present (Eph. 3:2), and (3) what was to him the future (Eph. 1:10). These three periods, they say, require two more: an era before the Law, which is divided into (4) one before the Fall, and (5) one after the Fall. The normal number of dispensations then becomes seven with (6) one after Noah's flood and (7) one with the call of Abraham.

Divorce ■ The legal dissolution of a marriage. In the OT, teaching about divorce is found in Deuteronomy 24:1–4; in the NT, in Matthew 19:3–12 (also 5:32) and Mark 10:2–12. While there is no question that God intended marriage to last for a lifetime (Rom. 7:1–3; 1 Cor. 7:10), the evangelical Christian community disagrees if and when divorce and/or remarriage is permissible.

It would seem from passages like Matthew 5:32, "for the cause of unchastity," and 19:9, "for immorality," that divorce is permissible on those grounds. In 1 Corinthians 7:15, Paul seems to allow divorce at least in some circumstances as a result of desertion (see also v. 11).

The Church has an obligation to minister to families in a way that builds strong relationships—we often do more to separate families than to unite them. People should find in the Church models of love and faithfulness, and the Church should provide quality marriage counseling for families in need. The sin of divorce is no different from any other sin: When a marriage ends in failure the Church has an obligation to minister to the divorced person, striving to meet the needs of sinners with a view toward restoring them in their relationship with God.

See: J.E. Adams, *Marriage, Divorce and Remarriage in the Bible* (Presbyterian and Reformed, 1980); G.R. Collins, *Make More of Your Marriage* (Word, 1976); J. Murray, *Divorce* (Baker, 1961); H. Norman Wright, *Communication: Key to Your Marriage* (Regal Books, 1974).

Docetism ■ From the Greek *dokein*, "to appear," "to seem." Docetism teaches that the humanity of Jesus was not real; He was a divine being who only seemed to have a human body. The belief was widespread among those who held that Christ could not suffer and still be Divine, and also among those who believed that Christ's having a material body would have tainted Him with sin. Docetism was opposed by the framers of the Apostles' and Nicene Creeds and soundly defeated at the Council of Chalcedon in 451, where it was affirmed that Jesus was "truly God and truly man." See: **Apostles' Creed; Chalcedon, Council of; Nicene Creed.**

Doctrine ■ From the Greek *didache* and the Latin *doctrina*, meaning "teaching," or "teacher." A principle, or a body of principles, in a branch of knowledge or system of belief. In theology, that which is taught as a formal truth or belief of the faith. See: Matthew 7:28; Mark 4:2; Romans 16:17; Titus 1:9; and Revelation 2:14–15.

Dogma ■ From a Greek word meaning "decree," "ordinance," "decision," or "command" (Luke 2:1; Acts 16:4; 17:7; Eph. 2:15; Col. 2:14; Heb. 11:23). It came to mean a doctrinal statement expressing the official position of the Church. Because of certain abuses in Church history, the word has come to have a negative connotation. See: **Doctrine.**

Donatism ■ A separatist movement centering around Donatus, bishop of Carthage (313–347), in fourth-century Africa. Donatists had a high view of the role of the priest in the sacraments and a great respect for every word of Scripture as the Word of God. They considered Christians who had surrendered the Scriptures under persecution to the Romans to be heretics. Donatism grew out of the teachings of Tertullian (c. 155–220) and Cyprian (c. 200–258). Donatists survived until the seventh century.

Dort, Synod of ■ An international church assembly held in the Netherlands from 1618–1619 to treat theological issues within the Reformed Church. It formulated the Reformed position on election, and dealt with such issues as the control of the church by the state, humanism, and predestination. See: **Remonstrance.**

Doxology ■ From the Greek word *doxologia*, meaning "glory." One form is known as the *Gloria Patri* or "Lesser Doxology": "Glory be to the Father, and to the Son, and to the Holy Ghost: As it was in the beginning, is now, and ever shall be, world without end. Amen." This "Lesser Doxology" is often used as part of the worship service in churches that have a more formal, or high, liturgy, such as Lutheran and Anglican churches. One form of the doxology is used in worship services of many denominations: "Praise God from who all blessings flow; Praise him, all creatures here below; Praise him above, ye heavenly host: Praise Father, Son, and Holy Ghost. Amen."

Dualism ■ From the Latin *duo*, "two." The idea that reality has two fundamental parts or principles, often seen as opposing factors, such as matter and spirit or good and evil. Theological dualism is the belief that there are two gods fighting for control of the universe. See: **Manichaeism, Zoroastrianism.**

Eastern Orthodox ■ The name given to the Eastern (Greek) churches that broke in A.D. 1054 from the Western (Roman) churches in what is known as "the Great Schism." The Eastern Church was centered in Constantinople and headed by patriarchs; the Western church, centered in Rome, remained under the pope. The Eastern Church considers itself the first Christian Church. Originally there were five Patriarchates in the Orthodox Church: Constantinople, Alexandria, Antioch, Jerusalem, and Cyprus. Each traced its origin to one of the twelve Apostles. Today, several divisions exist within the Eastern Orthodox Church, mainly along national lines: Albania, Bulgaria, Rumania, Russia, Poland and Finland, for example, each has its own Orthodox Church. Most of these have their own patriarch, or head.

The Eastern Orthodox Church differs from the Roman Catholic Church on several points: (1) It does not recognize the Roman pope as infallible or as a supreme authority. (2) It believes that the Holy Spirit proceeds only from the Father; the Catholic Church, holding to the Nicene Creed, teaches that the Holy Spirit proceeds from both Father and Son. (3) It believes in heaven and hell, but not purgatory. (4) It does not believe in the Immaculate Conception; Mary's sin was purged at the Annunciation. (5) It does not believe in the physical assumption of the Virgin Mary. (6) Its priests may marry. (7) The laity partake of both the wine and leavened bread during communion. See: **Immaculate Conception, Purgatory, Roman Catholicism.**

See: W. Niesel, "The Gospel and the Orthodox Church," in *The Gospel and the Churches: A Comparison of Catholicism, Orthodoxy, and Protestantism* (Westminster, 1962); S. Runciman, *The Great Church in Captivity* (Cambridge: The University Press, 1968); A.P. Stanley, *Lectures on the History of the Eastern Church* (London: Murray, 1884).

Easy Believism ▪ A modern term that refers to the teaching that all a person needs to do to be saved is to believe. Easy believism expects no real-life commitment to follow from faith. See: **Disciple.**

See: G.R. Collins, *Beyond Easy Believism* (Word, 1982); Dietrich Bonhoeffer, *The Cost of Discipleship* (Macmillan, 1963).

Ebionite ▪ Probably from the Greek word *ebyonim*, "poor men." A Jewish-Christian sect in early Church history that taught Jesus was human, not divine; that Christians should be obedient to the Law of Moses; and that Jesus was the Messiah, though not God. Origen (c. 185–254) describes one group of Ebionites who accepted the virgin birth but rejected Christ's preexistence, and another group that said Jesus was a prophet fathered by Joseph. The following scriptures were important to their teaching: Deuteronomy 18:15; Matthew 5:3; Luke 4:18; 7:22; Romans 15:26.

Ecclesiology ▪ From the Greek *ekklesia*, "church," and *logos*, "the study of." In theology, an examination of the Church with particular concern to her origin, distinctive nature, mission, function, government, offices, ordinances and destiny. See: **Church.**

See: F.J.A. Hort, *Christian Ecclesia* (Macmillan, 1900); W. Robinson, *The Biblical Doctrine of the Church* (St. Louis: The Bethany Press, 1955).

Ecumenical ▪ From the Greek *oikoumenikos*, "the inhabited world" (Matt. 24:14; Acts 17:6; Heb. 2:5). Today the word refers to the Church as a whole, to the Christian community (John 17, especially v. 21; Eph. 4:3–5). The term is frequently associated with a modern-day movement that attempts to bring about institutional unity of denominations. Some trace its beginnings to the 1910 International Missionary Conference at Edinburgh, Scotland, which resulted in the establishment of three organizations: The International Missionary Council (New York, 1921), Conference on Life and Work (Stockholm, 1925), The Conference on Faith and Order (Lausanne, 1927).

In 1937 the Stockholm group and the Lausanne group suggested a worldwide organization of churches be founded; and shortly after World War II, the World Council of Churches was established in Amsterdam. The confessional statement reads: "The World Council of Churches is a fellowship of Churches which confess the Lord Jesus Christ as God and Savior according to the Scriptures and therefore seek to fulfill together their common calling to the glory of one God, Father, Son, and Holy Spirit." Evangelicals have long been critical of the WCC because of its emphasis of the federal model (desire for institutional union) and for its weakness on evangelism.

See: R.P. Beaver, *Ecumenical Beginnings in Protestant World Mission: A History of Comity* (Thomas Nelson, 1962); G.W. Bromiley, *The Unity and Disunity of the Church* (Eerdmans, 1958); J.D. Douglas, *Evangelicals and Unity* (Abingdon, 1965); R. Rouse and S.C. Neill, *A History of the Ecumenical Movement: 1517–1948* (Westminster, 1967); H.E. Fey, *A History of the Ecumenical Movement: 1948–1968* (Westminster, 1970); D. Hedegard, *Ecumenism and the Bible* (London: Banner of Truth Trust, 1964); J.W. Montgomery, *Ecumenicity, Evangelicals, and Rome* (Zondervan, 1969).

Ekklesia ■ In the NT the Greek word *ekklesia* is translated "church." See: **Church.**

Elder ■ From the Greek *presbyteros*, "an old man," in the NT variously referred to as bishops (Titus 1:7), overseers (Acts 20:17, 28), pastors or shepherds (1 Peter 5:1–4), and teachers (1 Cor. 12:28; Eph. 4:11). They are called elders because of their superior wisdom and experience; bishops or overseers because they watch over all that pertains to the edification and welfare of their congregation; pastors or shepherds because they are required to have a shepherd's care over their flock; and teachers because they instruct those under their charge.

Elders were to care for and spiritually oversee the churches. The plan throughout the NT was for a group of elders to be appointed in each church (Acts 14:23; 20:17; Phil. 1:1; 1 Tim. 5:17; Titus 1:5). Qualifications for the office are found in Titus 1:5–9; 1 Timothy 3:1–7 and 1 Peter 5:2. See also: 1 Timothy 5:17; Hebrews 13:7, 17; 1 Timothy 3:5; 1 Thessalonians 5:12. See: **Deacon, Deaconess.**

Election ■ In the NT, election is to choose for service or an office (Luke 6:13; John 6:70; 15:16; Acts 9:15; 15:7); it can also mean predestination to salvation (Eph. 1:3–11; Rom. 8:28–11:36).

Some believe in a general predestination in which Christ died for all, and all who accept the message of the Gospel are "predestined" to be saved. Some, on the other hand, hold to the definition of election adopted at the Synod of Dort (1618–1619): "The unchangeable purpose of God whereby, before the foundations of the world, out of the whole human race, which had fallen by its own fault out of its original integrity into sin and ruin, He has, according to the most free good pleasure of His will, out of mere grace, chosen in Christ to salvation a certain number of specific men, neither better nor more worthy than others but with them involved in a common misery." This double predestination, the belief that some individuals are chosen for salvation and some individuals are chosen for damnation, is standard Reformed doctrine. See: **Arminianism, Atonement, Calvinism, Predestination, Supralapsarianism.**

See: G.C. Berkouwer, *Divine Election* (Eerdmans, 1960); D. Engelsma, *Hyper-Calvinism and the Call of the Gospel* (Reformed Free Publishing Association, 1980); A.P.F. Sell, *The Great Debate: Calvinism, Arminianism and Salvation* (Baker, 1982); R. Shank, *Elect in the Son: A Study of the Doctrine of Election* (Westcott, 1970).

Elohim ▪ One of the OT names of God (Gen. 1:1—2:42; Ex. 3; Deut. 2:30, 33; 3:22; Isa. 44:7; 45:5–21; 52:10). Always used in the singular when it refers to the true God, it is also used for false gods, judges, and kings.

Emanation ▪ From the Greek *aporroia* and the Latin *emanare*, "to flow out of," or "down from." Emanation is a theory of creation that teaches that all reality proceeds from God's own being, a view just the opposite of the biblical teaching that God created all that exists from nothing (creation *ex nihilo*). Emanation implies that the further a thing is from God, the less perfection it possesses. Therefore, pure matter being the furthest from God, it is considered the most evil. This idea has Neoplatonic roots. See: **Creation.**

Emmanuel (Immanuel) ▪ A name for Jesus that means "God with us." The name is recorded three times in the Bible: Isaiah 7:14; 8:8; Matthew 1:23. See: **Christ, Jesus, Lord, Savior.**

Empiricism ■ In philosophy, an epistemology (a theory of how we gain knowledge) which holds that all knowledge comes from the five senses. The mind at birth is viewed as a *tabulae rasae*, a blank slate, and knowledge is said to be learned or "written" on that blank slate solely through sense experience. In theology, empiricism sometimes refers to natural theology, the view that one can gain at least some knowledge of God from nature (Rom. 1:18–23). See: **Rationalism.**

See: N.L. Geisler and P.D. Feinberg, *Introduction to Philosophy: A Christian Perspective* (Baker, 1980), pp. 83–166; P.K. Moser, *Empirical Knowledge: Readings in Contemporary Epistemology* (Rowman and Littlefield, 1986).

Enhypostasis ■ From the Greek *en*, "in," and *hypostasis* "substance." The teaching that the part of the Divine Trinity which became incarnate in Jesus contained all the properties of human nature in a perfect state. The person of Jesus is thus both wholly divine and wholly human. Upholding this completeness of both natures is important because both natures are necessary for Christ to atone for our sins.

Envy ■ Envy is "sadness because of another's good." It is a sin against love, because we should be pleased at the good of others. One of the Bible's most pointed examples of envy is Saul's hatred of David (1 Sam. 18:5–30).

The words "envy" and "jealousy" often mean the same thing, though jealousy can at times have good connotations, as in God's jealousy for His children (Ex. 20:5). Envy is always a negative term and is forbidden in several places in Scripture (Ps. 37:1; Prov. 3:31; 14:30; 23:17; 1 Cor. 13:4; Gal. 5:26). In Roman Catholic theology, envy is one of the Seven Deadly Sins. See: **Sins, Seven Deadly; Sins, Mortal and Venial.**

Epiphany ■ A transliteration (a word brought from one language to another by merely changing the spelling) of the Greek *epiphaneia*, "appearance" or "manifestation." It refers to the first coming of Christ—the Incarnation—or to the Second Coming of Christ. It is also a Christian festival celebrated on January 6 to commemorate the coming of the Magi to proclaim Jesus King. See: **Incarnation.**

Episcopalian ■ From the Greek *episkopos*, "a bishop." The Protestant Episcopal Church is a self-governing American branch of the Anglican Church (Church of England). An important part of American colonial history, the church separated from the Church of England in 1789, shortly after the Revolutionary War. The Episcopal Church places primary authority in the office of bishop. The church is also known for its stress on liturgical worship. See: **Anglicans, Bishop.**

See: *The Church's Teaching* (Seabury Press) in six volumes.

Epistle ■ From the Greek *epistole*, a "letter" or "message." A letter written to a person or group. In the NT it refers to books that were originally written as letters to people or churches, such as *The First Epistle of Paul to Timothy* or *The Epistle of Paul to the Romans*.

Epistemology ■ From the Greek *episteme*, "knowledge," plus *logos*, "theory." A theory of knowledge. In philosophy, epistemology examines how we gain knowledge, investigating the origin, structure, methods and validity of knowledge. It studies how we know what we know. See: **Empiricism, Philosophy, Rationalism.**

See: R.M. Chisholm, *Perceiving: A Philosophical Study* (Cornell University Press, 1957), and *Theory of Knowledge* (Prentice-Hall, 1977); P.K. Moser, *Empirical Knowledge: Readings in Contemporary Epistemology* (Rowman and Littlefield, 1986); L.M. Regis, *Epistemology* (Macmillan, 1959).

Eschatology ■ From the Greek *eschatos*, "the last," "last things," and *logos*, "the study of." In theology, eschatology is the study of the doctrine of future or last things. This involves analyzing God's dealings with Israel, the Church and the nations, taking into account distinctive promises to each and their ultimate fulfillment. In general, it treats beliefs associated with final events such as death, immortality, judgment day, heaven and hell, the end of the earth, and the end of human history. See: **Millennialism.**

See: J.E. Adams, *I Tell You the Mystery* (Prospective Press, 1966); H.A. Hoyt, *The End Times* (Moody Press, 1969); C.C. Ryrie, *The Basis of the Premillennial Faith* (New York: Loizeaux Brothers, 1953).

Essence ▪ From the Latin *essentia*, "the whatness of a being." In philosophy, essence is what makes a being precisely what it is, as opposed to something else—its qualities, attributes, and nature. The essence of a thing is its nature considered independently of its existence. See: **Metaphysics.**

Esthetics. See: Aesthetics, Axiology.

Eternal Life ▪ From the Greek *zoe*, "life," and *aionion*, "eternal." Some define "eternal life" as the life given to the believer in heaven, but eternal life can actually refer to the eternal destiny of either the saved or the damned. For the Christian, eternal life begins with salvation, not after death, and consists of knowing God (John 17:3). See: John 3:15–16, 36; 5:24; 6:27; 17:3; Acts 17:25. See: **Salvation.**

Eternity ▪ From the Latin *aeternus*, "age," a transcendence of time, everlasting, without beginning or end. Eternity can have a quantitative meaning, time without end; or a qualitative meaning, a character superior to the temporal. In philosophy, to be eternal is to have infinite duration in both directions, without beginning or end. God, then, is the only Being who is eternal in this strict sense. In theology and philosophy, eternity is also used to refer to God's infinite nature. God transcends the limitations of time and succession of events, existing all at once. He is unchanging and timelessly present.

Ethics, Christian ▪ A practical science that investigates the personal and social rules or laws of human conduct. It is the discipline that deals with what is good and bad, with moral duty and obligation. Christian ethics is a system of right and wrong based on principles drawn from the Bible. The foundation of ethics for the believer is found in Jesus' Sermon on the Mount (Matt. 5–7).

Many in today's diverse theological world argue that everything is relative. Discussions of conflicting ethical choices are seldom rooted in objective ethical norms, rights or wrongs that are right or wrong in every situation. Instead, actions are based on changing human understanding of what would be the most loving thing to do in the situation in which one is found. This "situation ethics"—an ethical relativism that suggests that any action, including murder or adultery, could be righteous in a given situation—is a total denial of Christian ethics.

Ultimately, for the Christian, ethics must be based on the absolute nature and character of God. Our "choosing" and "doing" must be based on our understanding of His character as revealed to us in His Word. See: **Sermon on the Mount.**

See: J. Fletcher and J.W. Montgomery, *Situation Ethics* (Bethany House Publishers, 1972); N.L. Geisler, *The Christian Ethic of Love* (Zondervan, 1973), *Ethics: Alternatives and Issues* (Zondervan, 1971), and *Options in Contemporary Christian Ethics* (Baker, 1981); C.F.H. Henry, *Christian Personal Ethics* (Eerdmans, 1957); C.S. Lewis, *The Four Loves* (Harcourt, Brace, and World, 1960); E.W. Lutzer, *The Morality Gap: An Evangelical Response to Situation Ethics* (Moody Press, 1972); P.T. Jersild and D.A. Johnson, *Moral Issues and Christian Response* (Holt, Rinehart and Winston, 1983).

Ethics, Social ■ The study of ethics (questions of good and evil, right and wrong, obligation and prohibition) regarding personal interaction with others and with society. Social ethics deals with issues such as crime, ecology, economics, education, poverty, politics, public policy, racism, war and our obligation to understand, interpret, and reinforce ethical values within a social context.

See: R.G. Clouse, *Wealth and Poverty: Four Christian Views of Economics* (InterVarsity Press, 1984); C.F.H. Henry, *Aspects of Christian Social Ethics* (Baker, 1964); G.W. Forell, *Christian Social Teachings* (Augsburg, 1971); R.N. Longenecker, *New Testament Social Ethics for Today* (Eerdmans, 1984); T.L. Miethe, *The Philosophy and Ethics of Alexander Campbell: From the Context of American Religious Thought, 1800–1866* (University Microfilms, 1984).

Eucharist ■ From the Greek word *eucharistein*, "to give thanks." The Eucharist is a service of thanksgiving for the believer's redemption by Jesus' death on the cross and His subsequent resurrection. In the Roman Catholic Church, the Eucharist is a sacrament (it gives grace) by which the person who partakes of the Eucharist is spiritually changed and united into the community of Jesus' spirit and body: the Church. See: 1 Corinthians 11:23–29; Luke 22:19. See: **Communion, Lord's Supper, Sacrament.**

See: B.J. Kidd, *The Later Medieval Doctrine of the Eucharistic Sacrifice* (London: SPCK, 1958); J. Jeremias, *The Eucharistic Words of Jesus* (Oxford: Basil Blackwell, 1955).

Eudaimonism ■ Also spelled "eudemonism." From the Greek word, *eudaimonia*, "happiness." A theory of ethics that evaluates actions by their ability to produce personal well-being or happiness, the chief end of human beings. A life controlled by reason, however, is emphasized, rather than the mere pursuit of pleasure, as in hedonism.

Euthanasia ■ From the Greek *eu*, "good," and *thanatos*, "death," literally meaning "good death." In ethics, the act of inducing the painless death of a person for reasons assumed to be merciful. The term sometimes refers to direct, deliberate killing or hastening of death of one in great pain, a practice traditionally considered to be murder. It can also refer to "passive" euthanasia, the omission of treatment. This practice is common in situations where there is no medical hope of recovery or of improvement—when the person is a "vegetable"—but can be kept alive by mechanical means.

Evangelical Christians fall on both sides of the passive euthanasia issue. Some argue against any form of euthanasia on the basis of the sanctity of life, that life is a gift from God and only God has the right to give or take it. Others maintain that God delegated to human beings the right to make moral decisions even regarding life (for example, in capital punishment, self-defense, war, and so on), and that people have a right to die with dignity. Christians often differentiate between ceasing to preserve a life through "heroic measures" when there is no justified medical hope for recovery, and "active" euthanasia, taking direct steps to terminate a life.

Eutychianism ■ From the teaching of Eutyches (c. 378–454) which stated that Jesus had only one nature, the divine, clothed in human flesh. Condemned at the Council of Chalcedon. See: **Chalcedon, Council of; Monophysitism.**

Evangelicalism ▪ A modern movement in Christianity that transcends denominational lines. Evangelicals emphasize the Gospel of forgiveness and regeneration through personal faith in Jesus Christ, affirm orthodox doctrine and the truth of historical biblical Christianity, regard the Scriptures as the inspired and infallible Word of God for every generation, and believe in the urgency of missionary outreach.

Although there are many distinctives among evangelical groups, all evangelicals generally accept Christ's Incarnation, sinless life, death on the cross, bodily resurrection and Second Coming; the doctrines of the Trinity and the virgin birth; and the reality of miracles, a final judgment and the ultimate destruction of this world.

Evangelicals became distinct from fundamentalists after 1947, when Harold J. Ockenga coined the term the "new evangelicalism." Among others, Ockenga, Edward J. Carnell, Carl F. H. Henry, and Billy Graham took issue with older fundamentalism. These "New Evangelicals" thought that the fundamentalists had (1) an incorrect attitude (a suspicion of everyone who did not conform on every minor point); (2) a wrong strategy (separatism); and (3) bad results (ineffectiveness in changing social, political, and economic structures). Evangelicals further thought that fundamentalists were isolationist and anti-intellectual. Today, evangelicals and fundamentalists are beginning to work together in theological, political, and social arenas.

Evangelicals can be found in almost any denomination, and whole denominations can be referred to as "evangelical." There are several associations of evangelicals, including the National Association of Evangelicals (NAE, founded in 1942), the Evangelical Theological Society (1949), and the Evangelical Philosophical Society (1976). *Christianity Today* (1956) is perhaps their most important magazine. See: **Fundamentalism.**

See: D.G. Bloesch, *The Evangelical Renaissance* (Eerdmans, 1973); Kenneth Kantzer, *Evangelical Roots* (Thomas C. Nelson, 1978); C.F.H. Henry, *Evangelicals at the Brink of Crisis* (Word, 1967), and *A Plea for Evangelical Demonstration* (Baker, 1971); George Marsden, *Reforming Fundamentalism: Fuller Seminary and the New Evangelicalism* (Eerdmans, 1987); D.F. Wells and J. D. Woodbridge, *The Evangelicals: What They Believe, Who They Are, Where They Are Changing* (Abingdon, 1975).

Evangelism ▪ From the Greek noun *euangelion*, "good news," and the verb *euangelizomai*, "to proclaim good news." Evangelism is the active preaching or presentation of the Gospel with the goal of bringing the hearer, through the power of the Holy Spirit, to faith in Jesus Christ and thus into a right relationship with God. (See: Luke 15; John 3:16; Rom. 5:8; 10:14–15; 2 Peter 3:9.) God has given all believers the privilege and responsibility of being ambassadors of Christ, ministers of reconciliation in the world (2 Cor. 5:17–21).

See: J.C. Aldrich, *Life-Style Evangelism: Crossing Traditional Boundaries to Reach the Unbelieving World* (Multnomah Press, 1978); R.E. Coleman, *The Master Plan of Evangelism* (Fleming H. Revell, 1963); M. Green, *Evangelism: Now and Then* (InterVarsity Press, 1979); J. Petersen, *Evangelism for Our Generation* (NavPress, 1985); T.L. Miethe, "Sharing Your Faith," in *The Christian's Guide to Following Jesus* (Bethany House Publishers, 1984), pp. 111–116; and "Free to Win Souls to Christ," in *A Christian's Guide to Faith and Reason* (Bethany House Publishers, 1987), pp. 60–69.

Evidentialism ■ The position in apologetics which teaches that the truth claims of Christianity can be verified by appealing to historical evidence available to believer and unbeliever alike. Unlike some Protestant theologians, evidentialists do not reject natural theology, but think a valid attempt can and must be made to know and prove God by studying nature and relying on human reason. This viewpoint is based on the belief that the God who gave us the Bible also created the universe, made man in His image, and authored language, truth and logic. Thus there must be truth and evidence shared by believer and unbeliever alike. They disagree with those who believe that one can only appeal to presuppositional starting points such as biblical revelation. Proponents of evidential apologetics include Norman L. Geisler, Gary R. Habermas, Terry L. Miethe, John Warwick Montgomery, J. P. Moreland, Clark Pinnock, John Gerstner and others. See: **Apologetics, Presuppositionalism.**

See: J.H. Gerstner, *Reasons for Faith* (Baker, 1967); T.L. Miethe, *A Christian's Guide to Faith and Reason* (Bethany House Publishers, 1987); J.P. Moreland, *Scaling the Secular City: A Defense of Christianity* (Baker, 1987); J.W. Montgomery, *Faith Founded on Fact: Essays in Evidential Apologetics* (Thomas Nelson, 1978); C.H. Pinnock, *A Case for Faith* (Bethany House Publishers, 1980), and *Set Forth Your Case* (Moody, 1971); R.C. Sproul, J. Gerstner, and A. Lindsley, *Classical Apologetics: A Rational Defense of the Christian Faith and a Critique of Presuppositional Apologetics* (Zondervan, 1984).

Evil, The Problem of ■ There are several dimensions to the Christian explanation of why evil and pain exist in the world: (1) God lovingly created the best of all possible ways to obtain the best of all possible worlds. This world, with its free creatures and their responsibility for evil, is the best way to ultimate good. (2) Evil is inherent in the risky gift of free will. Real freedom demands the potential for either good or evil. (3) Much of the suffering in our world can be traced directly to the evil choices people make. Even natural evil can be traced to human free choices and the resulting fall of the natural world. (4) Scripture tells us of the reality of Satan, who is free to do evil until God's final judgment. (5) God has himself entered into our pain and has become the great sufferer. In giving His Son, Christ Jesus, God allows each of us to be eventually redeemed if we so choose.

See: N.L. Geisler, *The Roots of Evil* (Zondervan, 1978); C.S. Lewis, *The Problem of Pain* (Macmillan, 1962); T.L. Miethe, "The Problem of Evil," in *The Christian's Guide to Following Jesus* (Bethany House Publishers, 1984), pp. 127–132; J. Wenham, *The Goodness of God* (InterVarsity Press, 1974).

Evolution ▪ From the Latin *evolvere*, "to unroll," the act or process of unfolding or developing, change in one direction. Evolution usually refers to the biological theory that all life forms have gradually developed from simpler forms.

Nothing in the Bible opposes what is called the "special theory of evolution," that great change is possible within fixed kinds. It is the "general theory of evolution," the amoeba-to-human-being theory, that many Christians oppose. Change is undeniable; the question is how and why it takes place. Christians are concerned with upholding the biblical truths of God's work not only in creating the world, but in sustaining and governing it. The crucial problems for the Christian can be reduced to three areas: the origin of the universe, the origin of life, and the origin of human beings and their sociological institutions. Evolutionary theories are typically schemes of natural causation with no room for God. See: **Creation, Creationism.**

See: N. Macbeth, *Darwin Retried: An Appeal to Reason* (Gambit, 1971); T.L. Miethe, "The Limits of Science," in *A Christian's Guide to Faith and Reason* (Bethany House Publishers, 1987), pp. 95–111; B. Nelson, *After Its Kind* (Bethany House Publishers, 1967); C.B. Thaxton, W.L. Bradley and R.L. Olsen, *The Mystery of Life's Origin: Reassessing Current Theories* (Philosophical Library, 1984); J.C. Whitcomb and H.M. Morris, *The Genesis Flood: The Biblical Records and Its Scientific Implications* (Baker, 1970).

Evolution, Theistic ▪ The idea that God began creation and then used evolution to produce the universe as we know it, at times possibly entering into the process to modify what was developing, but usually using the evolutionary process He had started. In this view, one of the most important ways God entered into the process was to directly create the human spirit and then infuse it into pre-Adamic man, who had evolved naturally and was not fully human.

Ex Cathedra ■ From the Latin meaning "from the throne." When the Roman Catholic Pope makes an official pronouncement from his throne dealing with matters of faith or morals, it is said to be made "ex cathedra." His judgment is regarded as infallible, and all who call themselves Roman Catholics must abide by such pronouncements since they are essential matters of the faith. See: **Infallibility.**

Excommunication ■ From the Latin *excommunicare*, meaning "to cut off communication." Excommunication is the exclusion of a sinner from communion with the faithful. It has two goals: (1) to bring the sinner to repentance; and (2) to safeguard the community's purity.

In the Roman Catholic Church, when a person breaks the faith—for sins such as idolatry, murder, impurity, loss of faith, denunciation of church doctrine—they are cut off or expelled from the fellowship of the church and all privileges and rights of membership. Though the Reformers, especially John Calvin, believed excommunication was an important part of church discipline, today it is rarely practiced in Protestant churches, though it is still accepted in the canons of the Church of England revised in 1969. See: Matthew 16:19; 18:18; John 20:23. See: **Absolution, Penance.**

Exegesis ■ From the Greek meaning "interpretation," from *ex*, "out," and *hegeisthai*, "to guide." Exegesis is a method of attempting to understand a Bible passage. The reader of Scripture studies the word meanings and grammar of the text to discern what the Holy Spirit was communicating, drawing the meaning out of the text rather than reading what he wants into the text. It attempts to elicit the true teaching of a biblical text for spiritual growth in Christian living.

Existence ■ The state or quality of being, reality as opposed to appearance. Existence can refer to total reality, the universe as it is, rather than as we know it. In this case it must include the spiritual as well as the purely physical or material. See: **Metaphysics, Philosophy.**

Existential ■ Of, relating to, or affirming existence; empirical, having being in space and time; personal, daily. See: **Empiricism.**

Existentialism ■ In philosophy, a school of thought which stresses that existence is prior to essence—the fact that something exists is more important than what that something is, and the concrete and individual are more important than the abstract and universal. Important themes in existentialism are human freedom of choice, personal responsibility for actions, and the subjectivity and irrationality of human life.

Existentialism contends that neither traditional metaphysics nor the natural sciences are adequate for understanding life's deepest truths. Existentialism is strictly non-metaphysical and anti-hypothetical, claiming to give only a simple description of existent psychological realities. Some prominent modern existentialists are Martin Heidegger, Jean-Paul Sartre, Albert Camus, Karl Jaspers and Gabriel Marcel.

See: P.F. Sanborn, *Existentialism* (Pegasus, 1968); J.P. Sartre, *Essays in Existentialism* (The Citadel Press, 1974), and *Existentialism and Human Emotions* (Philosophical Library, 1957).

Faith ■ From the Greek *pistis*, "firm persuasion." The word "faith" appears only 2 times in the OT (Deut. 32:20 and Hab. 2:4). It appears 307 times in the NT. Biblical faith has two essential components: (1) trust or acceptance, belief that Jesus is Lord with acknowledgement of His resurrection, and (2) intellectual content, the revealed truth that is firmly believed and is reflected in the life of the believer.

John Stott explains faith as "a reasoning trust, a trust which reckons thoughtfully and confidently upon the trustworthiness of God." The NT in no way teaches we should have a blind faith. Hebrews 11:1 reads: "Now faith is the substance of things hoped for, the evidence of things not seen" (KJV). The Greek word translated as "evidence" in the King James literally means "proof," or "proving." The New International Version (NIV) brings out this meaning when it says: "Now faith is being sure of what we hope for and *certain of what we do not see*" (emphasis added). Even the aspect of trust in faith is not blind; there is proof, evidence for belief. In the Christian sense, faith may be defined as a conscious mental desire to do the will of the God of Scripture. See: **Fideism.**

See: T.L. Miethe, "What is Faith," in *The Christian's Guide to Following Jesus* (Bethany House Publishers, 1984), pp. 21–26, and "What is Faith, Really?" in *A Christian's Guide to Faith and Reason* (Bethany House Publishers, 1987), pp.15–25.

False Cause, Argument from ■ A logical fallacy that mistakenly draws a causal connection between two events simply because one event follows the other in time or succession. The mere fact that incident "A" preceded incident "B" does not prove that A *caused* B. An example of the fallacy: "Yesterday, I told a lie about my age. Today, I woke up with several new wrinkles in my face. I am being punished for telling that lie." See: **Logical Fallacies.**

Fast, Fasting ■ Refraining from an activity—such as eating food—either totally or partially for a limited period of time. In the NT, fasting allowed an individual to engage in more concentrated spiritual activity, for example, prayer. In 1 Corinthians 7:5 we read: "Stop depriving one another [in regard to marital relations], except by agreement for a time that you may devote yourselves to prayer. . . ." Fasting is a means ordained by God to prepare the soul, body and spirit on important occasions for all types of spiritual endeavors. For the Christian who loves God and wants to serve Him with all his heart, soul, mind and strength, fasting should be considered more a privilege than a duty. See: Matthew 6:16–18; 9:14–15; 17:21; Acts 13:3; 14:23.

Fatalism ■ From the Latin *fatum*, meaning "that which the gods ordain to happen." The belief that God, because He is all-knowing and all-powerful, foresees and causes according to His divine foreknowledge every event in a person's life and in the universe. These events must occur; they cannot *not* happen. When God's sovereignty is taken to be so wooden, the resulting fatalism is devastating to evangelism, missions, and ultimately to the nature of God and human beings created in His image. See: **Arminianism, Atonement, Calvinism, Freedom of the Will, Predestination, Sovereignty.**
See: T.L. Miethe, "The Universal Power of the Atonement," in *The Grace of God/The Will of Man*, edited by C. Pinnock (Zondervan, 1989), and "God's Image Shines in Us," in *The Christian's Guide to Faith and Reason* (Bethany House Publishers, 1987), pp. 42–53.

Fideism ■ In Christian apologetics the term refers to an exclusive reliance on irrational faith (belief without evidence) as well as a belittling of the rational assessment of philosophical and religious truth. In Christian theology, this school holds that the ultimate ground for accepting the claims of the Bible is the testimony of the Holy Spirit, received by faith, which itself (the faith) is a gift of God.

In one sense, all perspectives are fideistic because they all must start with presuppositions. There is, however, a great difference between a "presupposition of method," the assumption that a real, factual world exists and that it is possible to investigate it, and "presuppositions of content," an assumed body of truth that must be accepted as true before truth can be known. See: **Apologetics, Evidentialism, Faith, Presuppositionalism.**

Force, Appeal to ■ In Latin, *Argumentum ad Baculum*. This fallacy is committed when one appeals to force or the threat of force to have his argument accepted. The motto "might makes right" epitomizes this reasoning. A lobbyist, for example, commits this fallacy when he reminds a representative that he (the lobbyist) represents thousands of votes. One nation threatening war against another as a political bargaining chip is another example of appeal to force. See: **Logical Fallacies.**

Foot Washing ■ In the days of open sandals and dusty roads, foot washing was a Middle Eastern courtesy. It was a symbol of a host's honor and respect for the one whose feet were being washed, and a symbol of humility, love and servanthood in the one who did the washing. Jesus washed the feet of His disciples and said: ". . . Do you know what I have done to you? You call me Teacher, and Lord; and you are right for so I am. If I then, the Lord and the Teacher, washed your feet, you also ought to wash one another's feet. For I gave you an example that you also should do as I did to you. Truly, truly, I say to you, a slave is not greater than his master; neither is one who is sent greater than the one who sent him. If you know these things, you are blessed if you do them" (John 13:1–17). Some Christian groups still practice foot washing as a symbol of these virtues.

Foreknowledge ■ In theology, the teaching that God knows everything that will occur in the future of the universe. Because God is not a part of the space/time continuum, He can know what human beings will experience as future in a way that does not destroy human freedom. How God experiences time is similar to how human beings experience it: Just as it is always *now* for us—we experience the past only in our memories, and the future only in our hopes—thus God sees everything in one eternal now, or present. What He knows as present, we experience

as past, present and future. Jesus seemed to have this foreknowledge even during His Incarnation (Matt. 24:35–44; Mark 9:1ff.; Luke 12:40, 21:20ff.).

Foreordination ■ In theology, the belief that God has set some or all events before they actually happen, for example, an individual's salvation. Throughout history most Christians have believed that God can and does rule human history, but not to the extent that He must destroy human freedom, an important part of what it means to be created in His image. See: **Calvinism, Fatalism, Freedom of the Will, Predestination, Sovereignty.**

See: T.L. Miethe, "God's Image Shines in Us," in *A Christian's Guide to Faith and Reason* (Bethany House Publishers, 1987), pp. 42–53.

Forgive, Forgiveness ■ Forgiveness is one of the most significant characteristics of God in Christian theology. Christian theology teaches that when a person accepts Jesus as Lord and Savior his or her sins are wiped clean, forgiven by God, never to be held against him or her again (Heb. 10:17). Jesus' death on the cross was God's gracious gift whereby our sins are forgiven. That promise is sealed in the further gift of eternal life. Just as Jesus rose from the dead, so we too will live eternally (Rom. 6:1–11). We are told that because God forgave us, we should also forgive others (Matt. 18:22, 35; Luke 17:4). See: Hosea 14:4; Luke 15:11–32; Colossians 2:13; Ephesians 4:32. See: **Cross, Crucifixion, Resurrection of Jesus.**

Form Criticism ■ A method of interpreting the Bible by attempting to get behind the written sources to what was actually said and done. It attempts to identify and evaluate material added as a result of oral transmission, and recognizes the existence of literary units and analyzes these units according to their form. Some theologians think this approach has been helpful in studying the parables and sayings of Jesus. See: **Biblical Criticism, Heilsgeschichte, Higher Criticism, Lower Criticism, Redaction Criticism.**

Freedom of the Will ■ The freedom to act and to be responsible for our actions. In creating us in His own image, God made us rational creatures, which necessarily means that He has delegated sovereignty to us. Our very experience of life tells us we have free choice: We can consciously deny ourselves even to the extent that we can willfully starve to death. Human freedom places no restriction on God's power. Exactly the opposite is true: We are free only because God chose to give us free will. A God who is truly sovereign must be able to create free creatures. It would be a greater threat to God's power were He unable to delegate freedom. Erasmus (1466–1536) wrote *Freedom of the Will* (1524) to answer Martin Luther (1483–1546), who stated that the will was in bondage to sin. See: **Calvinism, Fatalism, Foreknowledge, Predestination, Sovereignty.**

See: D. and R. Basinger, *Predestination and Free Will: Four Views of Divine Sovereignty and Human Freedom* (InterVarsity Press, 1986); W.L. Craig, *The Only Wise God: The Compatibility of Divine Foreknowledge and Human Freedom* (Baker, 1987); T.L. Miethe, *The Christian's Guide to Faith and Reason* (Bethany House Publishers, 1987); R. Rice, *God's Foreknowledge and Man's Free Will* (Bethany House Publishers, 1985).

Friends, Society of ■ Also known as "Quakers" or the "Religious Society of Friends." A Christian group founded by George Fox (1624–1691). The name "Friends" comes from John 15:14: "You are My friends, if you do what I command you." The Friends emphasize simplicity of life, reject all formalism and liturgy in worship, and reject all creeds. They accept pacifism, democracy in church government and an inner light (inner voice) of revelation, which God gives to individuals to guide them to truth and righteousness. For the Friend, the essence of worship is silence. In the midst of quiet, God reveals His direction; then one is moved to speak and to act. They encourage women to be ministers.

The first Friends to come to America were Mary Fisher and Anne Austin, who came to Massachusetts in 1656 and were later sent away. In 1659–1660 some Friends were hanged on Boston Common. William Penn (1644–1718) is perhaps the best known Friend in American history; their greatest philosopher and theologian has certainly been David Elton Trueblood.

See: D.E. Trueblood, *The People Called Quakers* (1966).

Fundamentalism ■ A modern, conservative Christian movement that emphasizes adherence to certain "fundamentals" or basic doctrines of Christianity. During the spread of problems that would mark the twentieth century, fundamentalism arose to protect orthodox biblical Christianity and to combat liberal theology—including higher criticism—and Darwinian evolutionary theory.

The inerrancy of Scripture, the virgin birth of Christ, Christ's substitutionary atonement, His bodily resurrection, and the historicity of miracles are one list of the "five fundamentals" used as early as 1910. These lists of fundamentals varied somewhat; the World's Christian Fundamentals Association, founded in 1919 in part by premillennial Baptists, tended to replace the historicity of miracles with belief in the Second Coming or with premillennialism. Another group listed the deity of Christ as a fundamental in place of the virgin birth. *The Fundamentals: A Testimony to the Truth*, a series of twelve volumes published from 1910–1915 and sent to almost every pastor in America, are the movement's foundational documents.

Fundamentalists today generally believe in the inerrancy of Scripture, ecclesiastical separatism, moral separatism, premillennial views of prophecy, dispensational views of theology, active evangelism, opposition of neo-evangelicalism, opposition of the charismatic movement, insistence on private religious education, and political conservatism. In 1941 the ecclesiastically separatist American Council of Christian Churches came into being. In later years this group became associated with a legalistic mindset, and only recently, starting with political activism, have some fundamentalists begun to work with evangelicals on theological, social and political issues. See: **Evangelicalism.**

See: E. Dobson and E. Hindson, *The Fundamentalist Phenomenon: The Resurgence of Conservative Christianity* (Doubleday, 1981); C.L. Feinberg, *The Fundamentals for Today*, 2 vols. (Kregel, 1958); J.G. Machen, *Christianity and Liberalism* (Eerdmans, 1923); E.R. Sandeen, *The Roots of Fundamentalism* (University of Chicago Press, 1970).

Gehenna ■ From the Greek transliteration of the Aramaic *gehinnam*, which in turn comes from the Hebrew *ge hinnom*, "Valley of Hinnom" (2 Chron. 28:3; 2 Kings 23:10). The Valley of Hinnom outside of Jerusalem was used as a refuse dump and was kept continually burning to prevent pestilence. In the NT, Gehenna represents the final spiritual state of the ungodly, the place of punishment for sins (Matt. 10:28; Mark 9:43). See also: Matthew 25:41; Revelation 20:4. See: **Eternal Life, Hades, Hell, Sheol.**

Generation ■ From the Latin *generatus*, "to generate," and from *genus*, "birth." In theology the word refers to several ideas: (1) The act of begetting. In the case of Jesus, He is the only begotten Son of God the Father (John 1:14). (2) An age in time (Gen. 2:4). (3) A group of individuals living at one time (Ex. 1:6; Num. 32:13; Judg. 2:10). (4) A group or family related by a common ancestor (Gen. 50:23; Deut. 23:2).

Gentiles ■ From the Greek *ethnos*, "heathen," and from the Latin *gentilis*, "of the same birth or race." For the Jews, one who is not Jewish. For a Christian, one who is neither a Jew nor a Christian. Synonymous with "heathen," or "pagan." See: Matthew 4:15; Romans 3:29; 11:11, 13; 15:10; 16:4; Galatians 2:8, 12, 14; Ephesians 3:1. See: **Pagan.**

Glossolalia ■ From the Greek *glossa*, "tongue," and *lalia*, "chatter." The word is commonly used to refer to "speaking in tongues." See: Mark 16:9–20; Acts 2:4–13, 22, 36–39, 43; 10:44–48; 11:13–18; 19:1–7; 1 Corinthians 12:4–11; 14:2. Some Christians claim that this gift of the Holy Spirit was meant not just for the first-century Church but for today as well. See: **Holy Spirit.**

See: Larry Christenson, ed., *Welcome Holy Spirit: A Study of Charismatic Renewal in the Church* (Augsburg, 1987); J.D.G. Dunn, *Baptism in the Holy Spirit* (A.R. Allenson, 1970); D.L. Gelpi, *Pentecostal Piety* (Paulist Press, 1972), and *Pentecostalism: A Theological Viewpoint* (Paulist Press, 1971); C.G. Hummel, *Fire in the Fireplace: Contemporary Charismatic Renewal* (InterVarsity Press, 1978); J.F. MacArthur, Jr., *The Charismatics: A Doctrinal Perspective* (Zondervan, 1978); T.L. Miethe, "The Holy Spirit and Knowledge," in *The Christian's Guide to Faith and Reason* (Bethany House Publishers, 1987), pp. 78–84; S.M. Shoemaker, *With the Holy Spirit and With Fire* (Word, 1960); F. Stagg, E.G. Hinson, and W.E. Oates, *Glossolalia: Tongue Speaking in Biblical, Historical, and Psychological Perspective* (Abingdon, 1967); M. Ramsey, *Holy Spirit: A Biblical Study* (Eerdmans, 1977).

Gluttony ■ An excessive use of things that are in themselves legitimate. A person should eat, for example, in proper quality and quantity to maintain well-being, but without exceeding the limit set by prudence. Paul severely condemns gluttony in Philippians 3:18–19: Many "are enemies of the cross of Christ, whose god is their appetite. . . ." In Roman Catholic theology, gluttony is one of the Seven Deadly Sins. It is usually a venial sin, but can be mortal if serious injury to health or if drunkenness results. See: **Sins, Seven Deadly; Sins, Mortal and Venial.**

Gnosticism ■ From the Greek *gnosis*, "knowledge," "wisdom." A group in the first and second century A.D. which taught that there was a special, higher truth that only the enlightened receive from God. They maintained that matter is evil; that the world was made by the "demiurge," God's created spirit; and that Christ was not human. The gnostics were influenced by Platonic dualism and Eastern religious thought. See: 1 Corinthians 1:22—2:16.

See: R.M. Grant, *Gnosticism and Early Christianity* (Columbia University Press, 1959), and *Gnosticism: A Source Book of Heretical Writings from the Early Christian Period* (Harper and Brothers, 1961).

God ■ The Supreme Being, or the Ultimate Reality, whose nature is to exist. God is the living, personal, loving, and merciful Creator and Sustainer of all that exists. In every way that He exists, He exists in perfection, without limit. He is eternal, all-powerful, all-knowing and perfectly good. The only Being worthy of worship. In Christian theology, He is the first person of the Trinity, the Father. See: John 3:16; Romans 5:8; 8:32; Ephesians 2:4–10; 1 John 4:9–21. See: **Attributes of God, Holy Spirit, Jesus, Metaphysics, Trinity.**

See: H. Bavinck, *The Doctrine of God* (Eerdmans, 1951); J. Collins, *God in Modern Philosophy* (Henry Regnery, 1959); W.L. Craig, *The Existence of God and the Beginning of the Universe* (Here's Life Publishers, 1979); C. Hartshorne and W.L. Reese, *Philosophers Speak of God* (University of Chicago Press, 1953); H. Kung, *Does God Exist?* (Doubleday, 1980); J.B. Phillips, *Your God Is Too Small* (Macmillan, 1967); A. Plantinga, *God and Other Minds* (Cornell University Press, 1967).

God, Arguments for the Existence of ■ Philosophical arguments that attempt through human reason to prove that God exists. In the history of thought there have been four classical arguments for God's existence. See: **Cosmological Argument, Moral Argument, Ontological Argument, Teleological Argument.**

Gospel ■ From the Anglo-Saxon *god-spell*, "God-story," a translation of the Greek *euangelion*, "good news." The Gospel is the good news of the message of salvation offered by God to all who believe in His Son, Jesus, as Lord and Savior. The word also refers to the first four books of the NT because they recount the life and teachings of Jesus. See: Matthew 4:23; 9:35; 24:14; 26:13; Mark 1:14–15; 10:29; 13:10; Romans 15:19; 1 Corinthians 9:12; 2 Corinthians 2:12; 9:13; 10:14; Galatians 1:7; Philippians 1:27; 1 Thessalonians 3:2. See: **Atonement, Salvation.**

Grace ■ From the Greek *charis*, "graceful," "agreeable." The gift of God, the unmerited favor of forgiveness or mercy given to sinners. An outpouring of God's love and mercy. It is also used to refer to a Christian virtue. See: John 3:16–21; 1 Corinthians 15:10; 2 Corinthians 5:17–20; 8:9; Ephesians 2:8.

Grace, Common ■ The grace extended to all mankind through God's general providence. Its benefits are experienced by the whole human race: the beauty of creation, the sun and the rain, the harvest (Matt. 5:45; Heb. 1:2–3; John 1:1–4).

Grace, Irresistible ▪ Grace which cannot be rejected, since God always achieves His aims: "The work of the Holy Spirit in bringing men to faith never fails to achieve its object." The doctrine of irresistible grace teaches that a person cannot resist God's choice to save him, a choice determined before the foundations of the world. Also known as "Effectual Calling," irresistible grace is one of the five points of Calvinism (Irresistible Grace.) See: **Atonement; Calvinism; Calvinism, Five Points of; Fatalism; Predestination.**

Greek ▪ The language in which the NT was written. The particular Greek dialect used, Hellenistic or *Koine* Greek (*he koine dialektos*), was the popular language of the people of the day, as opposed to the classical Greek of the philosophers and poets. It employs popular idiom and favors directness and simplicity. It was also much influenced by Hebrew and Aramaic. See: **Abba, Aramaic, Hebrew.**

Habit ▪ From the Latin *habitus* (from *habere*, "to have"), meaning "condition" or "character." Habit is the manner one uses in conducting oneself, the prevailing disposition or character of a person's thoughts and feelings. It can also be a behavior pattern, which by frequent repetition has become nearly or completely involuntary. "Habit" often has a negative meaning, connoting a flaw in character, but habits can also be good, the result of proper discipline in Christian living. See: Philippians 4:4–9.

See: T.L. Miethe, "Renewing the Mind: Key to Christian Living," in *A Christian's Guide to Faith and Reason* (Bethany House Publishers, 1987), pp. 85–90.

Hades ▪ From the Greek *hades*. The term used in the Greek translation of the OT (LXX) as a synonym for the Hebrew *Sheol*, the abode or place of the dead. The Greek saw Hades as a place within the earth ruled by the god Pluto, the enemy of all life. In the NT the term rarely appears. Jesus only used it four times (Matt. 11:23; 16:18; Luke 10:15; 16:23). In Luke 16:19–31, Jesus sets forth the account of the rich man and Lazarus. Lazarus is in Abraham's bosom, while the rich man is in Hades. Lazarus was in a conscious state and was being comforted. The rich man was also conscious, but he was in physical and mental torment. See: Matthew 11:23; 16:18; Luke 10:15; 16:23; Acts 2:27, 31; 1 Corinthians 15:55; Revelation 1:18; 6:8; 20:13–14. See: **Gehenna, Hell, Sheol.**

Hallelujah ▪ From a Hebrew word that can be translated "Oh Lord, save me," or "Praise the Lord." It appears as a short doxology in the Psalms, usually at the beginning or end, as in Psalm 104, 105, 106, 111, 112 and 135. Because of this, some scholars have suggested that the Levites might have had a special responsibility for uttering it, possibly as a summons to praise. In the NT, "Hallelujah!" is the triumphant shout of praise raised by the elect of God in heaven (Rev. 19:1, 3–4, 6). See: **Doxology.**

Hasty Generalization ■ Also referred to as the "Fallacy of Converse Accident." In seeking to understand and characterize all cases of a certain kind, one can usually give attention to only some of them. To gain the greatest understanding of all cases, those examined should be typical rather than atypical. If someone considers only unusual cases and hastily draws a conclusion that fits these unusual cases alone, he commits the fallacy of converse accident, or hasty generalization. See: **Logical Fallacies.**

Health and Wealth, Gospel of ■ A dangerous teaching in the modern church that the faithful of God will be rewarded with physical health and material wealth. The one who is sick or poor is judged to have little faith. This teaching is nothing more than humanistic materialism cloaked in alleged spirituality.

The NT stands radically opposed to the Gospel of Health and Wealth. Money in itself is not wrong—"the *love of money* is a root of all sorts of evil" (1 Tim. 6:10)—but we are also repeatedly warned against the dangers of material wealth (1 Tim. 6:5–11). Christ called us to be wealthy in doing good deeds (1 Tim. 6:17–18), "not to fix [our] hope on the uncertainty of riches, but on God. . . ." Luke 12:15 tells us, "Beware, and be on your guard against every form of greed; for not even when one has an abundance does his life consist of his possessions." And we are further warned in Luke 12:21 not to be like "the man who lays up treasure for himself, and is not rich toward God."

Nowhere in the NT are we called to success by the standards of this world. We are rather called to be faithful to God's revelation. The NT clearly portrays Jesus as faithful because He—God incarnate—was willing to become the suffering servant. Scripture repeatedly describes the life to which God calls Christians: "For to you it has been granted for Christ's sake, not only to believe in Him, but also to suffer for His sake" (Phil. 1:29); ". . . if you should suffer for the sake of righteousness, you are blessed . . ." (1 Peter 3:14). Paul warns us sharply: "For many walk, of whom I often told you, and now tell you even weeping, that they are enemies of the cross of Christ, whose end is destruction, whose god is their appetite, and whose glory is in their shame, who set their minds on earthly things" (Phil. 3:17–19). See: Matthew 5:12; Acts 9:16; 14:22; 1 Thessalonians 2:14; 2 Thessalonians 1:5; 2 Timothy 1:12; 1 Peter 3:17; 4:1; 5:10; Revelation 2:10.

See: Florence Bulle, *"God Wants You Rich" and Other Enticing Doctrines* (Bethany House Publishers, 1983); Ken L. Sarles, "A Theological Evaluation of the Prosperity Gospel," *Bibliotheca Sacra* (Oct./Dec. 1986) pp. 329–352.

Heart ■ Several OT expressions referring to "the innermost part" or "hidden part" are translated as "heart." Heart is used as the seat of physical life (Gen. 45:26), of wisdom (Prov. 2:10), of confidence (Prov. 3:5), of diligence (Prov. 4:23), of lust (6:25), of understanding (Prov. 8:5), and of knowledge (Prov. 15:14). In the NT, the Greek word *kardia*, "heart," came to refer to the center of a person's consciousness: rational, moral, and emotional makeup. Only those who are pure in heart can see the Father (Matt. 5:8).

The scriptural heart is (1) the intellect, the part of a man that thinks, reasons, understands and believes (Matt. 9:4; Heb. 4:12; Gen. 6:5; Matt. 13:15; Rom. 10:9–10); (2) the seat of the emotions and affections (Matt. 22:37; Mark 2:30–34; 2 Cor. 2:4); (3) the will (Acts 11:23; 1 Cor. 7:37; 2 Cor. 9:7); and (4) the conscience (1 John 3:19–21). It is clear in the NT that the person who truly has a changed heart has experienced a change of intellect, affections, will and conscience (Rom. 12:1–2; Phil. 1:9–11; 4:4–9; 1 Peter 3:15).

Heaven ■ From the Greek *ouranos*, "to lift" or "to heave." In the NT the word is used of the aerial heavens (Matt. 6:26; 8:20; Acts 10:12; 11:6), and the place from which the Son of God came to be born (John 3:13, 31; 6:38, 42). Heaven is where God lives (Matt. 5:16; 12:50; Rev. 3:12; 11:13; 16:11; 20:9). It is the place Christ prepares for believers—there they will be in His presence; there will be no pain or sorrow, but only complete happiness. The Holy Spirit descended from heaven at Pentecost (1 Peter 1:12). The angels also live in heaven (Matt. 18:10; 22:30; Rev. 3:5). See: Ephesians 2:6; Luke 16:26; 23:43; Matthew 25:1.

See also: Wilbur M. Smith, *The Biblical Doctrine of Heaven* (Moody Press, 1968).

Heavenlies, The ■ The place where God, Christ, and believers exist together. This phrase (*en tois epouraniois*) occurs only in Ephesians, and there only five times (1:3, 20; 2:6; 3:10; 6:12). Some theologians believe the heavenlies are a spiritual place where believers, though still alive in the physical world, are at the same time "seated" with the risen Christ. There they enjoy spiritual blessings and engage with the powers of Satan in a real battle for their souls.

Hebrew ■ "Hebrew" is the original name for Abraham and his descendants. With the exception of Aramaic in Ezra 4:6–8; 7:12–26; Daniel 2:4–7, 28; and Jeremiah 10:11, Hebrew is the language of the OT.

The word also refers to the language these people used. The Hebrew language is pictorial, poetic and simpler than Greek. It consists of a series of guttural sounds. Originally written without vowels, Hebrew now uses vowel points, a series of dots above consonants, to show vowels, an innovation introduced in A.D. 600–800 by Masorete scholars, notably at Tibereas in Palestine. Some of the Dead Sea Scrolls were written in Hebrew. See: **Aramaic, Dead Sea Scrolls, Greek.**

Heilsgeschichte ■ A German word which means "salvation history," denoting a school of theological thought that sees the ongoing story of God's redemptive activity as a central theme in interpreting the Bible. Johann Albrecht Bengel (1687–1752) is considered the father of *heilsgeschichte*. It was further developed by J. J. Beck (1804–1878) of Tubingen and J.C.K. von Hofmann (1810–1877). Certain famous theologians of this century—Oscar Cullmann, Gerhard von Rad, W. G. Kummel, D. P. Fuller, C. H. Dodd—also see the Bible as redemption history.

Calvinist scholar John H. Gerstner judges Jonathan Edwards' posthumous *History of Redemption* to be the first work of the American *Heilsgeschichte* school. No evidence suggests that Edwards (1703–1758) knew of Bengel's work.

Hell ■ The place of eternal punishment for those who reject Jesus as Lord and Savior. Scripture calls hell a place of everlasting punishment (Matt. 25:46), of everlasting fire (Matt. 18:8), of everlasting chains (2 Thess. 1:8–9), of eternal fire (Jude 7), of outer darkness (Matt. 8:12), of the wrath of God (Rom. 2:5), and a lake that burns with fire and brimstone (Rev. 21:8), a place prepared for Satan and his angels (Matt. 25:41).

In recent years conservative Christians have developed several differing views of hell. Some believe that hell must have literal flames since the Bible teaches this; this follows the view of Augustine (A.D. 354–430), who says in his *City of God* that hell is composed of physical fire. Others maintain that such language is figurative, but that hell will be fully hell no matter what the physical characteristics of the place. Those in hell, they say, will suffer eternal mental torture because they will be fully conscious that they rejected God. Some evangelicals are teaching a view of hell which states that each sinner will cease to exist after paying for his or her sins. See Matthew 18:18; 25:41–46; Mark 3:29; Hebrews 6:2; Jude 6. See: **Hades, Gehenna, Sheol.**

Henotheism ■ The worship of one god without denying the existence of other gods; the belief that there are many finite gods with one supreme among them.

Heresy ■ From the Greek *hairesis*, which denotes a "choosing" that leads to division and the formation of sects (1 Cor. 11:19; Gal. 5:20). Heresy is a teaching or belief that contradicts the teaching of the Bible, a deliberate denial of truth revealed by God. In the Roman Catholic Church, heresy can be either "formal," in which a baptized Roman Catholic holds to false doctrine, or "material," in which a non-Catholic believes false doctrine out of ignorance. See: 2 Peter 2:1. See also: **Apostasy, Arianism, Docetism, Gnosticism, Manichaeism, Nestorianism, Schism.**

Hermeneutics ■ From the Greek *hermeneutikos*, "interpretation." Hermeneutics is the science of the study and interpretation of Scripture, the branch of theology that prescribes rules by which the Bible should be interpreted. Biblical hermeneutics strives to formulate guidelines for studying Scripture that help recover the meaning a biblical text had for its original hearers. See: **Exegesis.**

Higher Criticism ▪ A method of interpreting the Bible from the standpoint of literature. Higher criticism seeks to determine the authorship, date and underlying literary documents of books of the Bible, as well as their historical dependability. Higher criticism is different from lower criticism, which tries to determine the Bible's correct text at the points where copied manuscripts of the Bible vary slightly. See: **Form Criticism, Lower Criticism.**

Hinduism ▪ The dominant cultic religion of India. It emphasizes dharma, an individual's duty fulfilled by observing custom or law. Central among its teachings are reincarnation; karma, the force generated by a person's actions that determines his destiny in his next existence; and nirvana, absorption of the individual into the whole of reality. The absorption ends reincarnation, cycles of birth and rebirth. See: **Reincarnation.**

See: E.G. Parrinder, *Upanishads, Gita and Bible* (Association Press, 1962); M. Pitt, *Introducing Hinduism* (Friendship Press, 1965).

Holiness Movement, American ▪ A movement growing out of the teaching of John Wesley (1703–1791), the founder of the Methodist Church. The American Holiness Movement came into being in the United States in the 1840s and 1850s. Emphasizing total sanctification and a life of separation and godliness, preachers in this tradition taught a process of salvation in two phases: (1) conversion, or justification, which frees the individual from sins committed in the past; and (2) sanctification, or full salvation, which frees the individual from "the flaw in the moral nature" that causes the person to sin. During this period Charles Grandison Finney (1792–1875) and others contributed to the movement, and the Wesleyan Methodist Church (1843) and the Free Methodist Church (1860) became the first two church groups organized on the basis of holiness as a central doctrine.

After the Civil War, a major revival focusing on holiness broke out in Methodism, causing a breach between the Holiness leaders and more traditional Methodist leaders. By the 1880s the first independent Holiness denominations had come into being: the Church of God, Anderson, Indiana (1880); the Church of the Nazarene (1908); and Pilgrim Holiness Church (1897), which later merged with the Wesleyan Methodists to form the Wesleyan Church in 1968.

But the Holiness Movement spread beyond the Methodist groups to a Mennonite group, for example, which was formerly called the United Missionary Church, and since 1969 has been known as the Missionary Church, to the Brethren in Christ (1863), to the Evangelical Friends Alliance (1947) and to the Salvation Army. The Christian and Missionary Alliance Church has Wesleyan ideas, though they never accepted the doctrine that believers could in this life be freed from all willful sin. The CMA's two most famous theologians, A. B. Simpson and A. W. Tozer, are still esteemed in Holiness groups. Pentecostalism also has roots in the Holiness Movement. See: **Perfection, Christian; Perfection, Theological; Pentecostalism; Wesleyanism.**

See: Charles E. Jones, *A Guide to the Study of the Holiness Movement* (Scarecrow Press, 1974); Donald W. Dayton, *The American Holiness Movement: A Bibliographic Introduction* (Asbury Theological Seminary, 1971); Melvin E. Dieter, *The Holiness Revival of the Nineteenth Century* (Scarecrow Press, 1980).

Holy ▪ From the Greek *hagios*, "separated," separated from sin and therefore consecrated to God, set apart for a sacred use. God, the Father, is the absolutely Holy One (Luke 1:49; John 17:11; 1 Peter 1:15–16; Rev. 4:8; 6:10). Jesus, the Son, is said to be holy (Luke 1:35; Acts 3:14; 4:27, 30; 1 John 2:20). The word is used of the Holy Spirit throughout the NT (Matt. 1:18; 2 Tim. 1:14; Titus 3:5; 1 Peter 1:12; 2 Peter 1:21; Jude 20). People are considered holy when they are devoted to God (2 Tim. 1:9; 1 Peter 3:15; 2 Peter 3:11).

Holy Spirit ▪ The third Person of the Trinity. The Holy Spirit is equal with the Father and Son (Matt. 28:19; 2 Cor. 13:14). Christians are reborn through the Holy Spirit (Acts 2:38). The Holy Spirit gave Christians gifts, such as the ability to speak in tongues, to prophesy, to heal and to work miracles (1 Cor. 12 and 14). Jesus promised that when He departed the Holy Spirit would come and dwell with every believer (John 14:16–26). He is called the Comforter, or Helper (John 14; 15:26; 16:7). He would guide and teach the Church (John 14:25–26), bear witness to Christ and glorify Him (John 15:26), and convict the world of sin (John 16:7–14) and judgment (Luke 24:49; John 7:37–39; 14:25–26; Acts 1:8).

It is in the NT that the personality of the Holy Spirit is truly revealed. The Holy Spirit is involved in the miraculous conception of Jesus (Matt. 1:18–20), in Jesus' baptism (Matt. 3:16; Mark 1:10; John 1:32) and on the day of Pentecost at the birth of the Church (Acts 2:4). He dwells within us (John 14:17; Acts 2:38). The Holy Spirit inspired the Scriptures and speaks through them (Acts 1:16; 2 Peter 1:21). The Holy Spirit can be grieved (Eph. 4:30) and blasphemed against (Matt. 12:31). See: **Pneumatology; Trinity; Sin Against the Holy Spirit; Tongues, Speaking in.**

See Also: M. Green, *I Believe in the Holy Spirit* (Eerdmans, 1975); T.L. Miethe, "The Holy Spirit and Knowledge," in *A Christian's Guide to Faith and Reason* (Bethany House Publishers, 1987); L. Morris, *Spirit of the Living God* (InterVarsity Press, 1960); C.F.D. Moule, *The Holy Spirit* (Eerdmans, 1978); D.M. Howard, *By the Power of the Holy Spirit* (InterVarsity Press, 1973); B.L. Ramm, *The Witness of the Spirit* (Eerdmans, 1959); W.H. Griffith Thomas, *The Holy Spirit of God* (Eerdmans, 1913); J.R.W. Stott, *The Baptism and Fullness of the Holy Spirit* (InterVarsity Press, 1964).

Homiletics ■ From the Greek *homiletikos*, "to deal with others." The discipline that examines methods of constructing, preparing and delivering sermons. Also used to refer to the study of preaching in general. See: **Homily, Preaching, Sermons.**

See: A.W. Blackwood, *The Preparation of Sermons* (Abingdon, 1948); D. Martyn Lloyd-Jones, *Preaching and Preachers* (Zondervan, 1971); T.H. Pattison, *The Making of the Sermon* (Judson Press, 1941); J.R.W. Stott, *The Art of Preaching in the Twentieth Century: Between Two Worlds* (Eerdmans, 1982).

Homily ■ From the Greek *homilia*, "to converse" or "sermon." "Homily" is another word for sermon. See: **Preaching, Sermon.**

Homoiousios ■ Semi-Arians used this term to say that Jesus was not the *same* as the Father, but was *similar* in nature. Jesus was of a substance like the Father. Orthodox Christianity saw this as a watering-down of Christ's full divinity. See **Homoousion.**

Homoousion ■ Athanasius (293–373), bishop of Alexandria, used this term to refer to the theological teaching that Jesus is of the same nature, or substance, as the Father. The term was used by the Council of Nicea in 325 to condemn Arianism. See: **Arianism; Nicea, Council of.**

Hope ■ The belief that God will keep His promises for the future. We base this hope on the evidence of His faithfulness in the past. Hope includes confidence in all Christian promises not yet a reality in the life of a believer. Certainly, life after death and an eternity in heaven is an important one. In 1 Corinthians 15:19 Paul says: "If we have only hoped in Christ in this life, we are of all men most to be pitied."

Christians should be able to defend their hope: In 1 Peter 3:15, the Christian is told to ". . . sanctify Christ as Lord in your hearts, always being ready to make a defense to every one who asks you to give an account for the hope that is in you, yet with gentleness and reverence." In 1 Peter 3:15 the word "heart" refers to the center of our being, our minds. We are told to be able to give a defense of our hope in the Gospel because of the evidence for the truth of Christianity. See: **Apologetics.**

Hosanna ■ The Greek equivalent of a Hebrew greeting that means "save us we pray" (see Ps. 118:25). This greeting occurs only six times in the NT, all with regard to Christ's triumphal entry into Jerusalem (Matt. 21:9, 15; John 12:13). This word subsequently came to be used at an early date as an expression in Christian worship of joy and praise.

Humanism ■ In one sense, Jesus Christ is the greatest humanist of all time. In this use of the word, "humanism" refers to caring for mankind and making an effort to improve the lives of human beings. This should also characterize the wishes and actions of all Christians.

But another use of the word "humanism"—the belief that human beings are the ultimate standard by which to judge all things—flatly contradicts Christ's teaching. This humanism ascribes to human beings the highest value in the universe, making human beings gods and denying the existence of any Being beyond mankind. Some Christians use the term "secular humanism" today to refer to this second sense. Neither the term nor the belief system it represents, however, are inventions of Christians. Self-proclaimed secular humanists often represent a world view militantly anti-Christian. Although all Christians must be humanists in the first sense, we cannot be influenced by this idolatrous second view.

See: A statement of basic beliefs by a leading secular humanist: Paul Kurtz, *In Defense of Secular Humanism* (Prometheus Books, 1983); Terry L. Miethe, "The Humanity of Jesus," in *The New Christian's Guide to Following Jesus* (Bethany House Publishers, 1984), pp. 43–46; T.M. Kitwood, *What is Human?* (InterVarsity Press, 1970).

Hypocrite ▪ One who pretends to possess virtues or qualities he does not have, from the Greek *hupocrites*, a stage or play actor, which is in turn from the Greek *hupokrinein*, "to play a part." Greek and Roman actors used large masks with mechanical devices that increased the volume of the voice, hence the idea that they portrayed something they did not actually possess. In His condemnation of Pharisees, Jesus makes the point that while on the outside hypocrites seem religious, on the inside and in the sight of God they are profane and ungodly people. In Mark 7:6, Jesus calls the Pharisees "hypocrites" and quotes Isaiah 29:13, "This people honors Me with their lips, but their heart is far away from Me." See: Matthew 24:51; Mark 12:15; Luke 6:42; 11:44; 12:56; 13:15, 46.

Hypostasis ▪ A transliteration of the Greek word for "self-subsistence," "substance," or "nature." In theology, this means the real or essential nature of a thing as distinguished from its attributes. The Nicene Creed (325) holds that the substance (*hypostasia*) and the essence (*ousia*) of God the Father and Jesus the Son are one and the same. This is in opposition to Arianism, which views God the Father and Jesus as one in substance, but different in essence. See: **Arianism; Nicea, Council of; Nicene Creed.**

Hypostatic Union ▪ In theology, hypostatic union refers to the union of Jesus' divine and human natures in one person. In the Incarnation Jesus' human nature was forever inseparably united with His divine nature, yet the two natures remain distinct and whole without mixture. Thus Jesus Christ is at once fully God and fully human. This was first put forth officially in the statement of faith produced by the Council of Chalcedon (451), and rules out several historical ideas about the Incarnation. See: John 1:1–14; Romans 1:2–5; 9:5; Philippians 2:6–11; 1 Timothy 3:16; Hebrews 2:14; 1 John 1:1–3. See: **Arianism; Adoptionism; Apollinarianism; Chalcedon, Council of; Docetism; Eutychianism; Monophysitism; Nestorianism; Socinianism.**

"I Am" sayings of Jesus ■ Some theologians say that these NT sayings of Jesus show His equality with God the Father because they reflect Exodus 3:14, where God the Father, "Yahweh" or "I am," identifies himself. Only John 8:58 and 13:19, however, undeniably match the absolute statement of Exodus 3:14 in both form and content. See: John 4:25–26, "I am the Messiah"; John 6:35–36, "I am the bread of life"; John 8:12, "I am the light of the world"; John 8:23, "I am from above, not of this world"; John 8:58, "Truly, truly, I say to you, before Abraham was born, I am"; John 9:5, "I am the light of the world"; John 10:7, "I am the door of the sheep"; John 10:11, "I am the good shepherd; the good shepherd lays down His life for the sheep"; John 10:36, Christ indirectly says "I am the Son of God"; John 11:25, "I am the resurrection, and the life"; John 13:13, "I am the Teacher, and Lord"; John 13:19, ". . . you may believe that I am"; John 14:6, "I am the way, the truth, and the life"; John 15:1, "I am the true vine"; John 18:5–6, "I am."—Christ's hearers drew back and fell to the ground; Mark 14:62, "I am the Christ, the Blessed One"; Revelation 1:8, "I am the Alpha and the Omega"; Revelation 1:17, "I am the first and the last." See also: **Yahweh.**

I—Thou ■ An important concept in the religious thought of Martin Buber (1878–1965), a Jewish philosopher. Buber tells us in his popular book *I and Thou* that we exist in dimensions of relationship: "I—It" and "I—Thou." The first refers to our relationship with objects, the second to our relationship with persons. For Buber, we meet God in I—Thou relationships. God is the eternal Thou. Buber's concept of the "I—Thou" relationship has been adopted by several Christian theologians, including

Karl Barth (1886–1968), Dietrich Bonhoeffer (1906–1945), and Rudolf Bultmann (1884–1976).

Idolatry, Idols ■ In the OT the word "idol" means "vanity" (Jer. 14:22; 18:15); idols were made of wood, stone and precious metal (Isa. 40; Jer. 10). While such idols continued into NT times, especially in Greek culture, the NT also recognizes that anything treasured more than God is an idol. In Romans 1:22–25, idolatry is a sin against God and an idolater is a slave to whatever has taken the place of God. See: Acts 17:16; 1 Corinthians 5:11; 10:7, 14; Galatians 5:20; Philippians 3:18–19; Colossians 2:18; 3:5; Titus 3:3.

Ignorance ■ A state of lack of knowledge or comprehension. In the Bible, ignorance is never honored by God and can even be the basis of sin. See: Acts 3:17; 1 Peter 2:15; Hebrews 9:7; 1 Corinthians 14:16, 23–24.

Ignorance, Argument from ■ In Latin, *Argumentum ad Ignorantiam*. An example: there must be ghosts because no one has ever shown that they do not exist. The fallacy of Argument from Ignorance is committed whenever a person asserts that a proposition is true simply because it has not been proven false, or that it is false merely because it has not been proven true. This mistaken logic often occurs in arguments where there is no clear-cut evidence either for or against an issue. See: **Logical Fallacies.**

Illumination ■ From the Greek *photizo*, which comes from the word for "light." In Protestant theology, illumination is the work of the Holy Spirit that allows human beings to understand Scripture when it is heard or read. Jesus, through the Gospel, enlightens (John 1:9; 2 Tim. 1:10). In Ephesians 1:18, a form of the Greek word is translated as "enlightened," which refers metaphorically to spiritual understanding. See John 1:9; Ephesians 3:9; Hebrews 6:4; Revelation 22:5.

Imago Dei ■ A Latin phrase frequently used in theology meaning "image of God." In Genesis 1:27, we are told that human beings are created in God's image. Some Protestant Reformers taught that this image of God had been lost in the fall of Adam.

Immaculate Conception ▪ This Roman Catholic doctrine is more formally known as "The Immaculate Conception of the Blessed Virgin Mary, the Mother of God." Immaculate Conception is the miracle of the removal of the sins of Mary, the mother of Jesus, at her conception. According to Catholic theology, original sin is passed from generation to generation by childbirth. Had Mary's sins not been removed, Jesus would have inherited original sin. The miracle of the Immaculate Conception thus explains how Christ could be completely without sin.

This teaching was proclaimed in the papal bull *Ineffabilis Deus* by Pius IX on December 8, 1854, which says that "the Blessed Virgin Mary, at the very moment of her being conceived, received immunity from all stain of original sin, due to the merits of Jesus Christ the Savior of humanity. . . ." See: Genesis 3:15 and Luke 1:28.

Immanence ▪ The idea that God, though sovereign and transcendent, is also present and active in both creation and human history.

Immersion ▪ From the Greek *baptizein*, "to dip in water," "immerse." A mode or form of water baptism. Christ's own baptism is a clear example of immersion: "And as soon as Jesus was baptized, he went up out of the water. At that moment heaven was opened, and he saw the Spirit of God descending like a dove and lighting on him. And a voice from heaven said, 'This is my Son, whom I love; with him I am well pleased' " (Matt. 3:16, NIV). See: **Baptism, Sprinkling.**

See: K. Barth, *The Teaching of the Church Regarding Baptism* (London: SCM Press, 1948); G.R. Beasley-Murray, *Baptism in the New Testament* (Eerdmans, 1962); P.K. Jewett, *Infant Baptism and the Covenant of Grace* (Eerdmans, 1978); Dale Moody, *Baptism: Foundation for Christian Unity* (Westminster, 1967); T.L. Watson, *Should Infants Be Baptized?* (Guardian Press, 1976).

Immortality ▪ From the Greek *athanasia* or the Latin *im*, "not," and *mortis*, "death." Literally, the state of not being mortal. The resurrection body is immortal, not subject to death (1 Cor. 15:53–

54). Stated positively, "immortality" is the condition of being able to live forever. This is possible only because of the sustaining power of God. See: **Eternal Life.**

Imprimatur ▪ Latin for "let it be printed." If this word appears on the back of the title page of a book (on the copyright page) it means that a bishop of the Roman Catholic Church or his delegate has licensed the book for publication. The Nihil Obstat and Imprimatur are official declarations that a book or pamphlet is free from doctrinal or moral error. See: **Nihil Obstat.**

Imputation ▪ From the Greek *logizomai* and the Latin *imputare*, "to reckon in," "to charge to one's account" (Phil. 1:8). To transfer one person's sin or righteousness to another. Imputation often refers to God's crediting Christ's righteousness to all who believe in Him. See: Genesis 15:6; Romans 4:3, 6, 11; 5:15; 9:22; Galatians 3:6. See: **Atonement, Sin.**

Incarnation ▪ From the Latin *in*, "in" and *caro*, "flesh." In theology, this is the doctrine that God, the Eternal Son—the second person of the Trinity—became man, or flesh, in the person of Jesus. This does not mean, however, that He gave up His deity in the process. See: John 1:14; Romans 1:3; 8:3; Galatians 4:4; Philippians 2:7–8; 1 Timothy 3:16; Hebrews 1; 1 John 4:2; 2 John 7. See: **Christ, Christology.**
    See: Athanasius, *The Incarnation of the Word of God* (London: A.R. Mowbray and Co., 1963); A.B. Bruce, *The Humiliation of Christ* (George H. Doran Co.); L. Cerfaux, *Christ in the Theology of St. Paul* (Herder and Herder, 1959); H.R. Mackintosh, *The Doctrine of the Person of Christ* (Edinburgh: T. and T. Clark, 1914); H.D. McDonald, *Jesus, Human and Divine* (Zondervan, 1968); J.F. Walvoord, *Jesus Christ Our Lord* (Moody Press, 1969).

Inerrancy ▪ The doctrine that the Bible, in all it teaches, is free from error. The best statement of what evangelicals mean by inerrancy is found in "The Chicago Statement on Biblical Inerrancy" (see: pages 493–502 of N. L. Geisler's *Inerrancy*, Zondervan, 1979). Article VI affirms: ". . . that the whole of Scripture and all its parts, down to the very words of the original, were given by divine inspiration." Article X affirms: ". . . that inspiration, strictly speaking, applies only to the autographic text of Scripture, which in the providence of God can be ascertained from available manuscripts with great accuracy." This doctrine does not assert that no errors in the copies were transmitted through history or that one does not have to study the text carefully in regard to textual problems and interpretation.

The view that the Bible is inerrant is rooted in our view of God. If there are good reasons to believe in a God who is Supreme Being, unlimited in His very nature (unlimited in power, knowledge, goodness, wisdom and so on), then there is little problem with the possibility of such a Being communicating with mankind in a way that would preclude the possibility of error. In fact, if such a God exists then one would expect this kind of revelation from Him. The real problem would be if no such communication existed! See: **Bible, Inerrancy and Infallibility of; Biblical Criticism.**

See: D.A. Carson and John D. Woodbridge, *Scripture and Truth* (Zondervan, 1983); N.L. Geisler, *Biblical Errancy: An Analysis of its Philosophical Roots* (Zondervan, 1981), and *Inerrancy* (Zondervan, 1979); Gordon Lewis and Bruce Demarest, *Challenges to Inerrancy: A Theological Response* (Moody Press, 1984); J.W. Montgomery, *God's Inerrant Word* (Bethany House Publishers, 1974).

Infallibility ■ From the Latin *in*, "not," and *fallere*, "to deceive." The doctrine that the Bible is free from mistakes, incapable of error, not liable to mislead, deceive, or disappoint. Often used interchangeably with the term "inerrancy." See: **Bible, Inerrancy and Infallibility of.**

The Roman Catholic and Eastern Orthodox churches have taught that the proclamations of doctrine or dogmas by their councils are infallible. The Roman Catholic Church also teaches that the pope is infallible when he speaks *ex cathedra*, "from the Chair" of St. Peter. The doctrine of papal infallibility was officially equated with the infallibility of the Roman Catholic Church at the First Vatican Council in 1870. See: **Ex Cathedra.**

Infralapsarianism ■ From the Latin *infra*, "below," "lower than," and *lapsus*, "a falling." The doctrine that God decrees election to salvation after the Fall. This can also mean that "God's decree of election contemplated the Fall as a past event," whether the event was in human perspective past or not. Infralapsarianism is one view of how God, according to Calvinistic teaching, chose some to be saved, elected, before they were born. See: **Sublapsarianism; Calvinism; Calvinism, The Five Points of; Election; Predestination; Supralapsarianism.**

Inspiration ■ From the Latin *inspirare*, "to breathe in." In theology, the Holy Spirit acting on the writers of the Bible in a way that protects the truth of its message, making it the Word of God. 2 Peter 1:20–21 reads: "But know this first of all, that no prophecy of scripture is a matter of one's own interpretation, for no prophecy was ever made by an act of human will, but men moved by the Holy Spirit spoke from God." See: 2 Timothy 3:16. See: **Bible, Inerrancy and Infallibility of; Inerrancy; Propositional Revelation.**

See: S. Custer, *Does Inspiration Demand Inerrancy?* (Craig Press, 1968); T.E.W. Engelder, *Scripture Cannot Be Broken* (Concordia Publishing House, 1945); F.S.R.L. Gaussen, *Divine Inspiration of the Bible* (Kregel); C.F.H. Henry, *Revelation and the Bible* (Baker, 1958); J. Orr, *Revelation and Inspiration* (Eerdmans, 1952); J.I. Packer, *God Speaks to Man: Revelation and the Bible* (Westminster Press, 1966); C.H. Pinnock, *A Defense of Biblical Infallibility* (Presbyterian and Reformed, 1967), *Biblical Revelation: The Foundation of Christian Theology* (Moody, 1971), and *The Scripture Principle* (Harper & Row, 1984).

Inspiration, Dictation Theory ■ The view that God dictated to the writers of the Bible the words they then recorded. This view is rejected by a vast majority of conservative Christians. Evangelicals generally hold to plenary (extending to all parts of the canonical books) and verbal (extending to the very words of the text) inspiration; this second view allows for the individual style of different writers to be seen in the texts of the Bible.

Intercession ■ An act of prayer, petition, or entreaty in favor of another. In Romans 15:30 Paul says: "Now I urge you, brethren, by our Lord Jesus Christ and by the love of the Spirit to strive [agonize] together with me in your prayers to God for me . . ." Some have correctly seen intercessory prayer as one of the most important ministries of a Christian. See: **Prayer.**

See: A. Murray, *The Ministry of Intercessory Prayer* (Bethany House Publishers, 1966).

Intercession of the Saints ■ From the Latin *intercessio*, "an intervention." The Roman Catholic belief that the prayers of the saints in heaven can affect God's judgment of those alive on earth. The Catholic Church has also taught that Christians can pray to, or through, saints for God's forgiveness for those alive.

Intermediate State ■ The period between a person's death and the resurrection and final judgment. See: Luke 16:19–31; 2 Corinthians 5:1–10; 1 Peter 3:18–22; 4:6. See: **Purgatory.**

Ipsum Esse ■ Latin for "being itself." In philosophy, "ipsum esse" is the phrase for "Being-in-Itself," the idea that God's essence is existence and His existence is His essence. See: **God, Metaphysics.**

Islam ■ With more than 500 million followers, Islam may well be the world's largest religion. Founded by Mohammed (c. 570–632), an Arab religious leader who was born at Mecca in the Arabian peninsula, Islam takes its name from the Arabic word for "devout submission to the will of God." "Allah," the name Muslims use for God, is the same term sixth-century Syrian Christians used for God.

Mohammed, who regarded himself as the last in a series of accepted prophets, believed he was to take up the prophetic task where his immediate predecessor, Jesus, left off. In A.D. 610 Mohammed claimed he had a vision in which the angel Gabriel appeared to him and said that he, Mohammed, was the last of God's prophets. Over a twenty-year period Gabriel dictated to him everything necessary to call mankind back to the true religion of Abraham.

Islam is based on Mohammed's teachings as found in the *Koran*, the *Sunna* and the *Consensus* (*ijma*). Mohammed did not write these down; his hearers recorded his messages, learned them by heart and related them to others. In the beginning the movement lacked an official text, but relatively soon after Mohammed's death four scholars assembled the recollections of early reciters.

Muslim observance is contained in "The five pillars of Islam": the declaration of faith (the *shahada*), prayer, fasting, almsgiving, and the pilgrimage to Mecca. Muslims must pray at set hours five times daily, with a special service on Fridays at the mosque. In Islamic society, the man has absolute authority over his wife (or wives), children (even when they are grown with families of their own), and slaves. Men can marry Jewish or Christian women, but Muslim women cannot marry outside the faith. Divorce, polygamy and the keeping of concubines (the man's right to sleep with his female slaves) are all allowed. Usury (interest on loans) is absolutely banned.

See: H.A.R. Gibb and J.H. Kramers, *Shorter Encyclopedia of Islam* (Cornell University Press, 1965); T.P. Hughes, *A Dictionary of Islam* (Reference Book Publishers, 1965); K. Cragg, *The Call of the Minaret* (Oxford University Press, 1956); E.G. Parrinder, *Jesus and the Qur'an* (Barnes and Noble, 1965), and *The Koran: The Eternal Revelation Vouch-safed to Muhammad* (Frederick A. Praeger, 1971).

ΙΧθΥΣ ▪ The Greek word *ichthys*, "fish." This acronym stood for the initial letters of the Greek phrase *Jesus Christ, Son of God and Savior*. Very early in Church history Christians used the insignia or symbol to designate those who were of the faith. See: Matthew 4:19; 13:47–49; Luke 5:4–10.

Jehovah's Witnesses ▪ A religious group founded in the 1870s by Charles Taze Russell (1852–1916). Though he had only seven years of schooling, Russell was a successful owner of a men's clothing store. He began studying the Bible with the help of Seventh-Day Adventist friends, and came to believe that Christ had invisibly returned to earth in 1874, that the saints were raised in 1878, and that the end of the "times of the Gentiles" would take place in 1914. Russell published the first book of his seven volume series, *Studies in the Scripture*, in 1886. The Witnesses' self-declared pastor, Russell was often lauded by his followers as the Apostle Paul's equal as a Bible expositor. In 1880 Russell married Maria Ackley. In 1897 she left her husband and in 1903 she sued for permanent separation (since Jehovah's Witnesses do not permit divorce) on the grounds of adultery. She won her case.

Jehovah's Witnesses reject the doctrine of the Trinity and view Jesus as the first son brought forth by Jehovah God. At some points they follow an extremely literal interpretation of the Bible; only 144,000 people, for example, will share in heavenly glory, while the others will enjoy the blessings of life down here on earth. They teach that Abel, Adam's son, was the first Jehovah's Witness. They have their own version of the Bible, *The New World Translation of the Holy Scriptures*, yet Russell thought it better to quit the Scriptures and read his books than to read the Scriptures and neglect his books.

A Jehovah's Witness takes courses in speech, Bible, and missionary methods, and spends a minimum of 60 hours per month witnessing. He cannot be a salesperson or shopkeeper, and cannot drink, smoke, attend movies, dance, hold public office, vote, salute the flag or enter the military. The name "Jehovah's Witnesses" was adopted in 1931. Though they meet in their Kingdom Halls, organizationally they are not a church.

See: J. Gerstner, *The Theology of the Major Sects* (Baker, 1971); A. Hoekema, *The Four Major Cults* (Eerdmans, 1963); W. Martin, *The Kingdom of the Cults* (Bethany House Publishers, 1985); R. Pike, *Jehovah's Witnesses* (The Philosophical Library, 1954).

Jesuits ▪ See: **Society of Jesus, The.**

Jesus ▪ From the Hebrew *Yehoshua, Y'shua,* meaning "Yahweh is salvation." The Hebrew name given to Jesus, the child conceived by the Holy Spirit and born to the Virgin Mary. Born in Bethlehem in Palestine around 4 B.C. (Matt. 1:18—2:12; Luke 1:26–27), Jesus began His ministry after His baptism by John the Baptist (Mark 1:1–15; Acts 1:21–22; 10:37). The Bible tells us that Jesus was a Jew (Gal. 4:4), a descendant of David (Rom. 1:3); he was tempted (Heb. 2:18; 4:15) yet sinless (2 Cor. 5:21); he was transfigured (2 Peter 12:17–18); he was crucified (1 Cor. 1:23), rose from the dead (1 Cor. 15:3–11) and ascended into heaven (Eph. 4:8). See: **Christ, Christology, Messiah, Resurrection of Jesus, Second Coming of Christ, Son of God, Son of Man, Virgin Birth.**

See: E. Brunner, *The Mediator* (Westminster, 1947); R.C. Foster, *Studies in the Life of Christ* in 3 vols. (Baker, 1962): *Introduction and Early Ministry* (505 p.), *The Middle Period* (604 p.), and *The Final Week* (345 p.); G.R. Habermas, *Ancient Evidence for the Life of Jesus* (Thomas Nelson, 1984); J. Pelikan, *Jesus Through the Centuries: His Place in the History of Culture* (Yale, 1985); J.W. Shepard, *The Christ of the Gospels* (Eerdmans, 1939).

Jew ▪ From the Hebrew *Yehudi,* which originally referred to an inhabitant of Judah (2 Kings 16:6). The word is commonly used by non-Jews in reference to the Hebrews, the descendants of Abraham (Jer. 34:9). By the NT period, "Jew" was popularly used for any Israelite (Gal. 2:14; Titus 1:14). Today the word refers to a person of Hebrew descent or to a convert to Judaism.

Joy ▪ In Greek, *chara,* "joy," and *chairo,* "to rejoice." In Christian usage, joy is more than a feeling. It is a quality of life (Ps. 16:11; Rom. 15:13), a sense of satisfaction or delight not affected by circumstances. Paul used the word *chara* in three contexts: (1)

Maturing in Christ is a cause for joy (1 Thess. 2:19–20; Phil. 2:2); (2) Christian joy may come out of suffering and sorrow for Christ's sake (Col. 1:24; 2 Cor. 6:10; 1 Peter 4:13; Heb. 10:34); and (3) Joy is a gift of the Holy Spirit (Gal. 5:22).

C. S. Lewis says of joy: ". . . it is that of an unsatisfied desire which is itself more desirable than any other satisfaction. I call it Joy, which is here a technical term and must be sharply distinguished both from Happiness and from Pleasure. Joy (in my sense) has indeed one characteristic, and one only, in common with them; the fact that anyone who has experienced it will want it again. Apart from that, and considered only in its quality, it might almost equally well be called a particular kind of unhappiness or grief. But then it is a kind we want. I doubt whether anyone who has tasted it would ever, if both were in his power, exchange it for all the pleasures in the world" (pp. 17–18 of *Surprised by Joy*).

Lewis further says: "I had hoped that the heart of reality might be of such a kind that we can best symbolize it as a place; instead, I found it to be a Person" (p. 230). See: Matthew 5:12; John 15:9–14; 2 Corinthians 12:9; 1 Thessalonians 5:16; Philippians 3:1; 4:4; 1 Peter 1:6–8.

See: C.S. Lewis, *The Joyful Christian* (Macmillan, 1977), and *Surprised by Joy: The Shape of My Early Life* (Harcourt, Brace and World, 1955).

Judaism ▪ Derived from the Greek *Ioudaismos*. The religion and culture of the Jewish people. See: Galatians 1:13–14. Modern Jewish faith has four foundations: (1) The Torah—the Law, the first five books of the OT; (2) God who is one, spiritual and eternal; (3) The people who were especially called by God; and (4) The land—today Eretz Yisrael—which they trace back to Abraham (Gen. 17:7–8). See: **Jew.**

Judgment, Final ▪ The event at the end of the world at which Jesus will judge the living and the dead. This will be the final triumph of God's will and justice. See: Matthew 10:15; 18:23–35; 24:43–51; 25:31–46; Mark 14:62; Luke 17:20–31; John 5:24–35; 1 Thessalonians 5:3; Galatians 5:5; Colossians 3:4; 1 Corinthians 6:1–5; Romans 8:31–39; 1 Peter 1:5–9. See: **Apocalypse, Eschatology, Parousia.**

Justice ▪ The biblical words translated "justice" are *sedaqa*, *sedeq*, *dike* and *dikaiosyne*. They are also rendered "righteousness." Justice is an aspect of God's character whereby He is infinitely righteous in himself and all He does. See: Psalm 89:14; 145:17; 2 Thessalonians 1:6. See: **Righteousness of God.**

Justification ▪ From the Hebrew *sadeq*, the Greek *dikaioo* and the Latin *justificare*, "to justify," "to pronounce, accept and treat as just." In theology, God's pardoning sinners and restoring them to a state of righteousness. Paul develops the doctrine of justification by faith in Romans and Galatians. See: Deuteronomy 25:1; Proverbs 17:15; Psalm 32:1–5; 130; Luke 7:47–50; 18:9–14; Acts 10:43; Romans 3:25, 28, 30; 8:33–34; Galatians 4:21—5:12; 1 John 1:7—2:2. See: **Salvation.**

See: G.C. Berkouwer, *Faith and Justification* (Eerdmans, 1954); J. Buchanan, *The Doctrine of Justification* (Baker, 1955).

Kantianism ■ Based on the thought of the German philosopher, Immanuel Kant (1724–1804). Kant set out to unite rationalism and empiricism. He declared that all knowledge comes from sense experience, but its structure is derived from the categories of the understanding, which are forms in the mind itself. In the *Critique of Pure Reason*, Kant addressed the three foundational questions in philosophy: (1) What makes mathematics possible? Science for Kant dealt with necessary connections and laws. (2) What makes physics possible? He took for granted that Sir Isaac Newton achieved necessary and true knowledge about physical nature. (3) Is metaphysics possible? Kant answered that metaphysics is not possible.

Kant, and empiricists in general, hold that there is no such thing as intellectual intuition. Intuition is any cognitive act that grasps an object immediately. The only kind of intuitive knowledge that Kant admitted was sense intuition. Kant provides the universal element or necessity in terms of forms of the mind itself, i.e., the categories of the understanding. For Kant, metaphysics dealt with three basic types of ideas: (1) the idea of the world in its unconditioned totality, (2) the idea of freedom, and (3) the idea of God.

Given Kant's system existence cannot be affirmed. He distinguished between the phenomena, that is appearance, and noumena, things that are Real with a capital "R." Experience can never disclose the thing in itself. Our total experience is of the phenomenal rather than the noumenal. There is no way in which Kant could define a causal relationship in which phenomena was based on noumena.

In the *Critique of Practical Reason*, Kant gave three postulates of practical reason: (1) the freedom of the will, (2) the immortality of the soul, and (3) the existence of God. These three are consequences of the reality of moral being. Even if man cannot prove these three by rational processes, man must live as if they exist to make sense out of the world. Kant simply took it for granted that appearance implies reality. Kant cannot merge the two worlds: nineteenth-century scientific world, mechanistic in nature; and a world of spiritual value, freedom, moral value, the immortal soul, and God. Mechanism on the one hand and freedom on the other will never meet. Yet, Kant thinks that they do meet somehow mysteriously in man. See: **Empiricism, Epistemology, Rationalism.**

See: F. Copleston, *A History of Philosophy*, vol. 6, *Modern Philosophy*, part 2, "Kant." (Doubleday, 1960); T.L. Miethe, "God In Kant," in *The Metaphysics of L.J. Eslick: His Philosophy of God* (University Microfilms, 1976), pp. 102–113.

Kenosis ▪ A Greek word meaning "an emptying," from *kenos*, "empty." The teaching that Christ "emptied" himself or limited His divine powers when He became human in the Incarnation. Paul tells us in Philippians 2:6–9: ". . . who, although He existed in the form of God, did not regard equality with God a thing to be grasped, but emptied Himself, taking the form of a bondservant, and being made in the likeness of men. And being found in appearance as a man, He humbled Himself by becoming obedient to the point of death, even death on a cross. Therefore also God highly exalted Him, and bestowed on Him the name which is above every name. . . ." See: 2 Corinthians 8:9. See: **Incarnation.**

Kerygma ▪ A Greek word meaning "that which is preached or proclaimed." In theology the word is used to refer to the early Christian message as preached by the disciples regarding what must be believed for salvation. The term can also refer to the Word of God as found in the Gospels (Mark 1:14–15). See: 1 Corinthians 1:21; 11:23; 15:3; 2 Corinthians 5:19–20.

See: J.I.H. McDonald, *Kerygma and Didache* (Cambridge University Press, 1980).

Kingdom of God ▪ A world that emulates heaven; God's reign as king over all the earth. The "kingdom of God" also refers to the "kingdom of Jesus" (Matt. 13:41; 16:28; Luke 22:30; John

18:36). Jesus says in Luke 22:29–30: ". . . and just as My Father has granted Me a kingdom, I grant you that you may eat and drink at My table in My kingdom, and you will sit on thrones judging the twelve tribes of Israel." (Also 1 Cor. 15:24–28). See: Matthew 5:3; 8:12; 12:28; 19:24; 21:31; 21:43; 25:34; Luke 12:32; John 3:3, 5; 18:36; Romans 14:17; Colossians 1:13; James 2:5; 2 Peter 1:11; Revelation 12:10.

Know, Knowledge ■ Three Greek words are translated into English words related to knowing. The Greek *ginosko* means "to come to know, recognize, understand, or to understand completely" (John 13:12; 15:18; 21:17; 2 Corinthians 8:9; Hebrews 10:34; 1 John 2:5; 4:2, 6, 7, 13; 5:2, 20). In the NT *ginosko* often links what is known and its value to the one who knows, especially with regard to knowing God (1 Cor. 8:3; Gal. 4:9).

The Greek *oida* means "to see," "to have seen or perceived," thus "to know," "to have knowledge of." In Matthew 6:8, 32; John 6:6, 64; 8:14; 11:42; 13:11; 18:4, it refers to divine knowledge. In 1 Thessalonians 1:4, 5; 2:1; 2 Thessalonians 3:7, it refers to human knowledge. *Ginosko* frequently implies progress in knowledge, while *oida* suggests fullness of knowledge (John 8:55; 13:7; 14:7).

Epiginosko denotes "to observe," "fully perceive," "notice attentively," to "discern." This word suggests a more advanced knowledge or special appreciation (Rom. 1:32). This word can refer to a special participation in the object known. See: Colossians 1:6; 1 Timothy 4:3.

Koinonia ■ The Greek word meaning "communion," "fellowship" or "participation." In the NT the word refers to a close-knit fellowship of its Spirit-filled membership. Inherent in the word is a sense of sharing and self-sacrifice (Rom. 12:13; 15:26; 2 Cor. 8:4; 9:13; 13:14; Gal. 6:6; Phil. 2:1; 4:15; Hebrews 13:16; 1 Peter 5:1; 2 Peter 1:4).

Laity ■ From the Greek *laos*, "people," or *laikos*, "belonging to the people." Originally the word referred to the whole Church, all the people of God. Today the word unfortunately contrasts those not ordained to professional ministry (laity) with the ordained (clergy). See: Acts 20:28; 1 Corinthians 3:5–9; 1 Peter 5:3–4. See: **Clergy, Ministry, Priesthood of All Believers.**

See: F.O. Ayres, *The Ministry of the Laity: A Biblical Exposition* (Westminster, 1962); L. Peabody, *Secular Work is Full Time Service* (Christian Literature Crusade, 1974).

Lamb of God ■ A title John the Baptist uses of Jesus in John 1:29, 36: "The next day he saw Jesus coming to him and said, 'Behold, the Lamb of God who takes away the sin of the world!' " This title specifically connects Jesus to the Father in the task of bearing the sins of a fallen humanity (Isa. 53:6).

Law and Gospel ■ A phrase used to compare and contrast the OT system of the Mosaic law with the NT system of the gospel of grace in Jesus Christ.

See: F.F. Bruce, *The Time is Fulfilled* (Eerdmans, 1978), and *The New Testament Development of Old Testament Themes* (Eerdmans, 1968); E.E. Ellis, *Paul's Use of the Old Testament* (Eerdmans, 1957).

Laying on of Hands ■ In the NT, the ceremonial act of setting aside or consecrating a person for a special purpose, as in ordaining an individual to the ministry (Acts 6:6; 13:3; 1 Tim. 4:14; 2 Tim. 1:6).

Jesus and the apostles also healed the sick by laying hands on them (Mark 1:41; 5:23; 6:5; 8:23, 25; Matt. 8:15; Luke 4:40; Acts

9:17; 28:8). See: Mark 10:16; Acts 6:1–6; 8:15–17; 19:5; Hebrews 6:2. See: **Ordination.**

Lectionary ∎ From the Latin *legere*, "to read." Today a "lectionary" is usually a book or table of readings from the OT and NT for each day of the year. It is commonly used for personal devotions or to guide a congregation during a worship service.

Liberal Protestantism ∎ Liberal Protestantism is a modern movement that reinterprets the biblical and historic doctrines and practices of Christianity. Reluctant to endorse orthodox doctrines such as the virgin birth, the bodily resurrection of Jesus, the need for renewal by the Holy Spirit and the infallibility of the Bible, liberal Protestants are more interested in adapting religious ideas to modern culture and thought. Though elements of liberalism exist in almost all denominations, those churches commonly called "mainline"—Methodist, Presbyterian, Lutheran—have been most severely affected by liberal Protestantism. These churches have also been active in the modern Ecumenical Movement.

Following theologians like Rudolf Bultmann (1884–1976), liberal Protestants insist that modern men and women cannot understand or accept the outdated teachings of Christianity in a world so changed by modern science. This is a thinly disguised naturalism—in Bultmann's case a strident anti-supernaturalism—which insists that the Bible must be "demythologized," freed of symbolic myths such as the atonement or miracles and reinterpreted to see what Jesus or the Bible's writers really taught. Biblical Christianity is precisely the story of a great miracle—the resurrection; this view destroys any real possibility of belief in God. See: **Ecumenical, Naturalism.**

See: H.O.J. Brown, *The Protest of a Troubled Protestant* (Arlington House, 1969); W.K. Cauthen, *The Impact of American Religious Liberalism* (Harper & Row, 1962); C.F.H. Henry, *Christian Faith and Modern Theology* (Channel Press, 1964); J.G. Machen, *Christianity and Liberalism* (Eerdmans, 1923); J.D. Murch, *The Protestant Revolt* (Crestwood Books, 1967).

Liberation Theology ∎ A term used to refer to a group of theological movements such as third-world liberation movements, feminist theology and black social theology. Since liberation theologies see sin as man's inhumanity to man—not as rebellion

against God—they emphasize deliverance from social, economic and political conditions, rather than reconciliation to God and the new birth. Nash, in *Liberation Theology*, says: "Liberation theology is the most widely discussed theological movement of the decade. While liberation theology has taken a variety of forms that speak to the oppression of several different classes of people (including blacks and women), [it has been predominately a] movement among Latin American Catholics and Protestants that seeks radical changes in the political and economic institutions of that region along Marxist lines. . . . Consequently, liberationists believe, the Christian church must become a part of the revolutionary process including its violence." See: **Born Again.**

See: C.E. Armerding, *Evangelicals and Liberation* (Presbyterian and Reformed, 1977); R.M. Brown, *Theology in a New Key: Responding to Liberation Themes* (Westminster, 1978); I. Ellacuria, *Freedom Made Flesh: The Mission of Christ and His Church* (Orbis, 1977); R.H. Nash, *Liberation Theology* (Mott Media, 1984), and *Social Justice and the Christian Church* (Mott Media, 1983).

Liberty, Christian ▪ The NT clearly shows that God gives Christians liberty, a freedom to choose that grows out of a person's own commitment to Christ and understanding of Scripture. Yet this freedom has obligations. Christians have a responsibility to learn of God from the Bible and to pattern their lives after His character, relating to others in a way that witnesses effectively to a lost world. In 2 Corinthians 3:17 we read: "Now the Lord is the Spirit; and where the Spirit of the Lord is, there is liberty." In Colossians 1:13–14 we read: "For He delivered us from the domain of darkness, and transferred us to the kingdom of His well-beloved Son, in whom we have redemption, the forgiveness of sins."

In 1 Corinthians 6:12 and 10:23, the Christian is told that "Everything is permissible, but not everything is beneficial" and that we should "not be mastered by anything." Christian liberty is vast, yet it is not license. It recognizes that not everything is constructive, for when we engage in activities harmful to ourselves or others, we actually destroy the freedom God has given us.

Light ▪ John 1:4 says of Jesus: "In Him was life; and the life was the light of men." In John 8:12 Jesus himself says: ". . . I am the light of the world; he who follows Me shall not walk in the darkness, but shall have the light of life" (see also John 12:35).

Jesus calls His followers "the light of the world" (Matt. 5:14). In the Bible, light is from God; darkness is of the evil one. Light symbolizes goodness, righteousness, and wisdom; darkness symbolizes evil, confusion, and ignorance. See: 1 John 1:5.

Limbo ■ From the Latin *limbus*, "border," "edge," meaning "on the border." In medieval theology, limbo was a place at the edge of hell. It was thought to have two parts: (1) *Limbus Patrum* (Limbo of the Fathers) is the residence of the spirits of OT people freed by Christ's descent into hell (1 Peter 3:18–20), or the place where they await Christ's Second Coming so they can enter heaven. (2) *Limbus Infantium* (or *puerorum*, Limbo of the Infants) was for infants who die without baptism. While these infants do not experience pain or punishment, neither do they enjoy salvation in God's presence. See: **Intermediate State, Purgatory.**

Logical Fallacies ■ In the study of logic, the term "fallacy" refers to an argument that may be psychologically persuasive, but is incorrect. See: **Accident, Fallacy of; Against the Man; Authority, Appeal to; Begging the Question; Complex Question, Fallacy of; False Cause, Argument from; Force, Appeal to; Hasty Generalization; Irrelevant Conclusion; Ignorance, Argument from; People, Appeal to the; Pity, Appeal to.**
    See: I.M. Copi, *Introduction to Logic*, Seventh Edition (Macmillan, 1986), and *Informal Logic* (Macmillan, 1986); S.M. Engel, *With Good Reason: An Introduction to Informal Fallacies*, Second Edition (St. Martin's, 1982); A.C. Michalos, *Improving Your Reasoning* (Prentice-Hall, 1970).

Logos ■ The most common Greek term for "word," and the source of the words "logic" and "wisdom." In ordinary Greek *logos* means "reason," though John used "Word" at the beginning of his gospel to refer to Jesus: "In the beginning was the Word, and the Word was with God and the Word was God. He was in the beginning with God" (John 1:1–2). John is saying that Jesus was and is God, the "Logic of God" or the "Wisdom of God" incarnate. See: John 1:9, 14. See: **Incarnation.**

Lord ■ From the Anglo-Saxon *hlaford*, "bread keeper," one who has power or authority over others. The term often translates the OT term "Yahweh" (Jehovah), and thus is used as a name for God. Christians also use the term as a name for Christ, God the Son (Phil. 2:11). Paul says in 1 Corinthians 8:6 that there is only ". . . one Lord, Jesus Christ, through whom are all things, and we exist through Him." See: John 20:28; Acts 2:36; Romans 5:11; 14:8; 1 Corinthians 12:3; 16:22.

Lord's Day ■ The phrase in Greek *te kyriake hemera*, "the Lord's Day," appears only once in the entire NT, in Revelation 1:10. Some Christians confuse the OT "Sabbath" (the seventh day of the week, Saturday), the day of rest, with the NT Lord's Day (Sunday, the first day of the week), the day on which Jesus rose from the dead. It is clear in the NT that Christians did not believe Saturday should be observed by worship and rest (Rom. 14:5–6; Gal. 4:8–11; Col. 2:16–17), and most Christians have regarded the Sabbath as part of the ceremonial law of Israel and thus not applicable to the Church.

So for the Christian, Sunday is the Lord's Day. The day is important as a united witness to the world of the resurrection of Jesus, a day of worship of God, fellowship in the Spirit, and biblical teaching and encouragement in resurrection living (Eph. 4:11–16). See: Acts 20:7; Romans 1:12; 1 Corinthians 16:2; Hebrews 10:25. See: **Sabbath.**

See: D.A. Carson, *From Sabbath to Lord's Day* (Zondervan, 1982); C.L. Feinberg, *The Sabbath and the Lord's Day* (Van Kampen Press, 1952); P.K. Jewett, *The Lord's Day: A Theological Guide to the Christian Day of Worship* (Eerdmans, 1971).

Lord's Prayer, The ■ The name given to the model prayer given by Jesus in Matthew 6:9–13 as part of the Sermon on the Mount: "Pray, then, in this way: 'Our father who art in heaven, Hallowed be Thy name. Thy kingdom come. Thy will be done, On earth as it is in heaven. Give us this day our daily bread. And forgive us our debts, as we also have forgiven our debtors. And do not lead us into temptation, but deliver us from evil. [For Thine is the kingdom, and the power, and the glory, forever. Amen.]' "

This last clause (in brackets) is omitted in the earliest manuscripts.

Most theologians do not believe Jesus intended us to repeat this prayer by memory—though there is certainly nothing wrong with doing so—but that it was intended as a model of how people should pray. The Lord's Prayer tells us some important concerns:

(1) Prayer should consist of praise to God. (2) In prayer we should be concerned that the human city become God's city. (3) We should pray that God's will, His way, becomes our mark as individuals and as a society. (4) We can pray for our specific daily physical needs. (5) Prayer for forgiveness of our sins, our shortcomings, is important. (6) We should pray about our attitudes. (7) We should pray for the Holy Spirit's leadership in everyday life. See: Luke 11:2–4. See: **Prayer, Sermon on the Mount.**

See: D.M. Lloyd-Jones, *Studies in the Sermon on the Mount*, 2 vols. (Eerdmans, 1960); T.L. Miethe, "On Prayer," in *The New Christian's Guide to Following Jesus* (Bethany House Publishers, 1984), pp. 85–90.

Lord's Supper ■
In theology, the "Lord's Supper" is another name for communion, or the eucharist. The term also refers to the last supper Jesus ate with the apostles before His crucifixion. The Lord's Supper is recorded in Matthew 22:26–30; Mark 14:22–26; Luke 22:14–20 and 1 Corinthians 1:23–26. See: **Communion, Eucharist.**

See: J. Jeremias, *The Eucharistic Words of Jesus* (Blackwell's, 1955); E.F. Kevan, *The Lord's Supper* (London: Evangelical Press, 1966); A. Murray, *The Lord's Table* (Christian Literature Crusade, 1962); J.B. Phillips, *Appointment with God* (Macmillan, 1967).

Love ■
In Christian theology, the ability to love is a vital aspect of being created in God's image and regenerated by the Holy Spirit's power. In 1 John 4:7–11 we read: "Beloved, let us love one another, for love is from God; and every one who loves is born of God and knows God. The one who does not love does not know God, for God is love. By this the love of God was manifested in us, that God has sent His only begotten Son into the world so that we might live through Him. In this is love, not that we loved God, but that He loved us and sent His Son to be the propitiation for our sins. Beloved, if God so loved us, we also ought to love one another."

Love is also one of God's most important attributes.

Four of the most common Greek words for "love" are: (1) *philia*, usually translated "friendship," "tender affection"; (2) *eros*, which often refers to sexual or physical passion (never used in the NT); (3) *storge*, "family affection" (also not found in the NT); and (4) *agape*, which is best defined as "intelligently, intentionally willing the best for another," the attitude of God toward

His Son and toward us (John 3:16; 13:34–35; 14:21; 17:26; Rom. 5:8; 1 Thess. 3:12; 1 Cor. 16:14; 2 Peter 1:7; 1 John 4:18). See: Matthew 5:44–46; John 15:12–13; Romans 13:8–10; Galatians 5:6, 22; 1 John 4:7–20; Revelation 3:19. See: **Agape.**

See: N.L. Geisler, *The Christian Ethic of Love* (Zondervan, 1973); C.S. Lewis, *The Four Loves* (London: Geoffrey Bless, 1960); T.L. Miethe, "God's Love for Us" in *The New Christian's Guide to Following Jesus* (Bethany House Publishers, 1984), pp. 37–42.

Lower Criticism ■ Textual, or "lower," criticism is the attempt to restore the original wording of a text when altered in copying and recopying. See: **Biblical Criticism.**

Lust ■ From the Greek *epithumia*, "strong desire of any kind"; *hedone*, "pleasure," "enjoyment"; *orego*, "to desire"; *orexis*, "longing"; *pathos*, "passion"; and the Latin *lascivus*, "wanton." Originally, "lust" meant only strong desire or craving for an object, pleasure or delight. It did not have a negative or positive connotation. The word is used of a good desire in Luke 22:15; Philippians 1:23; and 1 Thessalonians 2:17. Today it is used negatively, as in Romans 6:12, where it refers to an evil desire, as it does in Romans 13:14; Galatians 5:16, 24; and Ephesians 2:3. In Roman Catholic theology, it is considered one of the Seven Deadly Sins. See: **Sins, Seven Deadly.**

Lutheran ■ The theology and churches that follow the thought of the German reformer and Augustinian monk Martin Luther (1483–1546).

Luther began studying law at the University of Erfurt in 1505. When a bolt of lightning threw him to the ground in July 1505, he vowed on the spot that if he were spared he would enter a monastery, and soon joined the monastery of the Hermits of St. Augustine. In 1512 he received his doctorate in Scripture. In classes he taught at the University of Wittenberg during 1515–1516, Luther concentrated on Paul's Epistle to the Romans. He was especially struck by Romans 1:17: "For in it the righteousness of God is revealed from faith to faith; as it is written, BUT THE RIGHTEOUS MAN SHALL LIVE BY FAITH." Luther called this passage "the gate of paradise."

Luther soon found himself at odds with the Roman Catholic

heirarchy. At that time the church had a pope—Alexander VI—that even Catholic scholars admit was "probably the worst occupant of the throne of Peter. . . . Clerical offices were bought and sold. The indulgence system became a gigantic scheme to funnel funds to the Vatican." On October 31, 1517, Luther nailed ninety-five theses to the door of the church in Wittenberg in protest of the sale of indulgences; and in 1520, Luther burned a papal bull excommunicating him from the Catholic Church.

Luther believed that people are by nature sinners. God gives the free gift of His grace through Jesus Christ and people accept the gift through faith. People are saved by faith alone, not by good works. For Luther three points were crucial: "God alone. Faith alone. The Scriptures alone." In 1519–1520, Luther wrote three famous treatises: (1) *An Address to the Nobility of the German Nation on the Reform of the Christian Estate*, (2) *On the Babylonian Captivity of the Church*, and (3) *On the Liberty of the Christian Man*. He gained such colleagues as Philipp Melanchthon (1497–1560), who authored the Augsburg Confession (1530), the standard doctrinal statement of all Lutheran churches, and Andreas Bodenstein von Carlstadt (1477–1541); he alienated, however, the humanist scholar Desiderius Erasmus (1466–1536), who broke with Luther over the issue of freedom of the will.

Lutherans generally emphasize *Sola Fide*, justification by faith alone, and *Sola Scriptura*, the Bible as the only source of Christian doctrine. They accept the Apostles' and Nicene creeds, recognize baptism and the Lord's Supper as means of grace, view salvation as a gift of God, and believe in Christ's real presence in communion (consubstantiation). In America, some of the larger Lutheran synods are the Lutheran Church in America (1962), the American Lutheran Church (1960), the Lutheran Church-Missouri Synod (1847). The first two bodies merged in 1988 with the American Evangelical Lutheran Church to become the Evangelical Lutheran Church in America, now one of America's largest denominations. See: **Consubstantiation.**

See: R.H. Bainton, *Here I Stand: A Life of Martin Luther* (Abingdon, 1951); V.E. Beck, *Why I Am a Lutheran* (Beacon Press, 1956); V. Ferm, *Cross-Currents in the Personality of Martin Luther* (Christopher Publishing House, 1972); J.W. Montgomery, *In Defense of Martin Luther* (Northwestern Publishing House, 1970); J.M. Todd, *Luther: A Life* (Crossroad, 1982); A.R. Wentz, *A Basic History of Lutheranism in America* (Muhlenberg Press, 1955).

Mammon ▪ The Aramaic word for riches or wealth. Even before the NT period the word referred to evils of money (Luke 16:9). Jesus used the word in Luke 16:9, 11, 13, and in Matthew 6:24, which reads: "No one can serve two masters; for either he will hate the one and be devoted to the other, or he will hold to one and despise the other. You cannot serve God and Mammon."

Man ▪ In Christian theology, man is the highest of God's living creation on earth. Created out of material elements (the dust of the earth), man received his spirit, or life force, when God breathed into him. The Scriptures teach that man alone is made in God's image (Gen. 1:27; 2:7–8; 5:1; 6:7). He has free will, can love and think abstractly, and has a personality because he was made in God's image. He could and did choose to rebel against God, that is, to sin. Thus man needs a Savior. Man's chief aim is to worship and serve God and to share God's love with others. See: Matthew 10:31; 12:12. See: **Arminianism; Calvinism; Evolution; Evolution, Theistic; Imago Dei; Sovereignty of God.**

See: G.C. Berkouwer, *Man: The Image of God* (Eerdmans, 1962); R.L. Harris, *Man: God's Eternal Creation* (Moody Press, 1971); J.G. Machen, *The Christian View of Man* (London: Banner of Truth Trust, 1965); R. Niebuhr, *The Nature and Destiny of Man* (Scribners, 1949); J. Orr, *God's Image in Man and Its Defacement in the Light of Modern Denials* (Eerdmans, 1948); L. Verduin, *Somewhat Less Than God: The Biblical View of Man* (Eerdmans, 1970).

Manichaeism ▪ A dualistic system of thought popular in the time of Augustine (354–430). Founded by Mani (216–c. 277), who combined Persian, Christian, and Buddhist elements, it emphasized asceticism (practice of self-discipline without certain bodily pleasures) and knowledge as a means of salvation. It also taught a doctrine of reincarnation. See: **Dualism.**

See: G. Widengren, *Mani and Manichaeism* (Holt, Rinehart and Winston, 1965).

Maranatha ▪ From two Aramaic words, *maran-atha*, which mean "Our Lord, come." It is found in 1 Corinthians 16:22: "If any one does not love the Lord, let him be accursed. *Maranatha.*"

Marriage ▪ From the Greek, *gamos*, "a marriage." The Christian view of marriage is that a man and woman shall leave their families and become one flesh (Gen. 2:24; Matt. 19:5; Eph. 5:31). Marriage is a union resulting in intellectual, emotional, spiritual and physical oneness. It is the deepest unity humanly possible and a unity God intends to endure for the lifetime of the couple (Matt. 19:6). It was at the marriage feast at Cana of Galilee where Jesus performed His first miracle (John 2:1–11). See: 1 Corinthians 7:4; 11:11–12. See: **Divorce.**

See: J.E. Adams, *Marriage, Divorce and Remarriage In the Bible* (Presbyterian and Reformed, 1980); E. White, *Marriage and the Bible* (Broadman, 1965); H.N. Wright, *Communication: Key to Your Marriage* (Regal, 1974).

Materialism ▪ In philosophy, materialism is the idea that the ultimate reality, or unifying principle of the world, is matter. All things are explained by examination of the matter of the physical universe.

Materialism is also the belief that things—money, possessions and so on—are more important than people. A dangerous, subtle form of materialism is invading the Church today in the form of the "Gospel of Health and Wealth." See: **Health and Wealth, Gospel of; Metaphysics.**

Mediator ▪ A title for Jesus that refers to His role as reconciler between God the Father and man. Because of the sin of mankind, God had to send His Son to reconcile lost man to himself. See: 2 Corinthians 5:18–21; Hebrews 8:6; 9:15; 12:24; 1 Timothy 2:3–6.

See: E. Brunner, *The Mediator* (Westminster, 1947).

Meekness ▪ From the Greek *prautes* or *praotes*, meaning "an inward grace of the soul." In Christian usage, meekness is humble, controlled strength and a gentleness in relating to others. Matthew 5:5 in the KJV reads: "Blessed are the meek: for they shall inherit the earth." See: 2 Corinthians 10:1; Ephesians 4:2; Colossians 3:12; Galatians 5:23; Titus 3:2.

Mennonites ▪ A Christian group with Anabaptist origins in Holland, Germany, and Switzerland. They teach believers' baptism, pacifism, and personal purity in Christian living, and reject oathtaking. Their basic doctrines were set out in the *Programmatic Letters* of Conrad Grebel (1524) and the *Seven Articles of Schleitheim* (1527), as well as in the writings of Pilgram Marpeck (d. 1556) and Menno Simons (1496–1561). The most conservative branch of Mennonites, the Amish, was founded in 1693 by Jacob Amman.

See: R.H. Bainton, *The Reformation of the Sixteenth Century* (Beacon Press, 1952); C. Browning, *Amish in Illinois* (By the author, 1971—Library of Congress CCN 73–163515); E.T. Clark, *The Small Sects in America* (Abingdon, 1937); W.R. Estep, *The Anabaptist Story* (Broadman, 1963); J. Horsch, *Mennonites in Europe* (Mennonite Publishing Co., 1942); *Mennonite Encyclopedia: A Comprehensive Reference Work on the Anabaptist-Mennonite Movement*, 4 vols. (Mennonite Publishing House, 1955–1959).

Merit ▪ From the Latin *meritum*, "to deserve." In theology, an act rewarded or punished by God. Most Christian groups hold that human beings can do nothing to merit salvation because it is a free gift from God. As result of sin, human beings merit only damnation, but God is a loving God who sent His Son so that all who believe would have salvation (John 3:16). See: **Atonement, Salvation, Works.**

Messiah ▪ The Hebrew *masiah*, the Aramaic *mesiha* or the Greek *christos* all mean "the anointed one." "Christ" is the Greek equivalent of the Hebrew "messiah." The OT referred to kings and other leaders in general terms as "anointed." In the NT, Jesus was the Messiah who at His baptism was "anointed . . . with the Holy Spirit and with power" (Acts 10:38). See: Mark 14:61–62; John 1:41; 4:25. See: **Christ, Christology.**

Metaphysics ■ The area of philosophy that studies the nature of being as being, or ultimate reality. Metaphysics is essentially a philosophy of God, because while some metaphysical systems purport to be agnostic or atheistic, all claim that they arrive at first principles. Metaphysics must be consummated by some kind of theory of God. See: **Kantianism, Ontology.**

See: E.A. Burtt, *The Metaphysical Foundations of Modern Physical Science* (Routledge and Kegan Paul Limited, 1932); N. Geisler, *Philosophy of Religion* (Zondervan, 1974); C. Hartshorne, *Creative Synthesis and Philosophic Method* (Open Court, 1970); G.P. Klubertanz, *The Philosophy of Being* (Appleton, Century, Crofts, 1963); G.P. Klubertanz and M.R. Holloway, *Being and God: Introduction to the Philosophy of Being and to Natural Theology* (Irvington, 1963); T.L. Miethe, *The Metaphysics of Leonard James Eslick: His Philosophy of God* (University Microfilms, 1976); S.M. Thompson, *A Modern Philosophy of Religion* (Henry Regnery, 1955).

Methodists ■ A denomination with roots in the teachings of John (1703–1791) and Charles Wesley (1707–1788), which stressed personal piety and inward heart religion. They started a "Holy Club" around 1725 along with University of Oxford classmate George Whitefield (1714–1770), and by 1729 they were known as "Methodists" because of their "insistence on exacting discipline in scholastic as well as spiritual matters." The doctrine of Christian perfection is the most distinctive teaching of the Methodist movement. Wesley regarded perfection, a "pure love reigning alone in the heart and life," as a real possibility for every Christian who had first been justified by faith.

Today, Methodist groups are found across the theological spectrum from conservative evangelicalism to extreme liberalism. Methodism has an episcopal form of church government. See: **Perfection, Christian; Perfection, Theological; Wesleyanism.**

See: *Cyclopedia of Methodism* (Everts and Stewart, 1878); *Who's Who in Methodism* (Marquis Who's Who, 1952); F.C. Gill, *Charles Wesley: The First Methodist* (Abingdon, 1964); L.C. Rudolph, *Francis Asbury* (Abingdon Press, 1966); H.A. Snyder, *The Radical Wesley and Patterns for Church Renewal* (InterVarsity Press, 1980); M. Schmidt, *John Wesley: A Theological Biography* (London: Epworth Press, 1962); R.L. Smith, *Why I Am a Methodist* (Beacon Press, 1955); J. Telford, *The Life of John Wesley* (London: Epworth Press, 1960); John Wesley, *The Works of John Wesley Complete and Unabridged*, 14 vols. (Baker, 1978).

Millennialism ■ From the Latin *milleannus* or the Greek *chiliasm*, "a thousand." In theology, the teaching that there will be a period of 1000 years when Christ will rule this earth as king.

Revelation 20:1–10 states that Satan will be thrown into a bottomless pit which will be sealed for 1000 years, and that during this period Christians who have been killed "because of the testimony of Jesus" will reign with Christ over an earth marked by prosperity, peace, freedom and a righteous rule. There is great debate regarding whether this idea should be taken literally. See: **Amillennialism, Postmillennialism, Premillennialism.**

See: D.H. Kromminga, *The Millennium in the Church: Studies in the History of Christian Chiliasm* (Eerdmans, 1945); A.J. McClain, *The Greatness of the Kingdom* (Zondervan, 1959); I.H. Marshall, *Eschatology and the Parables* (Tyndale, 1963).

Ministry ■ From the Greek *diakoneo*, "to serve," or *douleuo*, "to serve as a slave." In the NT, ministry is service to God and to other people in His name. Jesus provides the pattern for Christian ministry: He came not to receive service but to give it (Matt. 20:28; Mark 10:45; John 13:1–17). The Christian should minister by meeting people's needs with love and humility on Christ's behalf. See: Matthew 20:26; 22:13; Mark 10:43; John 2:5, 9; Acts 6:3; Romans 1:1; Galatians 1:10; Colossians 4:12; Ephesians 4:7–16; Philippians 2:7. See: **Clergy, Deacon, Deaconess, Foot Washing, Priesthood of All Believers.**

See: R.S. Anderson, *Theological Foundations for Ministry* (Eerdmans, 1979); T.L. Miethe, "Ministry and the Christian" in *The New Christian's Guide to Following Jesus* (Bethany House Publishers, 1984), pp. 103–110.

Miracle ■ Three Greek words are translated "miracle": *dynamis*, "powers," *terata*, "wonders," and *semeia*, "signs." An action of God or His messenger that runs counter to observed processes of nature. The miracles of Jesus are central to understanding who He is and to validating His claims. In the NT more than 30 miracles that Jesus performed are recorded (Matt. 9:18–26; 17:1–14; Mark 9:1–14; Luke 7:11–16; 9:12–17; John 2:1–11; 11:32–44).

Some modern theologians have tried to take the miracles out of the Bible to demythologize it, in order to make its message "understandable" to the modern mind. But the message of the Bible is a great miracle: the resurrection of Jesus. See: **Demythologizing, Liberal Protestantism.**

See: N.L. Geisler, *Miracles and Modern Thought* (Zondervan, 1982); C.S. Lewis, *Miracles: A Preliminary Study* (Macmillan, 1960); R. Swinburne, *The Concept of Miracle* (Macmillan, 1970); F.R. Tennant, *Miracle and Its Philo-*

sophical Presuppositions (Cambridge University Press, 1925); B.B. Warfield, *Miracles: Yesterday and Today, True and False* (Eerdmans, 1965).

Modalism ▪ A heresy stressing the radical unity of God. Modalism teaches that the three parts of the Trinity—Father, Son, and Holy Spirit—are merely different modes, or manifestations, of God, rather than three distinct persons who are at the same time one in substance. See: **Monarchianism, Synergism.**

Modernism ▪ The attempt in theology to update biblical doctrines to make them acceptable to the modern mind. Modernism assumes that only the modern mind can truly know reality since it alone has possessed modern advances in technology and understanding. Therefore, biblical teaching needs to be rewritten in terms tolerable to current ways of thinking. See: **Liberal Protestantism.**

Monarchianism ▪ The second and third century view that God is radically one. It took two forms: (1) "Dynamic monarchianism," the teaching that Jesus was only a man who had been given the Holy Spirit. This view was held by Theodotus of Byzantium (about A.D. 190) in Rome. (2) "Modalistic monarchianism," which saw the Trinity as different and successive revelations of God: the Father was the first revelation of God, the Son the second, and the Holy Spirit the third. This view was taught by Sabellius in the third century in Rome. See: **Modalism.**

Monergism ▪ The teaching that conversion is accomplished exclusively by the working of God. Monergism states that if a person is saved, it results entirely from the work of God.

Based on a misunderstanding of Ephesians 2:8, monergists see even faith as a gift from God, a special gift of God given only to those God has chosen. But in the Greek text of Ephesians 2:8 ("By grace you have been saved through faith, and that not of yourselves, it is a gift of God") there is only one pronoun, not two. It does not agree grammatically with the word "faith"; the pronoun is neuter in gender, while "faith" is feminine. According to all grammatical rules, the gift to which the verse refers cannot be faith.

The gift is salvation, which none can merit. See: **Arminianism, Atonement, Augustinianism, Calvinism, Faith, Synergism.**

Monophysitism ▪ From the Greek *monos*, "one," and *physis*, "nature." Monophysitism teaches that Jesus had only one nature. Though Jesus was clad in human flesh, the union of His two natures produced a unique, single *divine* nature. In other words, His humanity was absorbed into His deity. See: **Monotheletism.**

Monotheism ▪ From the Greek *monos*, "one" and *theos*, "God." The belief that there is one God and only one God. In the OT God strove to teach Israel that He alone was God; the NT clearly revealed that God was a Trinity, three in one. See: Acts 17:22–31; 1 Corinthians 8:4–6. See: **Atheism, Henotheism, Polytheism, Theism, Trinity.**

Monotheletism ▪ From the Greek *mono*, "one," and *thelein*, "to will." In an attempt to protect Christ's having only one will, this teaching, strong in the Eastern church in the seventh century, held that Jesus had only one nature. The Council of Chalcedon defended the doctrine of the two natures, and the Council of Constantinople declared that Christ had two wills, but that His human will was subject to His divine will. See: **Chalcedon, Council of; Constantinople, Councils of.**

Montanism ▪ A prophetic movement that grew from the teachings of Montanus in A.D. 172 in Phrygia (Turkey). The Montanists believed that the Holy Spirit continued to speak through prophecy in the second century; the prophetesses Prisca and Maximilla preached "the New Prophecy," which encouraged the people to prepare for the Second Coming of Jesus. Though they believed that the Holy Spirit spoke through them, often in the first person, many of their prophecies were not fulfilled. Tertullian (c. 155–220) was Montanism's most famous adherent.

Moral Argument ▪ One of the philosophical arguments used as a proof for God's existence. It was first used by Immanuel Kant (1724–1804) as a practical postulate of God's existence, not as a proof. The moral argument attempts to argue from the existence of an objective moral law—or the fact that human moral nature compels us to make moral assertions about the world and destiny—to the existence of a Moral Law Giver. A simple form of the argument is as follows: (1) There is an objective moral law independent of human consciousness, despite people's lack of conformity to it. (2) Yet ideas exist only in minds. (3) Therefore, there must be a supreme Mind beyond all finite minds in which this objective moral law exists. C. S. Lewis did much to popularize the argument in our world. See: **Cosmological Argument, Kantianism, Ontological Argument.**

See: N.L. Geisler, "Teleological and Moral Arguments," in *Philosophy of Religion* (Zondervan, 1974), pp. 104–132; C.S. Lewis, *Mere Christianity* (Macmillan, 1953); W.R. Sorley, "The Moral Argument" in *Philosophy of Religion*, pp. 201–211.

Moral Rearmament ▪ Founded by American Lutheran minister Frank Buchman (1878–1961), Moral Rearmament (M.R.A.) emphasized the importance of moral ideals and action. The group adopted its name in the late 1930s after beginning as the Oxford Group of Oxford, England. It aimed at "A New World Order for Christ, the King," and "a campaign for the renaissance of the practice among men of the truths of simple Christianity":

"The aims of the Oxford Group are to bring into the world the realization of the power of the Holy Spirit as a force for spiritual and material stability and betterment of the world; To awaken in us as individuals the knowledge that we are dissipating our spiritual inheritance and that sin is the frustration of God's Plan for us all."

Buchman believed social reform must be rooted in personal transformation. The Oxford Group stressed four keys to the spiritual life: (1) Absolute honesty; (2) Absolute purity; (3) Absolute unselfishness; and (4) Absolute love.

See: W.H. Clark, *The Oxford Group: Its History and Significance* (Bookman Associates, 1951); T. Driberg, *The Mystery of Moral Re-Armament* (Knopf, 1965); P. Howard, *Frank Buchman's Secret* (Doubleday, 1961); *What Is the Oxford Group?* by the Layman with a Notebook (Oxford University Press, 1933).

Moral Theology ▪ "Moral theology" is a Roman Catholic term equivalent to what Protestants call Christian ethics. Catholics define moral theology as: "The science of human acts considered in the light of man's supernatural destiny; consequently not only reason but also the light of faith is employed in establishing and applying the principles of the science." Moral theology treats subjects such as moral discernment; what is good and evil, right and wrong, sin and virtue; justice; sexuality; and the holiness or sanctity of life. In the Catholic Church, moral theology is based on reason and natural law, revelation, and the tradition and authority of the Church. See: **Ethics, Christian.**

See: J.M. Gustafson, *Protestant and Roman Catholic Ethics* (The University of Chicago Press, 1978).

Mormons—Latter-Day Saints ∎ A religious group

founded in 1830 by Joseph Smith. In 1827 Smith claimed to receive a set of golden plates upon which the *Book of Mormon* is alleged to have been written. Officially founded as a "new religious society" entitled "The Church of Christ," it came to be named the Church of Jesus Christ of Latter-Day Saints. From the state of New York the nucleus of the Mormon Church moved to Kirtland, Ohio, then to Jackson County, Missouri, on to Nauvoo, Illinois, and finally to Utah.

Aside from the King James Version of the Bible, the Mormons have added the *Doctrine and Covenants*, the *Pearl of Great Price*, and the *Book of Mormon* to the canon of what they call authorized scripture. Mormons claim to possess the priesthoods of Aaron and Melchizedek. Mormon theology is polytheistic, teaching in effect that the universe is inhabited by different gods who procreate spirit children which are in turn clothed with bodies on different planets. Though veiled in semi-orthodox terminology, Mormonism has never historically accepted the Christian doctrine of the Trinity. Salvation for the Mormon involves not only faith in Christ, but baptism by immersion, obedience to the teachings of the Mormon Church, good works, and keeping the commandments of God.

See: W. Martin, *The Kingdom of the Cults* (Bethany House Publishers, 1985); W. Martin, *The Maze of Mormonism* (Vision House Publishers, 1978); J. Tanner, *The Changing World of Mormonism* (Moody Press, 1981).

Mysticism ∎ The Greek *mysterion*, from *mystes*, "one initiated

in the secrets of a truer reality." Mystics stress direct apprehension of God, direct communication or revelation from God, and salvation on the basis of this direct relationship. One strand of mysticism tends toward occultism, stressing magic, parapsychology and a preoccupation with visions and supernatural powers and revelations. Historic biblical Christianity stands opposed to this type of mysticism, arguing that the text of Scripture is all any person needs to discover God's will for his or her life. God has objectively revealed the truth equally for all.

There is, however, a long history of Christian mysticism that has avoided occultic phenomena. From the beatific vision in Augustine (354–430) to modern day Christian mystics, this strand of mysticism has stressed God's peace, love, and tranquility. These mystics seek a more direct experience of loving and knowing God, but do not make this the norm for themselves or others. Some claim this tradition is as old as the Apostle Paul, Clement of Alexandria (c. 150–220), Origen (c. 185–254), Gregory of Nyssa (c. 330–395), Evagrius of Pontus (346–399) and John Cassian (c. 360–435).

See: N. Anderson, "Mysticism," in *Christianity and World Religions* (InterVarsity Press, 1984), pp. 37–45; M.L. Furse, *Mysticism: Window on a World View* (Abingdon Press, 1977); T. McCormick and S. Fish, *Meditation: A Practical Guide to a Spiritual Discipline* (InterVarsity Press, 1983); P. Means, *The Mystical Maze* (Campus Crusade for Christ, Inc., 1976); R.C. Petry, *Late Medieval Mysticism* (Westminster Press, 1957); A.W. Tozer, *The Knowledge of the Holy* (Harper & Row, 1961).

Myth ■ From the Greek *mythos*, "tale" or "fable." A story in a set literary form (such as poetic imagery or cultural narrative) with a truth or moral rather than historical narrative as its point. The word appears five times in the NT: 1 Timothy 1:4; 4:7; 2 Timothy 4:4; Titus 1:14; 2 Peter 1:16. In each case the term refers to a fable as distinct from a historical or factual truth. In 2 Peter 1:16 we read: "For we did not follow cleverly devised tales [*mythos*] when we made known to you the power and coming of our Lord Jesus Christ, but we were eyewitnesses of His majesty." The Bible makes an obvious distinction between actual facts and stories, fables and myths.

A large group of modern liberal theologians, following Rudolf Bultmann (1884–1976), insist that biblical accounts of miracles as well as concepts such as the atonement are myths needing reinterpretation to be understandable to the modern scientific mind. Bultmann's method begins with an assumption that supernatural events are impossibilities. See: **Liberal Protestantism.**

See: Morris Ashcraft, *Rudolf Bultmann* (Word, 1972); C.W. Kegley, *The Theology of Rudolf Bultmann* (Harper & Row, 1966); G.E. Ladd, *Rudolf Bultmann* (InterVarsity Press, 1964).

Name ▪ A word or symbol designating a thing is called a "proper name." In the Bible, names were not insignificant labels. Instead, a name usually indicated a promise parents made to God regarding their child-to-be. Later in life the name could be changed to signify the chief characteristic of the person. A name told something important about the person who bore it, often referring to his or her essential identity.

Naturalism ▪ The philosophical idea that the system of nature we observe and experience is the whole of reality, the sum total of existence. Everything that exists—matter, nature, life, mind, creativity—is explained in terms of a mechanistic materialism. To a naturalist the human mind, for example, is nothing more than an electrical-chemical machine, a product of the evolutionary process. Naturalism dismisses the existence of any spiritual realm, thus ruling out the existence of God, spirit, immortality, and human freedom. It is the foundational tenet of atheism. See: **Atheism, Evolution, Liberal Protestantism, Miracle, Secular Humanism, Spirit.**

See: A.G.N. Flew, *God and Philosophy* (Harcourt Brace and World, 1967), *The Presumption of Atheism* (Barnes and Noble, 1976), and *A Rational Animal* (Clarendon, 1978); N.L. Geisler, *False Gods of Our Time* (Harvest House Publishers, 1985); C.S. Lewis, *Miracles: A Preliminary Study* (Macmillan, 1947); R.A. Varghese, *The Intellectuals Speak Out About God* (Regnery Gateway, 1984).

Natural Law ▪ In ethics, the idea that there are, within each man, natural moral laws known by all, moral order divinely implanted, and accessible to all human beings by way of reason. All beings, potential or actual, come under the regulation of this

Eternal Law. Thus all things are inclined toward their proper acts and ends by divine Reason. Men and animals share in this divine regulation. To avoid confusion with the law of nature, we call the part of the Eternal Law which applied especially to the free acts of man, the "natural moral law." The Thomistic definition of this law is: "A participation of the Eternal Law on the part of a rational creature." "Natural Law" is not made by human reason, but is naturally implanted in the reason of man by God. See: **Natural Theology, Synderesis Rule.**

See: A. Battaglia, *Toward a Reformulation of Natural Law* (The Seabury Press, 1981); V.J. Bourke, *Ethics: A Textbook in Moral Philosophy* (Macmillan, 1951), and "Two Approaches to Natural Law," in *Natural Law Forum*, vol. 1 (1956), pp. 92–96; T.L. Miethe, "Natural Law, the Synderesis Rule and St. Augustine," in *Augustinian Studies*, vol. 11 (1980), pp.91–98.

Natural Revelation ■ Also known as "general revelation."

That which all people at all times can know about God apart from special revelation, the Bible. Through natural revelation we can know that God exists, that He is all-knowing, all-powerful, eternal, good, immanent, righteous and transcendent. We cannot know through natural revelation the atonement, the Incarnation, the Trinity or any part of the plan of salvation. There are two parts to natural revelation: (1) what we can know from an innate sense God puts within us, and (2) what we can know by examining nature and the external world. "Natural revelation" and "natural theology" greatly overlap. See: **Natural Law, Natural Theology, Synderesis Rule.**

Natural Theology ■ Knowledge about God that can be

gained from the natural world—apart from special revelation—because the nature of creation reveals something of the nature of the Creator. Thomas Aquinas argued that reason could prove God's existence through a proper understanding of the physical world. See: Romans 1:18–23. See: **Cosmological Argument, Thomism, Via Negativa.**

See: E. Gilson, *Christianity and Philosophy* (Sheed and Ward, 1939), and *God and Philosophy* (Yale University Press, 1941); G. Smith, *Natural Theology* (Macmillan, 1951).

Necessary Being ▪ In philosophy, that Being which must exist: Absolute Being, or Eternal Being. A Being that cannot *not* be, whose very essence is existence. See: **God, Metaphysics, Ontological Argument, Via Negativa.**

Neoorthodoxy ▪ A twentieth-century theological school of thought which broke with nineteenth-century liberalism, yet did not fully embrace orthodoxy because of its perceived conflict with the twentieth-century scientific world view. Neoorthodoxy emphasizes God's transcendence, the reality of sin, and revelation as a personal encounter with God through the Scriptures, though the text is not considered to be propositionally true (that is, the text of the Bible as written is not the Word of God, but becomes the Word of God as it transforms the individual). It is associated with the thought of Karl Barth (1886–1968) and Emil Brunner (1889–1966), and later with C. H. Dodd (1884–1973) and Reinhold (1892–1971) and H. Richard Niebuhr (1894–1962). See: **Liberal Protestantism.**

See: G.H. Clark, *Karl Barth's Theological Method* (Presbyterian and Reformed, 1963); A.B. Come, *An Introduction to Barth's Dogmatics for Preachers* (Westminster, 1963); L. Kliever, *H. Richard Niebuhr* (Word, 1977); B.E. Patterson, *Reinhold Niebuhr* (Word, 1977); H.R. Niebuhr, *Christ and Culture* (Harper & Row, 1951); R. Niebuhr, *The Nature and Destiny of Man: A Christian Interpretation* (Scribners, 1949).

Neoplatonism ▪ Literally, the "New Platonism." Neoplatonism was a resurgence of Greek philosophy in the third to the sixth centuries considered by many to be the last great effort of ancient pagan philosophy. Its exponents believed the movement was a direct continuation of Plato's thought. Ammonius Saccus (second century A.D.) and Plotinus (c. A.D. 204–270) were prominent neoplatonists. Plotinus taught that God, that is, "The Good" or "The One," was beyond being, essence, or knowledge.

See: T.L. Miethe, "God in Plotinus," in *The Metaphysics of Leonard James Eslick: His Philosophy of God* (University Microfilms, 1976), pp. 60–69; Plotinus, *The Enneads* (London: Faber and Faber, 1930).

Nestorianism ▪ From the teaching of Nestorius of Syria (exact dates unknown). Nestorius, who became patriarch of Constantinople in 428, was believed to have taught that the divine and human natures were not united or merged in Christ. Modern research has found a book written by Nestorius, the *Book of Heracleides*, in which he denies the heresy.

New England Theology ■ A theological tradition that grew from the work of Jonathan Edwards (1703–1758), a Congregational minister and theologian of the First Great Awakening, and continued well into the nineteenth century. Edwards was a minister in Northampton, Massachusetts, when he preached his famous sermon "Sinners in the Hands of an Angry God." He was also president of Princeton University for a few weeks before his death.

The movement was characterized by interest in the freedom of the human will and the morality of divine justice. Some of the more famous proponents of New England Theology were Joseph Bellamy (1719–1790), Samuel Hopkins (1721–1803), Timothy Dwight (1752–1817), Jonathan Edwards, Jr. (1745–1801), Nathaniel W. Taylor (1786–1858) and Edwards Amasa Park (1808–1900). See: **Freedom of the Will.**

See: J. Edwards, *The Freedom of the Will*, edited by P. Ramsey (Yale University Press, 1957).

Nicea, Councils of ■ The first ecumenical (church-wide) council in Church history, the Council of Nicea was convened by the Emperor Constantine in 325 in response to Arianism. More than 300 bishops, mostly from the East, almost unanimously condemned Arianism and declared that Christ was of one substance with the Father. The Second Council of Nicea (787), the seventh ecumenical council, accepted the veneration of images of Christ, Mary, the angels, and the saints as theologically correct. See: **Arianism, Veneration.**

Nicene Creed ■ This creed affirms that Christ is *homoousios*, "of the same substance as God," identical in substance with the Father. Formulated at the Council of Nicea in A.D. 325, the creed asserts that Christ is "very God of very God, begotten, not made, being of one substance with the Father." There are actually two versions of the creed. As revised and enlarged in 381 at the Council of Constantinople it reads:

"We believe in one God, the Father almighty, Maker of heaven and earth, and of all things visible and invisible. And in one

Lord Jesus Christ, the only-begotten son of God, begotten of the Father before all worlds, Light of Light, very God of very God, begotten, not made, being of one substance with the Father; by whom all things were made; who for us men, and for our salvation, came down from heaven, and was incarnate by the Holy Ghost of the virgin Mary, and was made man; he was crucified for us under Pontius Pilate, and suffered, and was buried, and the third day he rose again, according to the scriptures, and ascended into heaven, and sitteth on the right hand of the Father; from thence he cometh again, with glory, to judge the quick and the dead; whose kingdom shall have no end. And in the Holy Ghost, who is Lord and Giver of life, who proceedeth from the Father, who with the Father and the Son together is worshiped and glorified, who spake by the prophets. In one holy catholic and apostolic church; we acknowledge one baptism for the remission of sins; we look for the resurrection of the dead, and the life of the world to come. Amen."

The revised and enlarged version was accepted by the Council of Chalcedon in 451, though some groups in the Eastern Orthodox Church still use the original version. See: **Eastern Orthodox; Chalcedon, Council of; Constantinople, Council of; Homoousion.**

See: J.N.D. Kelly, *Early Christian Creeds* (Harper & Row, 1960); P. Schaff, *The Creeds of Christendom*, 3 vols. (Baker).

Nihil Obstat ▪ Also known as *Quominus Imprimatur*. Latin for "nothing hinders," "Nihil Obstat" is printed on the back of a book's title page (the copyright page) to show that the Roman Catholic censor of books certifies that he has inspected the work and found in it nothing contrary to faith or good morals. The Nihil Obstat and Imprimatur officially declares a book or pamphlet is free from doctrinal or moral error. See: **Imprimatur.**

Noetic Effects of Sin ▪ The darkening of the mind by sin that necessitates a special divine grace to understand and obey biblical truth. Some feel this teaching is supported by scriptures such as: 1 Corinthians 1:18; 2:12–14; 2 Corinthians 4:4; Ephesians 4:17–18. See: **Calvinism; Calvinism, Five Points of; Faith; Monergism; Sin.**

Omnificence ■ From the Latin *omni* plus *ficent*, meaning "unlimited in creative power." God's creative power is limited only by His nature, that is, He cannot do something that would contradict His nature or essence as God. See: **Attributes of God; God.**

Omnipotence ■ From the Latin *omnipotens*, "all powerful." God's attribute of infinite power. See: **Attributes of God, God.**

Omnipresence ■ From the Latin *omni*, "all," and *praesens*, "That is before one." In theology, the claim that God is wholly present in all places at any given moment in time. God is intimately related to all things and has access to all of reality. See: **Attributes of God, God.**

Omniscience ■ In philosophy and theology, the term "omniscience" refers to the fact that God has complete and perfect knowledge of all things, including himself and everything actual or potential in His creation, even though human beings and the rest of creation experience reality as past, present, and future. See: **Attributes of God, God, Foreknowledge.**

Ontological Argument ■ The argument devised by St. Anselm (1033–1109) of Canterbury for God's existence which claims that from our idea of God's essence we can conclude God must exist. The argument is based on pure logic rather than on sense knowledge of the physical world. Anselm had two versions of the argument: (1) one based on the *predictability* of existence to an absolutely perfect Being and (2) the other based on the *inconceivability* of the nonexistence of a necessary Being.

It is the second form that most scholars think is valid. It argues as follows: God is the greatest being one can conceive. If God—the greatest of all beings—exists only in the mind, He would not be the greatest of all beings, because the greatest of all beings must really exist. It follows, then, that this greatest of all conceivable beings must exist. In short, Anselm states that God must exist because we can imagine a perfect being, and a perfect being by definition must exist. See: **Cosmological Argument; God; God, Arguments for the Existence of; Moral Argument; Teleological Argument.**

See: A. Plantina, *The Ontological Argument: From St. Anselm to Contemporary Philosophers* (Doubleday, 1965); N.L. Geisler, "Ontological Arguments," in *Philosophy of Religion* (Zondervan, 1974), pp. 133–162; C. Hartshorne, *Man's Vision of God* (Harper & Row, 1941).

Ontology ■ From the Greek *on*, "being" and *logos*, "logic," or "the study of." Ontology is the part of philosophy that deals with the nature of being; being *qua* (as) being. For Aristotle, ontology was the science of the essence of things. The term is usually synonymous with metaphysics. See: **Metaphysics.**

Ordination ■ From the Latin *ordinare*, "to set in order." A service in which a person is set aside, or "ordained," for ministry or special service in the church. In Protestant churches ordination is little more than a public service recognizing a commitment an individual has already made before God and endorsing the individual's character and theology. This is usually done in a service where recognized officers of a denomination (ministers in good standing) or a church (through its elders) confer ordination on the candidate by the laying on of hands (Acts 6:1–7). In the Roman Catholic Church, ordination conveys special powers of ministry—to perform marriages, baptize, bury and hear confessions—and is considered a sacramental rite.

Orthodoxy ■ From the Greek *orthodoxos*, from *orthos*, "right," "straight," and *doxa*, "opinion," "belief." Belief in or acceptance of the truth of doctrines taught in Scripture: the preexistence of

Christ, the virgin birth, His sinless life, the bodily resurrection and the Second Coming. Today the word is used synonymously with historical biblical Christianity and is opposed to liberalism or neoorthodoxy. See: **Heresy, Liberal Protestantism, Neoorthodoxy, Schism.**

Pagan ▪ From the Latin *paganus*, "countryman," "peasant." Anyone who is not a Christian, who does not worship the true God and Jesus Christ His Son. Synonymous with heathen.

Panentheism ▪ From the Greek *pan*, "all," *en*, "in," and *theos*, "god." The world view that all is in God. God is to the world as a soul is to a body: The being of God includes the being of the universe, but also transcends it; God is in everything that exists, but God is more than the world. Panentheism attempts to mediate between the extreme immanence of pantheism and the extreme transcendence of some theistic models. Panentheism is the view of God in process philosophy and theology. See: **Process Theology.**

    See: N.L. Geisler and W. Watkins, "Pan-en-theism: A World in God," in *Perspectives: Understanding and Evaluating Today's World Views* (Here's Life Publishers, Inc., 1984), pp. 99–136; R.G. Gruenler, *The Inexhaustible God: Biblical Faith and the Challenge of Process Theism* (Baker, 1983); R.C. Neville, *Creativity and God: A Challenge to Process Theology* (Seabury, 1980).

Pantheism ▪ From the Greek *pan*, "all" and *theos*, "god." The world view that denies God's transcendence and teaches that the substance of God and the substance of the physical universe are in some sense identical; reality is composed of a single being of which all things are modes, moments, members, appearances or projections. Classical Hinduism is pantheistic, as were the philosophies of Benedict Spinoza (1632–1677) and G.W.F. Hegel (1770–1831). See: **Hinduism.**

    See: N.L. Geisler and W. Watkins, "Pantheism: A World That Is God," in *Perspectives: Understanding and Evaluating Today's World Views* (Here's Life Publishers, 1984), pp. 69–98; J.W. Sire, "Journey to the East:

Eastern Pantheistic Monism" in *The Universe Next Door: A Basic World View Catalog* (InterVarsity Press, 1976), pp. 128–149.

Parable ▪ From the Greek *parabole*, "a comparing," from *para*, "beside," and *ballein*, "to cast," "to throw." A parable is a short story embodying a message or moral by means of comparison. Jesus illustrated essential truths about the human condition in more than two dozen parables (though some scholars count a total of sixty parables), including the parable of the prodigal son (Luke 15:11–32), the parable of the good samaritan (Luke 10:25–37), the parable of the unmerciful servant (Matt. 18:23–35), the parable of the sower (Luke 8:4–15) and the parable of the talents (Matt. 25:14–30).

See: W. Barclay, *And Jesus Said: A Handbook on the Parables of Jesus* (Westminster, 1970); A.B. Bruce, *The Parabolic Teaching of Christ* (Armstrong, 1908); A.M. Hunter, *Interpreting the Parables* (Westminster, 1960); J. Jeremias, *The Parables of Jesus* (Scribners, 1963).

Paraclete ▪ From the Greek *parakletos*, "one called to someone's aid." A theological term used to refer to the Holy Spirit. In the Bible *parakletos* is often translated as "Comforter." See: John 14:16, 26; 15:26; 16:7. See: **Holy Spirit, Trinity.**

Paradise ▪ From the Greek *paradeisos*, "the place of blessedness." The NT uses the word three times: (1) the place promised to the thief (Luke 23:43); (2) the third heaven (2 Cor. 12:4); and (3) where the tree of life is located (Rev. 2:7). See: **Heaven.**

Paradox ▪ Two assertions—such as in theology—held in tension that seem to contradict each other. The teaching of the Incarnation, that Jesus was at the same time fully human and fully divine, is an example. See: Matthew 10:39; John 11:24; 2 Corinthians 6:9–10. See: **Antinomy, Christ, Christology, Incarnation.**

Parousia ▪ A Greek word meaning "a being present." In the NT the word refers to the Second Coming of Christ. See: Matthew 10:23; 16:27–28; 24:36; 25:31–46; Acts 1:11; 1 Corinthians 13:12; 1 Thessalonians 4:15; 2 Peter 1:16; 1 John 3:2; Revelation 1:7 See: **Second Coming of Christ.**

Patristics ■ From the Greek *pater*, "a father." The study in Church history of the teaching and lives of the Church fathers, the early leaders of the Church. The patristic age usually is dated from the end of the NT era to the end of the eighth century.

See: B. Altaner, *Patrology* (Herder and Herder, 1960); *The Early Christian Fathers*, ed. and trans. by H. Bettenson (Oxford University Press, 1963); J.B. Lightfoot, *The Apostolic Fathers*, 5 vols. (Macmillan, 1890); G.L. Prestige, *God in Patristic Thought* (London: SPCK, 1959); J. Quasten, *Patrology*, 3 vols. (Newman Press, 1950–1960).

Pelagianism ■ The teaching of Pelagius (360–420), a British monk and theologian who held that, like Adam, each human being is created with the power and freedom to choose good or evil. Pelagius argued that each soul is a separate creation of God, and hence is not corrupted by Adam's sin. He attributed sin not to corruption of the human will by Adam's sin but to the weakness of human flesh; people inherit not sin but the effects of sin, which impair the flesh. They are free to cooperate with God in the attainment of holiness, using the gifts God gives to them—the Bible, reason and the example set by Jesus Christ. Pelagius' positions that God would not necessarily condemn unbaptized infants and that human nature is essentially good brought him into conflict with Augustine.

Penance ■ From the Latin *poena*, "penalty." In theology, the act of showing sorrow for sins. In the Roman Catholic Church, penance, one of the seven sacraments, is the method prescribed for the forgiveness of mortal sins committed after baptism. A priest forgives sins upon the sinner's completion of acts that at least partially pay for the sins. Made mandatory once a year in 1215, penance was officially declared a sacrament at the Council of Trent (1545–1563). See: Matthew 6:12; 18:15; John 20:19–23; 2 Corinthians 2:5–11; 1 John 5:16; 1 Timothy 1:19, 20. See: **Fasting; Sacraments, The Seven; Trent, Council of.**

Pentateuch ■ From the Greek *pentateuchos*, "five-volumed." The first five books of the OT (Genesis, Exodus, Leviticus, Numbers and Deuteronomy), which are the books of the Law, the first section of the three-fold Jewish canon of the OT.

Pentecostalism ■ A twentieth-century movement that takes its name from the Holy Spirit's working at Pentecost (Acts 2), maintaining that similar workings are possible in the Church today. It emphasizes a baptism of the Holy Spirit after regeneration that is possible or normative for all Christians. This baptism of the Holy Spirit is accompanied by supernatural gifts such as speaking in tongues.

Pentecostalism's modern history began with a manifestation of speaking in tongues in Topeka, Kansas, in 1901. A student named Agnes Ozman first experienced the gift in January 1901 as part of a movement led by a Methodist minister, Charles Fox Parham (1873–1929). Although instances of speaking in tongues had occurred in England and America in the 1800s, these never grew into important theological movements. A second important series of events happened in the Azusa Street Revival in Los Angeles from 1906–1909. Out of this revival led by William J. Seymour, a holiness preacher from Houston and a student of Parham, came a variety of new church groups: the Pentecostal Holiness Church, the Church of God in Christ, the Church of God (Cleveland, Tennessee), the Apostolic Faith (Portland, Oregon), the United Holy Church. Later came the Assemblies of God (1914) and the International Church of the Foursquare Gospel (founded 1927 by Aimee Semple McPherson). Another group, the Full Gospel Business Men's Fellowship, was founded in 1948.

Pentecostal phenomena has subsequently spread to many denominations. In 1966 the Roman Catholic Church experienced the beginnings of Pentecostalism at Duquesne University. By 1973, 30,000 Catholic Pentecostals gathered at Notre Dame for a national conference, and by 1980 the movement had spread to Catholic churches in over 100 countries. Catholic Pentecostals (or "charismatics") have never insisted that speaking in tongues is *the* sign of the gift of the Holy Spirit, as older Protestant Pentecostalism has done. Catholics rather have turned to serious exegetical and doctrinal study. As a result, supernatural spiritual gifts, though important, have been less of a measure of devout Christianity. This movement in the Catholic church is representative of events in many mainline denominations. Most refer to the movement as one of "charismatic renewal." See: **Glossolalia; Holy Spirit; Tongues, Speaking in.**

See: D.L. Gelpi, *Pentecostal Piety* (Deus Books, 1972), and *Pentecostalism: A Theological Viewpoint* (Deus Books, 1971); C.E. Hummel, *Fire in the Fireplace: Contemporary Charismatic Renewal* (InterVarsity Press, 1978).

People, Appeal to the ■ In Latin, *Argumentum ad Populum*, or "to the gallery." By directing an emotional appeal to the people to win their assent to a conclusion unsupported by good evidence, one commits this fallacy. Or to put it more clearly, we may define this fallacy as the attempt to win popular assent to a conclusion by arousing the emotions and enthusiasms of the multitude, rather than by appeal to the relevant facts. See: **Logical Fallacies.**

Perfection, Christian ■ At several points the Bible commands perfection of the believer: "Therefore you are to be perfect, as your heavenly Father is perfect" (Matt. 5:48, NASB). "Jesus said unto him, If thou wilt be perfect, go and sell that thou hast, and give to the poor, and thou shall have treasure in heaven: and come and follow me" (Matt. 19:21, KJV). See also Ephesians 4:13–14 and Hebrews 13:21.

But what is perfection? Groups in Christian history have suggested different answers. In gnostic Christianity, perfection was the soul's release from the bondage of the flesh, a release attained through esoteric knowledge and illumination. In Pelagianism, perfection was the culmination of vigorous moral education and discipline. Still other movements have defined perfection as a mystical experience or as manifestation of ecstatic gifts of the Holy Spirit.

Church tradition since Augustine (354–430), however, has pictured perfection as perfect love, labeling it an impossibility in this life, except for saints. The Protestant Reformers went even further, saying perfection was possible for no one. John Calvin (1509–1564), for example, wrote: "There still remains in a regenerate man a fountain of evil, continually producing irregular desires. . . ." This warfare inside each human being "will be terminated only by death. . . ." The Reformers taught that progress was possible, although perfection was not.

John Wesley (1703–1791) was one of few leaders to work out the idea of perfection within an evangelical framework. Wesley regarded perfection—"pure love reigning alone in the heart and life"—as a real possibility for every Christian. While he viewed love as God's law, he also believed perfection was a gift of grace. Although a long period of effort might precede it, perfection was given instantly, freeing the perfected from "voluntary transgression of known law," although the perfected might still fall into "involuntary transgressions." See: **Calvinism, Gnosticism, Pelagianism, Wesleyanism.**

See: C.G. Finney, *Sanctification* (Christian Literature Crusade, 1963); R.N. Flew, *The Idea of Perfection in Christian Theology* (Humanities Press, 1968); H.G. Lindstrom, *Wesley and Sanctification: A Study in the Doctrine of Salvation* (London: Epworth Press, 1950); W.E.R. Sangster, *The Path to Perfection* (London: Hodder and Stoughton, 1943); J. Wesley, *A Plain Account of Christian Perfection* (London: Epworth Press, 1960).

Perfection, Theological ■ In the Bible, perfection is a state of ideal wholeness or completion. The most common Greek word for perfection, *teleios*, signifies having reached the appropriate or appointed *telos*, or end. The Bible speaks of perfection in three connections: (1) God's perfection. Scripture speaks of God (Matt. 5:48), His work (Deut. 32:4), His way (2 Sam. 22:31), and His law (Ps. 19:7; James 1:25) as perfect. What God says and does is wholly free from faults and worthy of all praise. (2) Christ's perfection. The incarnate Son is made "perfect through suffering" (Heb. 2:10). (3) Human perfection. This is wrought through God's covenant relationship with human beings and His work of grace within them.

The Bible speaks of God's perfecting of His people in the image of Christ (Gal. 3:14; Eph. 4:13; Col. 3:10; 4:12; Heb. 5:14; 6:1; 1 Peter 2:2). Believers are perfected only "in Christ" (Col. 1:28— See: Eph. 4:12–16; Phil. 3:10–14; Col. 3:4; 1 John 3:2). Nowhere does the Bible relate the idea of perfection to law or directly equate it with sinlessness. According to Scripture, the present perfection some Christians attain is not sinlessness, but strong faith, joyful patience and overflowing love.

Perichoresis ■ A Greek word meaning "penetration." This theological term refers to the relationship and interaction of Jesus' two natures, the divine and human. It also refers to the indwelling interpenetration, the relationship among the persons of the Trinity. See: John 10:38; 14:10–12; 17:21; 1 Corinthians 2:10–16.

Perseverance ■ From the Latin *perseverare*, "to persevere," "to persist in a thing." See: Ephesians 6:18. Perseverance is the doctrine that true believers will continue in the faith until death.

Calvinists and Arminians view the doctrine somewhat differently. Calvin taught that God's sovereignty guaranteed the salvation of the elect: His sovereignty worked in a way that would never allow someone He had saved to fall away. The saved can fall into sin, but not out of salvation. This view of assurance is not shared by Arminians, who argue that election was conditioned on God's foreknowledge of who would believe. Faith is not a gift of God, as it is in Calvinism; Arminians believe that true believers can lose salvation by failing to maintain their faith. Those who are free to accept God, they say, are also free to reject Him. See: Acts 1:14; 2:42, 46; 8:13; Romans 12:12; Colossians 4:2; 1 Peter 1:5. See: **Arminianism; Atonement; Calvinism; Calvinism, Five Points of; Faith; Foreknowledge; Election; Sovereignty.**

See: J. Calvin, *Institutes of the Christian Religion* (Eerdmans, 1953), 3.11–14; I.H. Marshall, *Kept by the Power of God: A Study of Perseverance and Falling Away* (Bethany House Publishers, 1969).

Philosophy ■ From the Greek words *philein*, "to love," and *sophia*, "wisdom." A philosopher, then, is a lover of wisdom. By historical definition a philosopher is an honest seeker of truth. Philosophy has been called the most general science, the underlying principle of any intellectual discipline.

At first, philosophy was seen broadly as the rational explanation of anything. Later it became known as the science of first principles of being (that is, metaphysics). The discipline of philosophy now comprises metaphysics (or ontology), epistemology (theories of how we know what we know), logic (investigation of the structure of propositions and of deductive reasoning), ethics (the study of systems of moral principles, right and wrong, good and bad), aesthetics (the qualities perceived in works of art, the idea of beauty), and the study of foundational issues in disciplines such as science, religion or history.

Thomas Aquinas listed three ways philosophy can benefit the Christian: (1) It logically establishes the preambles of faith—God's existence, His oneness and so on—helping both believer and unbeliever see evidence for a Christian world view; (2) It illustrates doctrine (Augustine, for example, used philosophy to explain the Trinity), helping the Christian better understand the essence of the faith; and (3) It demonstrates the falseness or inadequacy of arguments against the Christian faith, aiding in apologetics and showing Christianity's intellectual soundness. See: **Aesthetics; Axiology; Ethics, Christian; Metaphysics; Ontology.**

See: C. Brown, *Philosophy and the Christian Faith* (Tyndale, 1969); N.L. Geisler and P. Feinberg, *Introduction to Philosophy: A Christian Perspective* (Baker, 1980); J.V. Langmead Casserley, *The Christian in Philosophy* (London: Faber and Faber, 1949); T.L. Miethe, *The Christian's Guide to Faith and Reason* (Bethany House Publishers, 1987); Warren C. Young, *A Christian Approach to Philosophy* (Baker, 1954).

Philosophy of Religion ▪ The study of foundational issues in the field of religion, including the nature and purpose of religion, the existence of God, the problem of evil, the nature of religious language, freedom and determinism, revelation and faith, the problem of miracles, the problem of verification of religious truth claims, human destiny, immortality and resurrection, evidence of religious experience and objections to religious claims. Study of the philosophy of religion often revolves around explaining or defending a particular religious view or religion. In this respect, the field is similar to apologetics, which states and defends philosophical issues in the Christian religion. See: **Apologetics; Metaphysics; God, Arguments for the Existence of.**

See: C.S. Evans, *Philosophy of Religion* (InterVarsity Press, 1985); N.L. Geisler, *Philosophy of Religion* (Zondervan, 1974); S.M. Thompson, *A Modern Philosophy of Religion* (Henry Regnery, 1956); D.E. Trueblood, *Philosophy of Religion* (Harper & Row, 1957); Ninian Smart, *The Philosophy of Religion* (Oxford University Press, 1979).

Pity, Appeal to ▪ In Latin, *Argumentum ad Misericordiam*. This fallacy is committed when one persuades using pity when the question at hand concerns facts, not feelings. This argument is often used by lawyers who seek to gain settlement through a jury or judge's pity rather than through sound argument or proofs. See: **Logical Fallacies.**

Platonism ▪ A system of philosophy based on the thought of Plato (428/7–348/7 B.C.) of Athens. Plato, a student of Socrates (c. 470–399 B.C.), impacted western philosophy and theology more than any other philosopher. It was not until the thirteenth century that Aristotle (384–322 B.C.), Plato's most famous student, began to exert as formidable an influence in the West as Plato. It is often said that "there is no road one can travel in philosophy where one does not meet Plato coming back."

Plato is famous for his theory of the Forms. Neither physical objects nor simply logical symbols, these ultimate Forms of reality have objective existence. The physical world imperfectly imitates these forms, and is in constant flux. For Plato, Forms were unchanging points of reference that gave the world meaning and order. People are born with innate knowledge of the Forms, and by questioning—the Socratic method—they can remember the ultimate knowledge they already possess. See: **Aristotelianism, Neoplatonism.**

See: F. Copleston, "Part Three: Plato," in *A History of Philosophy* (Doubleday, 1962), vol. 1, pp. 151–291; G.M.A. Grube, *Plato's Thought* (Hackett, 1980); T.L. Miethe, "God in Plato" in *The Metaphysics of Leonard James Eslick: His Philosophy of God* (University Microfilms, 1976), pp. 36–46, 191–193; *Plato: The Collected Dialogues*, ed. E. Hamilton and H. Cairns (Princeton University Press, 1961); *The Republic of Plato*, trans. by F.M. Cornford (Oxford University Press, 1945).

Pneumatology ■ From the Greek *pneuma*, "wind," "spirit," and *logos*, "the study of." In theology, a comprehensive study of the person and work of the Holy Spirit. Pneumatology traces the activities of the Holy Spirit through the Old and New Testaments, often with special attention to His ministry to Christ, to the Church and to the individual Christian. See: **Holy Spirit.**

Polity ■ From the Greek *politeia*, "government," "constitution." The form of government of a church. Churches usually are either "episcopal," headed by a bishop above the congregation; "congregational," governed by elders at the congregational level; or "presbyterian," governed by a hierarchy of democratic assemblies. See: **Bishop, Congregationalism, Presbyterians.**

Polytheism ■ Belief in many different gods or deities. With the exception of Judaism, Christianity, and Islam, most of the world's religions are polytheistic. See: **Monotheism, Panentheism, Pantheism, Theism.**

See: J.N.D. Anderson, *The World's Religions* (Eerdmans, 1950); J. Ferguson, *The Religions of the Roman Empire* (Cornell University Press, 1970); E.O. James, *Comparative Religion: An Introductory and Historical Study*

(London: Methuen and Co., 1961); S.C. Neill, *Christian Faith and Other Faiths: The Christian Dialogue with Other Religions* (Oxford University Press, 1961); E.A. Nida and W.A. Smalley, *Introducing Animism* (Friendship Press, 1959); A.J. Toynbee, *Christianity Among the Religions of the World* (Scribners, 1956).

Postmillennialism ▪ In eschatology, the idea that Christ will return after the millennium, the 1000 or more years of peace on the earth that come about as a result of Christians' preaching and teaching. Their work in the world will bring many conversions, reducing evil to a minimum. After this period of the Church's greatness, Christ will come again, the dead will rise, and God will conduct the final judgment. See: **Eschatology, Amillennialism, Millennialism, Premillennialism.**

See: L. Boettner, *The Millennium* (Presbyterian and Reformed, 1958).

Prayer ▪ For the Christian, prayer is a lifestyle (1 Thess. 5:15–18: "pray without ceasing"). Prayer should involve the whole person: mind, will and emotion. Prayer is not a magical way of grabbing goodies, for it is more a way of asking God to give you what He wants than demanding from Him what you want. God uses prayer to teach us to depend on Him and to tune our desires and wishes to His will. Christians should pray in Christ's name (Matt. 7:7–11; John 16:23–24; 15:7, 16). See: **Lord's Prayer, The.**

See: O.C. Hallesby, *Prayer* (Augsburg, 1975); W. Law, *The Spirit of Prayer, The Spirit of Love* (Cambridge: James Clarke, 1969); T.L. Miethe, "On Prayer," in *The New Christian's Guide to Following Jesus* (Bethany House Publishers, 1984), pp. 85–90; L.J. Ogilvie, *Praying With Power* (Regal, 1983); G.C. Morgan, *The Practice of Prayer* (Baker, 1971); A. Murray, *The Inner Chamber, The Inner Life* (Zondervan, 1958), *Ministry of Intercessory Prayer* (Bethany House Publishers, 1981), and *Believer's School of Prayer* (Bethany House Publishers, 1982).

Preaching ▪ Declaring the truth of God from the Word of God to an audience. Though there are many different methods of preaching and numerous types of sermons, preaching should primarily be exegetical: a careful study of the grammar, words, and context of a particular passage of Scripture. Preaching should answer three questions about a text: (1) What does the text say? (2) Why does it say it, or what did the Holy Spirit want the passage to communicate? (3) How does this truth apply to life at home, work, or play? Any sermon or lesson should be

aimed at the heart, intended to motivate people to take action, as well as at the mind, able to persuade. See: **Exegesis.**

See: A. Blackwood, *The Preparation of Sermons* (Abingdon-Cokesbury, 1948); J.A. Broadus, *On the Preparation and Delivery of Sermons* (Harper & Row, 1943); M. Lloyd-Jones, *Preaching and Preachers* (Zondervan, 1971); T.H. Pattison, *The Making of the Sermon* (The American Baptist Publication Society, 1941); J.S. Stewart, *Exposition and Encounter: Preaching in the Context of Worship* (England: Berean Press, 1956), and *Heralds of God* (Scribners, 1946); C.H. Spurgeon, *Lectures to My Students* (Zondervan, 1955); J.R.W. Stott, *Between Two Worlds: The Art of Preaching in the Twentieth Century* (Eerdmans, 1982).

Predestination ■ From the Latin *pre*, "before," and *destinare*, "to destine." In theology, the teaching that God has decided, or foreordained, every event that has happened, is happening, or will happen (Ps. 2; Eph. 1:11). There are several understandings of predestination regarding salvation: (1) General predestination: God wills everyone to be saved and foreknows who will respond in faith. (2) Single predestination: God chooses those who will be saved. (3) Double predestination: God chooses who will be saved and who will be damned. See: Acts 2:23; 4:28; Romans 8:29–30; Ephesians 1:5, 11. See: **Arminianism, Atonement, Calvinism, Election, Freedom of the Will, Sovereignty of God.**

See: D. Basinger and R. Basinger, *Predestination and Free Will* (InterVarsity Press, 1986); L. Boettner, *The Reformed Doctrine of Predestination* (Presbyterian and Reformed Publishing Co., 1968); D.J.A. Clines, "Predestination in the Old Testament," in C.H. Pinnock, ed., *Grace Unlimited* (Bethany House Publishers, 1975), pp. 110–126; I.H. Marshall, *Kept by the Power of God* (Bethany House Publishers, 1969), and "Predestination in the New Testament," in C.H. Pinnock, ed., *Grace Unlimited* (Bethany House Publishers, 1975), pp. 127–143.

Preexistence of Christ ■ The teaching in theology that Christ is eternal God, the second person of the Trinity, and that He existed before the Incarnation. See: John 1:1–11; Acts 2:22–23; 10:38. See: **Christ, Christology, Jesus, Trinity.**

See: H.R. Mackintosh, *The Doctrine of the Person of Christ* (Scribners, 1931); O. Cullmann, *The Christology of the New Testament* (Westminster, 1963).

Preexistence of Souls ■ The teaching that the human soul or spirit existed before conception and birth. This idea, important to Platonism, was accepted by Origen (c. 185–254). In the history of the Church, most theologians have held to what is called the "creationist view," that is, that God creates each individual soul at the moment it is given to a body (Gen. 2:7; Eccles. 12:7; Isa. 42:5; Zech. 12:1; Heb. 12:9). See: **Platonism, Traducianism, Soul.**

Premillennialism ■ In eschatology, the teaching that Christ will return, set up an earthly kingdom, and rule for 1000 years.

According to the premillennialist view, Christ's return will be preceded by an increasingly evil world—more wars, famines, earthquakes—by the Gospel's being preached to all peoples, by the appearance of the Antichrist and by the great tribulation. Christ will then come and set up His kingdom and reign with the saints for the 1000 years. Jews will come to Christ in large numbers and will again take an important place in God's kingdom. After a millennium (1000 years), evil will again cause rebellion, but God will crush it. At that time God will raise unbelievers for eternal judgment in hell and create a new heaven and earth for believers. See: **Amillennialism, Eschatology, Millennialism.**

See: G.E. Ladd, *Crucial Questions About the Kingdom of God* (Eerdmans, 1952) and *Gospel of the Kingdom* (Eerdmans, 1959); J.F. Walvoord, *The Millennial Kingdom* (Dunham Publishing Co., 1965).

Presbyter ■ From the Greek *presbyteros,* "elder," "older." An elder. In the NT the term is translated as overseers (Acts 20:17, 28) and as pastors or shepherds (1 Peter 5:1–4). In Luke 22:66 and Acts 22:5, the word is used of Jewish elders, and in 1 Timothy 4:14 of Christian elders. See: **Elder.**

Presbyterians ■ A denomination that finds its roots in John Calvin, who provided his followers with a theology, a liturgy and a particular form of church government. This form, Presbyterianism, vests religious authority in groups of Christians who represent a number of congregations rather than in bishops (Episcopalianism) or in local congregations (Congregationalism).

Presbyterianism was elaborated under John Knox (c. 1514–1572), who studied under Calvin in Geneva. Taking the Reformed theology of Calvin back to Scotland in 1559, he helped to establish the new Presbyterian faith. The Puritans, who had been greatly influenced by Calvinism, dethroned and beheaded

Charles I and called a group of Presbyterian ministers to West-minster in 1643 to draw up a new confession of faith. Within five years they produced the standards of faith for Scottish, English, and American Presbyterians: the Westminster Confession, the Larger and Shorter Westminster catechisms and the directory of worship. When a group of Puritans landed in Salem in 1629, most of them became Congregationalists, but a few turned to Presbyterianism and settled in New York, New Jersey, Pennsylvania, Maryland, and Delaware. Later the arrival of thousands of Scots-Irish in the colonies established a firm base for Presbyterianism.

In the presbyterian form of church polity, or government, presbyters (elders) of a given local church form its "session," or council. The presbytery, the next level of authority, makes decisions for a local group of churches; the presbytery is composed of one lay elder from each local session and all the ministers of that area. Above the presbytery is a General Assembly. The largest Presbyterian body in America today is the Presbyterian Church (U.S.A.), a 1983 merger of the United Presbyterian Church (U.S.A.) (northern) and the Presbyterian Church in the United States (southern). See: **Calvinism, Reformed Theology.**

See: H. Cowin, *John Knox: The Hero of the Scottish Reformation* (AMS Press, 1970); *Encyclopedia of the Presbyterian Church in the United States of America* (Presbyterian Publishing Co., 1888); G. MacGregor, *The Thundering Scot: A Portrait of John Knox* (Westminster, 1957); P.H. Miller, *Why I Am a Presbyterian* (Beacon Press, 1956).

Presuppositionalism ■ Presuppositions, the initial assumptions on which all thought is based, are difficult to uncover or prove because they stand prior to proof and become the criteria or truth. In apologetics, presuppositionalism is the idea that biblical revelation is the presupposition upon which any coherent system of truth must be built. All true statements are either explicitly stated in Scripture, or derived by sound logical inference from the statements of Scripture.

The starting point of a presuppositionalist system is either the axioms of logic, God and the Bible (as Gordon Clark argues) or the autonomous Scripture and the Triune God (as Cornelius Van Til maintains). The common ground between believers and nonbelievers is either the thought-forms of the mind (Clark) or nothing, no common ground epistemologically (Van Til). The test for truth is consistency (Clark) or self-authenticating claims of the

Bible (Van Til). See: **Apologetics, Evidentialism, Fideism.**

See: G.L. Bahnsen and J.H. Gerstner, "On Apologetics: Classical or Presuppositional?" in *The Presbyterian Journal*, vol. 44 (Dec. 4, 1985), pp. 6–11; E.R. Geehan, *Jerusalem and Athens* (Presbyterian and Reformed, 1971); R.B. Mayers, *Both/And: A Balanced Apologetic* (Moody, 1984); R.C. Sproul, J. Gerstner, and A. Lindsley, *Classical Apologetics: A Rational Defense of the Christian Faith and a Critique of Presuppositional Apologetics* (Zondervan, 1984); C. Van Til, *Apologetics* (Presbyterian and Reformed, 1980).

Pride ▪ Pride is the exact opposite of humility. It consists of excessive love of self and is exhibited in three ways: (1) contempt for lawful authority; (2) contempt for equals and inferiors; and (3) desire to surpass one's equals. In Roman Catholic theology, pride is one of the Seven Deadly Sins. Thomas Aquinas put pride in a class by itself as the most deadly and devastating of all vices, because it is a part of every sin. Certainly the Bible warns against false pride (See: Prov. 8:13; 11:2; 16:18; 1 John 2:16; Mark 7:22; James 4:16). See: **Sins, Seven Deadly.**

Priest ▪ From the Greek *presbyteros*, "older, "elder." The title given in the Anglican, Eastern Orthodox and Roman Catholic churches to an ordained person set apart for a holy purpose and separated from the laity. The Roman Catholic Church divides priests into two grades: (1) "Priests of the second order by their ordination to the priesthood are given power to offer the sacrifice of the Mass, to baptize solemnly, and to administer Extreme Unction, but need jurisdiction for the valid administration of the sacraments of Penance and for valid assistance at the sacrament of Matrimony, and an indult for the valid administration of Confirmation." (2) "Priests of the first order, i.e., bishops, possess the additional power of administering the sacraments of Confirmation and Holy Order." See 1 Corinthians 4:1–2. See: **Clergy, Laity, Ordination.**

Priesthood ▪ The office, dignity, or character of a priest. In the OT human sinfulness made offering sacrifices necessary. From this practice arose the need for the Aaronic, or Levitical, priesthood (Heb. 7:11–25). The NT calls Christ our High Priest (Heb. 7:26–28; 10:10, 14). See: **Clergy; Minister; Ordination; Rabbi, Rabboni.**

Priesthood of all Believers ■ The NT teaching that Christ's mediation gives all Christians equal standing before God, with direct access to God and no need for another human to bridge the gap between themselves and God. Many NT passages teach the priesthood of all believers. In 1 Peter 2:5, 9 we find a clear statement of the doctrine: (1) *Christians* are the living Church, not a physical building. (2) We offer "spiritual sacrifices" as priests by giving our lives to God through Jesus Christ. This is worship. (3) Our message as priests is to "declare the praises of Him" who has enlightened us, to extend His call to others. The priesthood of all believers is an essential and distinctive teaching of the Christian faith. See Romans 12:1–2; 2 Corinthians 5:17–20; Ephesians 4:11–12; Revelation 1:6; 5:10; 20:6.

See: F.O. Ayers, *The Ministry of the Laity: A Biblical Exposition* (Westminster, 1962); R.L. Calhoun, *God and the Day's Work* (Fleming H. Revell, 1943); C.S. Calian, *Today's Pastor in Tomorrow's World* (Hawthorn Books, 1977); W.R. Forrester, *Christian Vocation: Studies in Faith and Work* (Scribners, 1953); T.L. Miethe, "Ministry and the Christian," in *The Christian's Guide to Following Jesus* (Bethany House Publishers, 1984), pp. 103–110; L. Peabody, *Secular Work is Full Time Service* (Christian Literature Crusade, 1974); E. Trueblood, *The Company of the Committed* (Harper & Row, 1961).

Process Theology ■ A twentieth-century view of God rooted in the thought of Alfred North Whitehead (1861–1947), in which God is part of the process of reality. All reality is engaged in change and evolution—that is, process—and God himself undergoes self-development and growth as He is continuously and creatively involved with the world. In this view God has two equal and opposite natures: (1) a transcendent nature which is timeless and perfect in character, and (2) an immanent nature by which He is part of the cosmic process itself. See: **Panentheism.**

See: J.B. Cobb, Jr., and D.R. Griffin, *Process Theology: An Introductory Exposition* (Westminster, 1976); D.R. Griffin, *God, Power, and Evil: A Process Theodicy* (Westminster, 1976); R.G. Gruenler, *The Inexhaustible God: Biblical Faith and the Challenge of Process Theism* (Baker, 1983); C. Hartshorne, *The Divine Relativity* (Yale University Press, 1948); R.C. Neville, *Creativity and God: A Challenge to Process Theology* (Seabury, 1980); A.N. Whitehead, *Process and Reality: An Essay in Cosmology* (Harper & Row, 1957).

Prolegomena ■ From the Greek *prolegein*, "to say beforehand." Introductory material. A formal essay or critical discussion introducing and interpreting an extended work.

Proofs of God's Existence ■ The use of reason and an analysis of the nature of reality to support God's existence. Scripture seems to acknowledge that human beings have natural knowledge of the Creator (Rom. 1:18–23). Since God is the Author of language, logic, and of all reality, it seems plausible that humanity could know something about the Creator from the creation. See: **Cosmological Argument, Moral Argument, Ontological Argument, Teleological Argument.**

See: J. Collins, *God in Modern Philosophy* (Henry Regnery, 1959); N.L. Geisler, *Philosophy* (Zondervan, 1974); Hans Kung, *Does God Exist?* (Doubleday, 1980); A. Plantinga, *God and Other Minds* (Cornell University Press, 1967); S.M. Thompson, *A Modern Philosophy of Religion* (Henry Regnery, 1955); R. Swinburne, *The Existence of God* (Oxford University Press, 1979).

Prophecy, Prophet ■ From the Greek, *prophetes*, from *pro*, "before," "for," and *phemi*, "to speak." In theology, a prophet is one who speaks for God. The prophet in the Bible had two roles: (1) to teach God's message regarding a contemporary situation, and/or (2) to relate a message about the future which God had revealed to the prophet. While we often stress the predictive role, the Bible emphasizes the teaching function.

Based on the length of their writings, the OT prophets are often divided into major prophets (Isaiah, Jeremiah, Ezekiel, and Daniel), and minor prophets (Hosea, Joel, Amos, Obadiah, Jonah, Micah, Nahum, Habakkuk, Zephaniah, Haggai, Zechariah, and Malachi). There were other OT prophets: Moses (Deut. 34:10–12), Samuel (Jer. 15:1), Gad (2 Sam. 24), Nathan (2 Sam. 12), Ahijah (1 Kings 11), Elijah (1 Kings 18–19), and Elisha (2 Kings 5–8). John the Baptist was the last prophet of the old covenant (Matt. 3:1–17; Luke 3:16–21; John 1:19–39).

In the NT, Agabus (Acts 11:27; 21:10), Jude and Silas (Acts 15:32), the four daughters of Philip (Acts 21:8–10) and Anna (Luke 2:36) are called prophets. The role of prophet in the NT was even more closely associated with the teaching function. See: Deuteronomy 18:18; Jeremiah 1:9; Acts 2:14–36; 11:27–28; 15:30–32; 21:10–14; 1 Corinthians 14:3, 24, 29, 31; 15:1–4; 1 Thessalonians 2:13; 4:8.

See: A.B. Davidson, *Old Testament Prophecy* (Edinburgh: T. and T. Clark, 1903); M.R. DeHann, *The Jew and Palestine in Prophecy* (Zondervan, 1950); J.B. Payne, *Encyclopedia of Biblical Prophecy* (Harper & Row, 1973); J.F. Walvoord, *Israel in Prophecy* (Zondervan, 1962), and *The Church in Prophecy* (Zondervan, 1962).

Propitiation ■ From the Greek *hilaskomai, hilasterion,* and *hilasmos* (Heb. 2:17; Rom. 3:25; 1 John 2:2; 4:10) and the Latin *propitus,* "favorable." The sacrifice of Christ—the atonement—satisfies God's wrath and was the "propitiation" for our sins. In 1 John 4:10 it is declared: "In this is love, not that we loved God, but that He loved us and sent His Son to be the propitiation for our sins." See: Isaiah 53:10; Matthew 27:46; Mark 15:34; John 10:17–18; Romans 1:18, 24, 26, 28; 3:25.

Proselyte ■ From the Greek, *proselytos,* "one who has come to a place." A member of one religious group who is persuaded to join another religious group.

Propositional Revelation ■ In theology, the idea that the Bible is direct revelation from God and is factually true in sentence form. In other words, the very sentence structure of the Bible is God's verbal special revelation to mankind and is therefore factually true. See: **Bible, Inerrancy and Infallibility of the; Inerrancy; Inspiration; Inspiration, Dictation Theory; Revelation.**

Providence ■ From the Latin *providere,* "to provide." The word "providence" does not occur in the Bible. It refers, however, to three biblical concepts: (1) In theology, providence is the general foresight, love, and care of God for people. Romans 8:28 reads: "And we know that God causes all things to work together for good to those who love God, to those who are called according to His purpose." Providence can also refer to the idea that (2) God has divinely ordained or preordained certain events, or that (3) the universe is under God's control so that ultimately good will be produced. See: **Predestination.**

Pseudopigrapha ■ Those Jewish writings included in neither the OT canon nor the Apocrypha. These writings never approached canonical status. They include: *The Psalms of Solomon, Testaments of the Twelve Patriarchs, Book of Jubilees, Testament of Job, Life of Adam and Eve, Martyrdom of Isaiah, Paralipomena of Jeremiah the Prophet, Book of Enoch, Book of the Secrets of Enoch, The*

Assumption of Moses, Apocalypse of Ezra, Apocalypse of Baruch, The Letter of Aristeas, Sibylline Oracles, 3 and 4 *Maccabees.* See: **Apocrypha.**
See: R.H. Charles, *The Apocrypha and Pseudopigrapha,* 2 vols. (Oxford: Clarendon Press, 1963); W.O.E. Oesterley, *An Introduction to the Books of the Apocrypha* (London: SPCK, 1946).

Publican ■ From the Greek *telones,* "a collector of tax or custom on behalf of the Romans." That these individuals had a bad reputation is evidenced by the NT expression "publicans and sinners." See: Matthew 9:10–13; 11:19; Mark 2:15–17; Luke 5:30; 7:34; 15:1.

Purgatory ■ From the Latin *pugare,* "to purge." The destination, according to Roman Catholic theology, of people who die and are not sufficiently holy to go directly to heaven, nor sufficiently evil to be permanently assigned to hell. Through a process of purging experiences, they are prepared for heaven; the length of purgation is determined by their acts of sin and penance while living. In addition, the faithful on earth can influence the condition and status of those in purgatory by prayers, intercessions, works of charity, and the mass. The doctrine of purgatory was officially declared at the Council of Florence (1439). It was also affirmed by the Council of Trent (1545–1563). See: Luke 16:19–31; 2 Corinthians 5:1–10; 1 Peter 3:18–22; 4:6. See: **Gehenna; Hell; Intermediate State; Soul; Trent, Council of.**

Puritanism ■ A movement that originated in the sixteenth century whose purpose was to purify the Church of England beyond what had been accomplished during the English Reformation. Puritans emphasized simplicity of worship, life, biblical and theological truth. Though the Puritans are often thought to have been rigid or strict in religious observances and conduct, Leland Ryken and others have recently shown that this assessment is not completely accurate.

Often the name "Puritan" is associated with an ethic that emphasized two points: (1) Hard physical work gives the highest rewards and values to the individual and community; and (2) The Christian way of life should stress discipline, honesty, moderation, temperance, devotion, humility, frugality, simplicity, self-sufficiency and dedication to the family and community. Some of the most famous Puritans were: John Jewel (1522–1571), James Ussher (1581–1656), John Preston (1587–1628), Richard Baxter (1615–1691), John Owen (1616–1683), Stephen Charnock (1628–1680), John Bunyan (1628–1688), Jonathan Edwards (1703–1758) and Samuel Hopkins (1721–1803).

See: G.R. Cragg, *Puritanism in the Period of the Great Persecution, 1660–68* (Russell and Russell, 1971); E. Hindson, *Introduction to Puritan Theology: A Reader* (Baker, 1976); Leland Ryken, *Worldly Saints: The Puritans As They Really Were* (Zondervan, 1986); E.S. Morgan, *The Puritan Dilemma: The Story of John Winthrop* (Little, Brown, and Company, 1958); P. Miller and T.H. Johnson, *The Puritans: A Sourcebook of Their Writings*, 2 vols. (Harper & Row, 1963).

Quadragesma [Dies] ▪ The fortieth day before Easter and a term that has become the liturgical name for the whole Lent season in Latin liturgical books. The day is a day of fasting.

Quakers ▪ See: **Friends, Society of.**

Quietism ▪ The mystical teaching of Michel de Molinos (1640–1696), who held that perfection consisted in complete passivity of the soul. His motto was "Let God act": Once the soul had made the act of full passivity it must make no other virtuous act, not even to resist temptations. This teaching was condemned by Pope Innocent XI in 1687. A modified form of Quietism taught by Mme. Guyon (1648–1717) and Fenelon (1651–1715) had none of the immoral consequences of pure quietism; it rather taught the possibility of a pure love of God in which the soul can be indifferent to salvation and can even surrender eternal happiness.

Quinquagesima ▪ The period of the church year between Easter Sunday and Pentecost. It celebrates the appearances of Jesus after the resurrection.

Qumran ▪ The production of the Dead Sea Scrolls is generally ascribed to the Essene community known as "Qumran." See: **Dead Sea Scrolls.**

Rabbi, Rabboni ■ From the Hebrew *rab*, "great." It meant "master," and later "teacher." At the time of Jesus, "rabbi" was a title of respect and reverence, and was used of both John the Baptist and Jesus. "Rabboni" is used to address Jesus in Mark 10:51 and John 20:16. A rabbi today is a person who has credentials to teach the Jewish law—the Jewish religion's counterpart to a minister, pastor or priest. See: **Clergy, Priest.**

Rationalism ■ In philosophy, a theory of epistemology—how we know what we know—that stresses reason or rational explanations. Rationalism maintains that true knowledge is gained through the mind and reasoning rather than through sense perception. Some form of belief in innate ideas is essential to rationalism, and in this sense Plato (427–347 B.C.) was a rationalist. These innate ideas are attributes of the mind and are created in the mind by God. God thus is ultimately the guarantor of the certainty of knowledge. Descartes (1596–1650), Spinoza (1632–1677) and Leibniz (1646–1716) were Enlightenment rationalists. See: **Epistemology, Platonism.**

   See: R. Descartes, *The Philosophical Works of Descartes*, 2 vols., trans. by E.S. Haldnae and G.R.T. Ross (Cambridge University Press, 1968).

Real Presence ■ One theory of Christ's presence in communion. Roman Catholics hold that in the bread and wine of communion the real body and blood of Christ "together with his soul and divinity are contained truly, really and substantially, and not merely in sign, figure, or virtue" (Council of Trent, sess. 13, can. 1). This Catholic statement of real presence condemned the views of Zwingli (1484–1531), who held that in communion the bread and the wine are only symbols of the body of Christ. See:

Communion; Eucharist; Last Supper; Lord's Supper; Transubstantiation; Trent, Council of.

Realism, Scottish Common Sense Philosophy ■ A philosophy that affirms that an ordinary person has the power to know the external world through his senses; it upholds "the power of knowledge in general, as it is possessed and employed by a man of ordinary development and opportunities." Thomas Reid (1720–1796) articulated this philosophy in response to David Humes's (1711–1776) skepticism in ethics and religion.

Reid said that the veneration and submission we owe God are self-evident to anyone who believes in God's existence, perfection and providence. Criticizing the view that we have no trustworthy knowledge about anything, Reid asked why we should reject beliefs common to all mankind, yet still accept the arguments of philosophers. The skeptic's assertion that he is certain he has no certain knowledge is contradictory and self-refuting. Reid developed three principal themes: (1) egalitarian epistemology, (2) a humble empiricism, and (3) a communitarian morality.

Dugald Stewart (1753–1828), Reid's student, friend and biographer, thought the term "common sense" too vague, and preferred to speak of "fundamental laws of human belief." These laws are basic facts we can know about ourselves and the world in which we live. Stewart listed the following as examples: (1) I exist. (2) I am the same person now as I was yesterday. (3) There is a real material world that exists outside of my mind. (4) The general laws of nature will operate in the future as they have in the past. (5) Other intelligent beings exist besides myself. Stewart argued that any philosopher who denies these self-evident truths winds up in complete skepticism.

See: T.L. Miethe, "Scottish Common Sense: Reid and Stewart," in *The Philosophy and Ethics of Alexander Campbell: From the Context of American Religious Thought, 1800–1866* (University Microfilms, 1984), pp. 73–78; D.S. Robinson, *The Story of Scottish Philosophy* (Exposition, 1961); *The Encyclopedia of Philosophy*, "Thomas Reid," vol. 7, pp. 118–21, and "Dugald Stewart," vol. 8, pp. 16–17; Dugald Stewart, *The Works of Dugald Steward*, 7 vols. (Cambridge: Hilliard and Brown, 1829).

Recapitulation ■ From the Greek *anakephalaiosis* and the Latin *recapitulatio*, meaning a "summing up." From the teaching of Irenaeus (A.D. c. 130–200). According to this view, Christ took

on a human nature and restored what was lost through Adam's disobedience, summing up, or "recapitulating," what God had intended for the human race. See: Ephesians 1:10.

Redaction Criticism ■ A recent idea in biblical criticism that views the writers of the Gospels not as mere compilers of the material but as people who creatively shaped their materials in keeping with their own understanding of the events and claims. See: **Biblical Criticism, Form Criticism, Higher Criticism, Lower Criticism.**

Redemption ■ From the Latin *redemptio*, from *redimere*, "to redeem," "to buy back again." In theology, the idea that Christ "redeemed" or "bought back" mankind by delivering us from sin and its punishment, therefore making salvation possible. Jesus came to redeem all of fallen creation and to pay the price for human sin. See: Mark 10:45; Luke 2:38; 24:21; Romans 3:24; 1 Corinthians 1:30; Galatians 3:13; 4:5. See: **Atonement, Propitiation, Salvation, Sin.**

See: J. Edwards, *The History of Redemption* (Sovereign Grace Book Club, 1959); R. Milligan, *The Scheme of Redemption* (Gospel Advocate Company); J. Murry, *Redemption: Accomplished and Applied* (Eerdmans, 1955).

Reformation, The ■ From the Latin *reformare*, "to reform." A movement that began in the early sixteenth century to reform the Catholic church. It resulted in roughly a third of the Catholic church being torn from the pope's hand. The movement can be grouped into three main parts: (1) The German Reformation, which gave birth to the Lutheran churches and centered around Martin Luther (1483–1546) and Philipp Melanchthon (1497–1560); (2) The Swiss Reformation, which gave birth to the Reformed Churches and centered around Ulrich Zwingli (1484–1531) and John Calvin (1509–1564); and (3) The English Reformation, which gave birth to the Anglican Church and centered around King Henry VIII (1491–1547), Bishop Hugh Latimer (1485–1555), Bishop Nicholas Ridley (1500?–1555) and Archbishop Thomas Cranmer (1489–1556), the last three of whom were burned at the stake outside Balliol College in Broad Street in Oxford.

The Reformers recognized the Bible as the sole rule of faith and practice and taught that justification was by faith alone. The Reformation rejected Roman Catholic teachings concerning the sacraments, grace, indulgences, purgatory and papal authority. See: **Anglicans, Calvinism, Lutherans, Presbyterians.**

See: R.H. Bainton, *The Reformation of the Sixteenth Century* (Beacon Press, 1952); O. Chadwick, *The Reformation* (Eerdmans, 1965); J.H.M. D'Aubigne, *History of the Great Reformation of the Sixteenth Century in Germany and Switzerland*, 5 vols. (London: D. Walther, 1837), and *The Reformation in England*, 2 vols. (London: Banner of Truth Trust, 1962–1963); R.L. Demaus, *Hugh Latimer: A Biography* (London: Religious Tract Society, 1903); H.J. Grimm, *The Reformation Era* (Macmillan, 1965); H.S. Lucas, *The Renaissance and the Reformation* (Harper & Brothers, 1934); S. Ozment, *The Age of Reform: 1250–1550* (Yale University Press, 1980); M. Spinka, *Advocates of Reform: From Wyclif to Erasmus* (Westminster, 1953).

Reformed Theology ■ The theology that emphasizes the teaching of John Calvin (1509–1564) and Ulrich Zwingli (1484–1531). Calvin wrote the first Reformed catechism in 1537 and rewrote it in 1541. See: **Calvinism; Calvinism, Five Points of; Election; Predestination; Salvation.**

See: R.H. Bube, *To Every Man an Answer* (Moody, 1955); C. Van Til, *The Defense of the Faith* (Presbyterian and Reformed, 1955).

Regeneration ■ The new birth or the process in which the sinner repents, accepts Jesus as Lord and Savior and is born again by the Holy Spirit. People are restored to a right relationship with the Father through the sacrifice of the Son, Jesus, and the work of the Holy Spirit. Regeneration is the beginning of the Christian life, and sanctification is the continuing growth (1 Peter 2:2; 2 Peter 3:18). See: John 3:5–8; Romans 6:3–8; 12:2; 2 Corinthians 5:17–20; Ephesians 4:23–24; Colossians 3:9–11; Titus 3:5. See: **Born Again, Election, Salvation, Sanctification.**

Reincarnation ■ From the Latin *re*, "again," *incarnare*, "to incarnate," from *in*, "in" and *caro*, "flesh." The belief that an individual spirit is reborn into a succession of new bodies, each time living as a different god, person, animal or plant. The desired end of reincarnation is a dissipation into a oneness with "ultimate reality." An important part of classical Buddhism, the idea seems to have originated in northern India around 1000–800 B.C in Hindu scriptures. All theories of reincarnation are based on a mystical or occultic world view. The Bible teaches that human beings live only once (Heb. 9:27). See: **Buddhism, Hinduism.**

See: R.A. Morey, *Reincarnation and Christianity* (Bethany House Publishers, 1980).

Remonstrance ■ A document produced in 1610 by the Remonstrants, a group who followed the teachings of James Arminius (1560–1609). It rejected major Calvinistic doctrines, affirming that Christ died for all and that God does not elect individuals to either salvation or damnation. It had five articles on (1) election, (2) the atonement, (3) the fall of man and the work of the Holy Spirit, (4) irresistible grace, (5) a subdued view of eternal security. The Remontrants rejected both supralapsarianism and sublapsarianism. J. D. Douglas says: "The Remonstrance was a modified form of Calvinism which, like the term Arminianism, has been wrongly identified with anti-Calvinist tendencies." See: **Arminianism; Calvinism; Dort, Synod of; Sublapsarianism; Supralapsarianism.**

Repentance ■ From the Greek *metanoia*, "a change of mind," and the Latin *re*, "again" and *poenitere*, "to make repent." In general usage, repentance is a feeling of sorrow for what one has done. In the NT, however, it means to turn away from sin and turn toward God and His will. Repentance radically transforms attitude and direction. See: Matthew 4:17; Luke 1:16; 24:47; Acts 2:38, 3:19; 9:35; 11:21; 14:15; 15:19; 26:18–21; 1 Thessalonians 1:9; 1 Peter 2:25.

See: H.A. Ironside, *Except Ye Repent* (Baker, 1970); W.D. Chamberlain, *The Meaning of Repentance* (Westminster, 1943).

Resurrection of Jesus ■ The Resurrection of Jesus Christ is the most important doctrine of the Christian faith. Christians since the NT have argued for the centrality of the doctrine, convinced that it proved Jesus' deity and the efficacy of His death for our sins. Paul, for example, considered the resurrection to be the cornerstone of the Christian faith: If Jesus did not rise from the dead, the whole structure of Christianity collapses. Paul tells us in 1 Corinthians 15:14–17: "And if Christ has not been raised, our preaching is useless and so is your faith. More than that we are then found to be false witnesses about God. . . . And if Christ has not

been raised, your faith is futile." The Christian faith—and its claim to be Truth—exists only if Jesus rose from the dead, because the heart of Christianity is a living Christ. See: Philippians 3:20–21; 2 Corinthians 5:1–5; 1 Thessalonians 4:16–17.

The fact that Jesus rose bodily (in a real physical body) from the grave has been fundamental to Christian teaching from the beginning. In the NT Jesus' appearance is depicted as spiritual—in the sense of being independent of the ordinary laws of nature—but also as material or physical. He invited them to touch His hands and feet "for a spirit does not have flesh and bones" (Luke 24:39–40; see also: Matt. 27:61–66; 28:1–20; Mark 16:1–20; Luke 24:1–53; John 20:10–31).

See: F.X. Durrwell, *The Resurrection: A Biblical Study* (Sheed and Ward, 1960); M. Green, *The Empty Cross of Jesus* (InterVarsity Press, 1984); Gary R. Habermas, *Ancient Evidence for the Life of Jesus: Historical Records of His Death and Resurrection* (Thomas Nelson, 1984), and *The Resurrection of Jesus: An Apologetic* (Baker, 1980); T.L. Miethe, ed. with G.R. Habermas and A.G.N. Flew, *Did Jesus Rise from the Dead: The Resurrection Debate* (Harper & Row, 1987); F. Morison, *Who Moved the Stone?* (London: Faber and Faber, 1958); J. Orr, *The Resurrection of Jesus* (Eerdmans, 1965); W.J.S. Simpson, *The Resurrection and the Christian Faith* (Zondervan, 1968).

Resurrection of the Dead ■ From the Latin *resurrectio*, from *resurgere*, "to rise again," from *re*, "again," and *sugere*, "to rise." Both the OT and NT teach that the dead will come back to life. For the Christian the resurrection will be a complete redemption, with a new body that will be immortal and incorruptible. See: Isaiah 25:6–8; 26:19; Daniel 12:1–4; 1 Corinthians 15; 1 Thessalonians 4:14–17.

See: R. Pache, *The Future Life* (Moody, 1962).

Revelation ■ From the Latin *revelare*, "to unveil," "to reveal." In general usage, to make known something previously unknown. Theological usage differentiates two types of revelation: (1) "Supernatural" or "special" revelation is direct communication from God to human beings through special messengers (prophets or angels), Jesus Christ, or Scripture. Certain theological knowledge—the doctrine of the Trinity, the plan of salvation—can come only through this method. (2) "Natural" or "general" revelation is information about God available to everyone through nature, history and God's image in mankind. See: **Natural Revelation, Natural Theology, Propositional Revelation.**

See: C.F.H. Henry, *Revelation and the Bible* (Baker, 1958); J.I. Packer, *God Speaks to Man: Revelation and the Bible* (Westminster, 1966); C.H. Pinnock, *Biblical Revelation: The Foundation of Christian Theology* (Moody, 1971), and *The Scripture Principle* (Harper & Row, 1984); M.C. Tenney, *The Bible: The Living Word of Revelation* (Zondervan, 1968).

Revival ■ From the Latin *revivere*, "to live again." To be revived is to become active or flourish again; revival thus is a period of renewed group or individual spiritual interest, commitment and growth. In American history some of the great leaders of revival have been Jonathan Edwards (1703–1758), George Whitefield (1714–1770), Barton W. Stone (1772–1844), Alexander Campbell (1788–1866), Charles G. Finney (1792–1875), Dwight L. Moody (1837–1899), and twentieth century evangelists William "Billy" Sunday and William Franklin "Billy" Graham.

See: C.G. Finney, *Finney on Revival* (Bethany House Publishers, 1969); W.G. McLoughlin, *Revivals, Awakenings, and Reform: An Essay on Religion and Social Change in America, 1607–1977* (University of Chicago Press, 1978); M.W. Randall, *The Great Awakenings and the Restoration Movement* (College Press, 1983).

Righteousness of God ■ In general, something is righteous if it agrees with divine or moral law, and is free from guilt or sin. The "righteousness of God," however, is more than fulfilling an exterior code of what is right: It is an attribute of God's very nature. God does not arbitrarily decide what is right or wrong, good or bad; rightness and goodness flow out of the character of God himself. See: Romans 1:17; 3:21; 4:3, 24. See: **God.**

Roman Catholicism ■ The body of Christians that recognizes the bishop of Rome as the pope, the vicar of Christ on earth. The pope has supreme authority over the Catholic church, which teaches he received this power by apostolic succession from Peter, who is said to have been the first pope. The Catholic church traces its origins to the apostolic church; it ruled all of Christendom until the Great Schism (A.D. 1054) split the church into Eastern and Western branches. The term "Roman Catholicism" arose during the Reformation, the second major exodus from the Catholic church. The church today claims close to 650 million members worldwide.

The Catholic church has several distinctives: (1) the supreme authority and infallibility of the bishop of Rome; (2) seven sacraments, including baptism and communion; (3) doctrine based on sacred Scripture, sacred tradition, and the teaching authority of the church (the pope); and (4) the worship of Mary and the saints. See: Matthew 16:16–19. See: **Eastern Orthodox; Trent, Council of; Sacraments, the Seven; Schism, the Great; Vatican Councils; Veneration.**

See: G. Barraclough, *The Medieval Papacy* (Harcourt, Brace and World, 1968); G.C. Berkouwer, *The Second Vatican Council and the New Catholicism* (Eerdmans, 1965); G. Carey, *A Tale of Two Churches: Can Protestants and Catholics Get Together?* (InterVarsity Press, 1985); W.E. Garrison, *Catholicism and the American Mind* (Willett, Clark and Colby, 1928); J.A. Hardon, S.J., *The Catholic Catechism: A Contemporary Catechism of the Teachings of the Catholic Church* (Doubleday, 1975); E.L. Heston, *The Holy See at Work* (Bruce Publishing Co., 1950); J.W. Montgomery, *Ecumenicity, Evangelicals, and Rome* (Zondervan, 1969); J. Pelikan, *The Riddle of Roman Catholicism: Its History, Its Beliefs, Its Future* (Abingdon, 1959).

Rosicrucians ■ A contemporary cultic group that mixes elements of pagan mythology, Judaism, Christianity, Hinduism and Buddhism. More formally known as AMORC (Ancient and Mystical Order Rosae Crucis) the group was organized in 1915 by occultist H. Spencer Lewis (d. 1939), who was succeeded by his son Ralph (b. 1904). They assert that they can help followers throw off the shackles of the body and become attuned to Infinite wisdom, promising to reveal the existence of mysterious cosmic laws by which a person can turn wishes and daydreams into reality. They believe that there is no supernaturalism, but that everything occurs by cosmic, natural law.

AMORC claims to trace its history from the Pharaoh Akhnaton in 1350 B.C. down through a group of seventeenth-century colonists who called themselves Rosicrucians. The group is enlarged through ads in popular periodicals. The secrets of the order are taught in a series of Masonic-type degrees, the first two by mail and last seven through Rosicrucian temples. The Rosicrucians are headquartered in San Jose, California.

See: J.K. Van Baalen, *The Chaos of Cults* (Eerdmans, 1960); W.J. Whalen, *Faiths for the Few* (Bruce, 1963).

Sabbath ▪ From the Hebrew *shabbath* and Greek *sabbaton*, "to rest from labor." In the OT the seventh day of the week, the day of worship and rest for the Jews (Ex. 20:8–11). The Sabbath is different from the Christian Sunday, though the two are often confused. The Christian Sunday is the first day of the week and is observed to acknowledge the resurrection of Jesus. There was no continuation from the OT Sabbath of the principle of rest. See: Genesis 2:1–3. See: **Lord's Day.**

See: C.L. Feinberg, *The Sabbath and the Lord's Day* (Van Kampen Press, 1952).

Sacred ▪ From the Greek *hieros*, meaning something consecrated, or dedicated, to God. Some versions of the Bible translate this word as "holy," from the Latin *sacer*. The Scriptures are sacred (2 Tim. 3:15), and 1 Corinthians 9:13 speaks of those who perform "sacred services." In Church history, calling something sacred meant it was divine or singled out for spiritual use. Such sacred things were viewed with great reverence.

In modern usage, "sacred" is often contrasted with "secular." Something sacred has a religious connotation or use, while something secular is "worldly" or "profane." See: **Holy.**

Sacerdotalism ▪ From the Latin *sacerdotalis*. The idea that ordination to the priesthood conveys the ability to dispense grace through the sacraments. In this view priests become the essential mediators—middlemen—between God and Christians. See: **Priesthood.**

Sacrament ■ From the Latin word *sacramentum*, a sacred pledge, military oath of enlistment or a legal term to denote a sum of money deposited by the parties involved in a court case, which was forfeited by the loser and appropriated to sacred uses; the word used to translate the Greek meaning "mystery." The word is applied by Christians to mean something that is set apart for religious purposes.

Christ appointed two sacraments: baptism and the Lord's Supper. Protestants often refer to these as "ordinances" because they do not believe they are means of extending salvation or grace as Roman Catholics do, but are important symbols and reminders of what God has done in the life of the believer. These "ordinances" are events practiced by believers, which are to be observed until Christ's return. See Matthew 28:19ff.; Acts 2:38; Romans 6:1–11; 1 Corinthians 11:23–29; Matthew 26:26–28; Mark 14:22–24; Luke 22:17–20. See: **Baptism, Communion, Eucharist, Immersion, Lord's Supper, Sprinkling.**

See: D.M. Baillie, *The Theology of the Sacraments* (Faber and Faber, 1957); G.C. Berkouwer, *The Sacraments: Studies in Dogmatics* (Eerdmans, 1969); P.T. Forsyth, *The Church and the Sacraments* (Alec R. Allenson, 1955).

Sacraments, The Seven ■ Roman Catholic theology lists seven sacraments: (1) Baptism; (2) Confirmation, a sacrament received at the age of reason at which the bishop prays for the indwelling of the Holy Spirit; (3) Holy Eucharist or Communion; (4) Extreme Unction, a rite conferred on a baptized person who is in danger of death; (5) Penance, which includes contrition, confession, acceptance of punishment and absolution; (6) Ordination; and (7) Matrimony.

See: N. O'Rafferty, *Instructions on Christian Doctrine*, vol. 1, *The Sacraments* (Bruce, 1938).

Saint ■ From the Greek *hagios*, "holy." In Psalm 85:8, "saint" seems synonymous with the people of God, and in the OT in general a person was a saint not based on character but on relationship to the covenant people, Israel. In the NT saint is the most common term for one who believes in Christ. The saints are the Church (1 Cor. 1:2). See: Ephesians 1:1, 15; 2:19; 3:8, 18; 4:12; 5:3; 6:18.

Sainthood ■ In Roman Catholic theology, deceased saints are not merely patterns of virtuous life. They are living, functioning members of the mystical body of Christ, and by prayer they are in vital contact with the Church on earth. Once someone is recognized as a saint by the pope, the Roman Catholic Church appoints a feast day, dedicates churches and altars and displays statues and pictures in his honor, venerates his relics, and prays to him publicly.

In beatification, the first step of the process of naming a person a saint, the church enquires into the holiness of the deceased person, reporting to Rome the life, writings and alleged miracles of the candidate. The pope then may make a declaration of beatification. In the second step, canonization, it must be proven that the candidate performed two miracles. The pope then officially declares a person's heroic virtue and includes his or her name in the canon of saints. The judgments reached in this process are infallible, according to Catholic theology. The first person sainted was St. Ulrich of Augsburg by Pope John XV in 993.

Saints, Invocation of ■ The practice in the Roman Catholic Church of calling upon saints to intercede on a person's behalf.

Saints, Perseverance of the ■ See: **Perseverance**.

Saints, Veneration of the ■ The Roman Catholic doctrine that saints are to be honored and their virtues imitated. Based on the belief that saints are living members of the body of Christ and that verbal communion with them is possible, Augustine (354–430) distinguished between *latria* (worship), which belongs only to God, and *dulia* (honor), which human beings can merit because of their office or deeds. *Dulia* is paid to the saints, and still greater veneration, *hyperdulia*, to the Blessed Virgin Mary. Public *dulia* can be paid only to the beatified, who may be venerated only where permitted by the pope, or the canonized, who may be venerated anywhere. Romans 13:7 is used to support this Catholic doctrine. See: **Sainthood**.

Salt ■ In OT times salt was used in both human and animal food (Job 6:6; Isa. 30:24); it was also part of the offering presented at the altar (Lev. 2:13). Because of salt's ability to preserve food from decay, it became a symbol representing purity before God. In the NT Christ commands Christians to be the "salt of the earth" (Matt. 5:13), to set an example, pointing out that if "the salt loses its saltiness," it is worthless. See also: Mark 9:50; Colossians 4:6.

Salvation ▪ The general meaning of the several Hebrew and Greek words translated into English as "salvation" is "safety" and "deliverance." In the OT salvation refers to deliverance, both physically (Ps. 37:40; 59:2; 106:4) and spiritually (Ps. 51:12; 79:9). OT prophecies focus on the complete salvation of God's people by the coming Messiah (Job 19:25–27); the NT teaches that these prophecies are fulfilled by Jesus Christ. Jesus brought salvation through forgiveness of sins (Matt. 1:21) and the gift of eternal life (Heb. 5:9). See: Acts 4:12; Hebrews 2:10. See: **Atonement, Forgiveness, Regeneration, Resurrection of the Dead, Sanctification.**

See: T.W. Brents, *The Gospel Plan of Salvation* (Gospel Advocate Company, 1957); A. Campbell, *The Christian System* (Gospel Advocate Company, 1956); L.S. Chafer, *Salvation* (Zondervan, 1965); O. Cullman, *Salvation in History* (Harper & Row, 1967); E.M.B. Green, *The Meaning of Salvation* (London: Hodder and Stoughton, 1965); R. Milligan, *The Scheme of Redemption* (Gospel Advocate Company); C. Pinnock, *Live Now, Brother!* (Moody, 1972).

Salvation Army, The ▪ A parachurch organization essentially evangelical in theology, the Salvation Army is known for its ministry and care of the poor, the sick and alcoholics, and for furnishing housing for transients and unmarried mothers. According to an official statement by the Army, "The primary object of the Salvation Army is the spiritual regeneration of mankind."

Founded in 1865 as a rescue mission in London's East End by William Booth (1829–1912), a Methodist minister, the Salvation Army began as the "Hallelujah Army." Booth, who modeled his religious organization after the British army and gave it the name "Salvation Army" in 1878, was himself known as the "General Superintendent." The Salvation Army does not administer either baptism or communion, because Booth saw these as divisive issues. They teach that at the Fall "man's spiritual powers were marred, but not destroyed." They believe strongly in Christ's deity, make the existence of heaven and hell important elements in their preaching, and take a strong stand against the Calvinistic doctrines of predestination and eternal security. Their churches are known as citadels.

See: E. Bishop, *Blood and Fire* (Moody, 1964); Sallie Chesham, *Born to Battle: The Salvation Army in America* (Rand McNally, 1965); H.E. Neal, *The Hallelujah Army* (Chilton, 1961).

Sanctification ▪ From the Greek *hagiasmos*, the separation or setting apart of the sacred from the sinful to make it holy. In the OT, periods of time (Gen. 2:3), people (Ex. 13:2) and things (Ex. 40:10–13) were sanctified. In the NT, sanctification mainly refers to individuals setting themselves apart from the sinful, and purifying themselves to be used by God (1 Peter 3:15). In Romans 12:1–2, Paul commands Christians to be sanctified, presenting themselves as living sacrifices to God. We are not to conform to the world's sin, but to purify ourselves by renewing our minds. See 1 Corinthians 6:11; 2 Corinthians 7:1; 2 Timothy 2:21.

See: Terry L. Miethe, *The New Christian's Guide to Following Jesus* (Bethany House Publishers, 1984), and *A Christian's Guide to Faith and Reason* (Bethany House Publishers, 1987).

Sanctuary ▪ From the Greek *hagios*, a place or building set apart to God. In the tabernacle of the OT was the "Holy of Holies," a place made holy because of God's presence. Under the Old Covenant only the high priest could enter this Holy of Holies, but in the NT Christ instituted the New Covenant, becoming our High Priest (Heb. 9:11) and opening the way for all believers to enter in and fellowship with God (Heb. 10:24). After Christ the worship of God was no longer tied to a physical place; believers are now called to worship in spirit and in truth (John 4:21–24). See: Hebrews 9, 10.

Satan ▪ The evil one, the Devil. Scripture uses many names for Satan, including "prince of darkness," "god of this world," "deceiver," "liar," and "tempter."

In the OT Satan caused the fall of Adam—and therefore of humanity—as "the serpent" in Genesis 3. In Job 1 and 2, Satan is before God among "the sons of God," and in Zechariah 3:1–2 the Lord rebukes Satan. The Hebrew word for "adversary," from which the name "Satan" is derived, can also refer to human beings, as in 1 Samuel 29:4; Psalm 38:20; 71:13; and 109.

In the NT Satan is the adversary of God and Christ (Mark 1:13; 3:23, 26; 4:15), of God's people (Luke 22:31; Acts 5:3; Rom. 16:20) and of mankind in general (Luke 13:16; Acts 26:18; Rev. 2:9). He is a person, not merely an evil influence, for he tested Jesus in the wilderness (Matt. 4:10), and is the leader of the kingdom of evil (Matt. 12:26). Scripture sees Satan as a genuine danger. Satan still tries to tempt Christians (2 Cor. 2:11). Peter warns: "Be of sober spirit, be on the alert. Your adversary, the devil, prowls about like a roaring lion, seeking someone to devour" (1 Peter 5:8). Paul alerts us that ". . . even Satan disguises himself as an angel of light" (2 Cor. 11:14). And James tells us: "Submit therefore to God. Resist the devil and he will flee from you" (James 4:7).

Yet Satan's powers are limited (Job 1:12; 2:6; 1 Cor. 10:13; Rev. 20:2, 7). Jesus saw Satan's defeat in Luke 10:18–20, and it is Jesus' death, burial, and resurrection that defeats Satan (John 12:31; 16:11; Heb. 2:14; 2 John 3:8). Paul was appointed as is each Christian today to be "a minister and witness . . . to open their eyes so that they may turn from darkness to light and from the dominion of Satan to God," so that they might receive forgiveness of sins and salvation (Acts 26:16–18). Believers are assured of victory over Satan (Rom. 16:20).

See: E.M. Bounds, *Satan: His Personality, Power and Overthrow* (Baker, 1963); R. DeHaan, *Satan, Satanism and Witchcraft* (Zondervan, 1972); F.C. Jennings, *Satan: His Person, Work, Place and Destiny* (New York: Our Hope).

Savior ■ From the Greek *soter*, "savior," "deliverer," "preserver" and the Latin *salvare*, "to save." In the OT the Savior was the anticipated deliverer of the people of Israel. By His death, burial, and resurrection, Jesus Christ became the Redeemer, the Savior who brings eternal salvation to the entire human race. The claim that ". . . there is salvation in no one else; for there is no other name under heaven that has been given among men, by which we must be saved" (Acts 4:12) gave serious offense in the first century and continues to do so today. See: Luke 2:11; John 4:42; Acts 5:31; 13:23; Ephesians 5:23; Philippians 3:20; Titus 1:4; 2 Peter 2:20; 3:2, 18; 1 John 4:14. See: **Christ, Lord Jesus.**

Schoolman ▪ See: **Scholasticism, Thomism.**

Schism ▪ A transliteration from the Greek, "schism" is a division or tearing apart. It is used in 1 Corinthians 12:25 in reference to the body of Christ. (See also: 1 Cor. 1:10; 11:18.) God allows for diversity in the Church, but diversity should not turn into division. In the essentials of Christianity we must be united in commitment and love.

Schism, the Great ▪ The division in A.D. 1054 that separated the Christian Church into East (Eastern or Greek Orthodox) and West (Roman Catholic). See: **Eastern Orthodox, Roman Catholicism.**

Scholasticism ▪ A form of Christian philosophy and theology that flourished in Europe from the eleventh to the fourteenth centuries. Notable scholastics were Anselm of Canterbury, 1033–1109), Peter Abelard (1079–1142), Peter Lombard (c. 1100–1160), Albertus Magnus (1193–1280), Bonaventure (1221–1274), Thomas Aquinas (1224/5–1274), John Duns Scotus (1266–1308), and William of Ockham (c. 1280–1349). Often referred to as the "medieval schoolmen," the scholastics attempted to synthesize the best of classical Greek and Roman thought with Christian Scripture. Their systematic study of the problems and questions of the world and Scripture aimed at indisputable answers. Thomas Aquinas' *Disputed Questions* exemplifies work of this nature.

The structure and order the scholastics set forth bored Italian Renaissance thinkers of the fourteenth through seventeenth centuries, who believed scholasticism was based solely upon a dogmatism they did not accept. They attempted to discredit it, and so from then until the twentieth century scholasticism has been studied by relatively few. Today, however, there is renewed interest in scholasticism, especially Thomism, in Roman Catholic and some Protestant circles. See: **Thomism.**

Scripture ▪ From the Latin *scriptura*, "a writing." The NT uses the Greek word *graphe* to refer to the OT writings (Matt. 21:42; 22:29; John 5:39; Acts 17:11; 18:24; Rom. 1:2; 1 Cor. 15:3–4). Paul regarded both Deuteronomy and Luke's Gospel as Scripture, quoting from Deuteronomy and from Luke 10:7 in 1 Timothy 5:18. The author of Scripture is the Holy Spirit (Acts 28:25), and Scripture is "God-breathed" (2 Tim. 3:16). See: **Bible, Inerrancy and Infallibility of; Canon, of the Old Testament; Canon, of the New Testament; Pentateuch; Word of God.**

Second Coming of Christ ■ The Bible clearly teaches that Jesus, the risen Christ, will come a second time. Jesus himself told the disciples that He was going away to prepare a place for His followers and that He would come again to gather them together for eternity (John 14:3). The Bible lists several characteristics of Christ's Second Coming: He will come unexpectedly (Matt. 24:32–51), personally (John 14:3), triumphantly (Luke 19:11–27), and with His angels to "recompense every man according to his deeds (Matt. 16:27; See also: Rom. 2:6; 14:12; 2 Cor. 5:10; Eph. 6:8; Col. 3:25; Rev. 2:23; 20:12; 22:12; compare 1 Cor. 3:13). Angels foretold these events at the time of Christ's ascension (Acts 1:10–11), and most of the NT writers refer to these happenings (Acts 3:19–21; 1 Cor. 15:51; Phil. 3:20; 1 Thess. 4:16; 2 Thess. 1:7–10; Heb. 9:28; 10:37; James 5:7; 1 John 2:28; 3:2). Some theologians, especially dispensationalists, believe in a pretribulation rapture, and assert that Christ's return will have two phases: (1) His coming in the air (1 Thess. 4:16), and (2) His coming to earth (Zech. 14:4; Acts 1:11). In the rapture, the first phase, Christ will rescue all believers from the tribulation, and in the second phase—at the end of the tribulation—Christ will come to establish His earthly millennial kingdom. Other theologians think this distinction is artificial and maintain that there will be only one return, at the end of the tribulation. See also: **Amillennialism, Postmillennialism, Premillennialism, Apocalypse, Epiphany, Parousia, Tribulation.**

See: G.E. Ladd, *Jesus Christ and History* (InterVarsity Press, 1963); L. Berkhof, *The Second Coming of Christ* (Eerdmans, 1953); G.C. Berkouwer, *The Return of Christ* (Eerdmans, 1972); R. Pache, *The Return of Jesus Christ* (InterVarsity Press, 1960).

Secular Humanism ■ See: **Humanism.**

Semi-Arianism ■ A theory of the nature of Christ's relationship to the Father developed by theologians who rejected the extreme position of Arius (c. 256–c. 336—a priest of Alexandria) as well as the orthodox formulation of the Council of Nicea (325). Semi-Arians held that Christ is similar to the Father, yet not of the same substance or nature. They used the term *homoiousios,* "of like substance," to describe their position. They were also called "Eusebians" after Eusebius, bishop of Nicomedia and later patriarch of Constantinople. Eusebius signed the creed at Nicea, (as did all but two bishops, though many had reservations), but later became a leader against it. Another Eusebius, the early Church historian, was the most prominent leader of the Semi-Arian position. See: **Arianism; Nicea, Council of.**

See: J.N.D. Kelly, *Early Christian Creeds,* 2nd ed., (Harper & Row, 1960); Philip Schaff, *The Creeds of Christendom,* 6th ed., 3 vols. (Baker, first published 1877, reprinted 1919).

Semi-Pelagianism ■ A term coined in the sixteenth century to describe a mediating position between the views of Pelagius (360–420) and Augustine (354–430) regarding the role of divine grace and the human will in the initial work of salvation. Some say the term was first used in the Lutheran Formula of Concord in 1577. The theological position it named was developed during the fifth and early sixth centuries. The term is sometimes applied to Arminianism. See **Arminianism, Pelagianism.**

Septuagint ■ A translation of the Hebrew OT into the Greek language made in Alexandria, Egypt, the residence of many Greek-speaking Jews. According to tradition, 70 skilled Jewish linguists traveled to Egypt and made the translation at the invitation of Ptolemy Philadelphus (205–247 B.C.). Greek was used in most of the world at that time, and this translation was used regularly in the time of Christ. Many NT writers took their OT quotations from the Septuagint. Septuagint is sometimes abbreviated LXX, the Roman numeral for seventy.

See: S. Jellicoe, *The Septuagint and Modern Study* (Clarendon Press, 1968); A. Rahlfs, *Septuaginta,* 2 vols. (Stuttgart: Privilegierte Wurttembergische Bibelanstalt, 1935); H.B. Swete, *An Introduction to the Old Testament in Greek* (Ktav Publishing House, 1968).

Sermon ■ From the Latin *sermo,* "discourse." A sermon is a message given by a preacher, normally as a part of a worship service, in order to instruct in the message of the Bible and/or

Christian living. There are many forms of sermons: topical (concerned with a particular theme), textual-topical (topical, but organized around certain biblical passages), expository (explanation of a biblical passage), and exegetical (word by word examination of the original intent of a Greek or Hebrew text of the Bible). Genuine preaching from the Bible occurs when the preacher explains what the Bible says, why it says it, and how it applies to life at home, work and play. In other words, biblical preaching is primarily expository, exegetical preaching. Jesus commands us to teach new believers everything we have learned from Him (Matt. 28:20). See: **Gospel, Preaching.**

See: C.E. Fant, Jr., and W.M. Pinson, Jr., *Twenty Centuries of Great Preaching: An Encyclopedia of Preaching*, 13 vols. (Word Books, 1971); C. Hodge, *Princeton Sermons* (London: Banner of Truth Trust, 1958); C.G. Finney, *Charles G. Finney Memorial Sermon Library*, 7 vols. (Kregel, 1967); G.C. Morgan, *The Westminster Pulpit*, 10 vols. (London: Pickering and Inglis, 1955–1956); C.H. Spurgeon, *The New Park Street Pulpit*, 6 vols. (London: Banner of Truth Trust, 1963–1964), *Metropolitan Tabernacle Pulpit* (London: Banner of Truth Trust, 1965), and *New Library of Spurgeon's Sermons*, 24 vols. (Zondervan); J.R.W. Stott, *Christ the Controversialist: A Study in Some Essentials of Evangelical Religion* (InterVarsity Press, 1975).

Sermon on the Mount ■ Christ's message recorded in Matthew 5–7. The Sermon on the Mount is as foundational for the NT as the Ten Commandments were for the OT, presenting the highest standard of Christian living. Called the original draft of essential Christianity, the sermon contains the Beatitudes (5:1–12); a comparison of Christians to salt and light (5:13–16); an explanation of Jesus' relationship to the law (5:17–48); teachings on giving alms, prayer, fasting, gathering treasure in heaven, and judging others; the golden rule; and a warning of the coming of false teachers (Matt. 6, 7).

See: J.M. Boice, *The Sermon on the Mount* (Zondervan, 1972); D.M. Lloyd-Jones, *Studies in the Sermon on the Mount*, 2 vols. (Eerdmans, 1959–1960); W. Fitch, *The Beatitudes of Jesus* (Eerdmans, 1961); H. Tholuck, *Commentary on the Sermon on the Mount* (Edinburgh: T. and T. Clark, 1869).

Servant ■ Several Greek words are translated "servant," including *doulos*, "in bondage" (Rom. 6:9), and *diakonos*, "deacon" or "minister" or "servant" (Matt. 22:13; Mark 9:35; John 2:5, 9; Rom. 16:1). Jesus came not as King but as a servant: He ". . . emptied Himself, taking the form of a bond-servant, and

being made in the likeness of men" (Phil. 2:7). He was the perfect pattern of the servant Christians should be. Indeed, Jesus said ". . . but whoever wishes to become great among you shall be your servant, and whoever wishes to be first among you shall be your slave; just as the Son of Man did not come to be served, but to serve, and to give His life a ransom for many" (Matt. 20:25–28). See also: Luke 17:10; John 12:26; Romans 1:1; 1 Corinthians 3:5; Colossians 1:23.

Seven Last Words, The ■ Jesus spoke seven times while on the Cross. What He said has come to be called the Seven Last Words. (1) The first concerned forgiveness, as recorded in Luke 23:24: "Father, forgive them; they do not know what they are doing." (2) The second word Christ spoke to a thief being crucified with Him. The thief asked for salvation, and it was granted (Luke 23:42, 43). (3) Third, Jesus spoke to His mother and to John, saying, "Woman, behold your son!" and "Behold, your mother!" (John 19:26, 27). (4) The fourth word Christ uttered as He acted as mediator for sinful humanity. He felt the separation between God and humanity and cried out, " 'ELI, ELI LAMA SABACHTHANI?' that is, 'MY GOD, MY GOD, WHY HAST THOU FORSAKEN ME?' " (Matt. 27:46). (5) His fifth word fulfilled a prophecy concerning Him being the Messiah (John 19:28; Ps. 21:16; 68:21, 22). The soldiers unknowingly performed this when they gave Him vinegar to drink. (6) Christ came to reconcile man to God. As Adam's sin separated, Jesus' righteousness reunited. Jesus fulfilled His purpose on earth and said His sixth word, "It is finished" (John 19:30). (7) After this He committed His spirit to the Father, which was His seventh word (Luke 23:46).

Seventh-Day Adventists ■ A Christian denomination known for their observance of the seventh day as the Sabbath and for their belief that Christ's return is imminent. The Seventh-Day Adventists began in the early 1840s around leaders including William Miller (1782–1849), a Baptist minister in New York; Hiram Edson; and Joseph Bates. Mrs. Ellen G. White (1827–1915) announced she had seen a vision of the Adventists marching straight into heaven and claimed other visions that verified Edson's and Bates' teachings. She became the leader of Adventism until her death.

Adventists believe that all Scripture, both OT and NT, were given by inspiration from God, though they accept the writings of Ellen White "as inspired counsels from the Lord." They maintain that all her visions and dreams harmonized with the Bible, and deny that Mrs. White ever fell into error. They believe in the Trinity, the deity of Jesus and His preexistence from all eternity, and reject the doctrines of eternal security or eternal punishment of the wicked. They believe in "soul-sleep," that at death a person enters a deep state of sleep; upon the righteous believer God will bestow immortality at the Second Coming. The wicked will also be raised from the dead at the end of the millennium, but only to be annihilated.

Seventh-Day Adventists maintain a worldwide private school system second in size only to that of the Roman Catholics. They insist on total abstinence from liquor, tobacco and narcotics. The majority of Adventists are vegetarians and certainly all observe OT prohibitions against eating pork, ham, and shell fish. They do not drink coffee or tea.

See: W.E. Biederwolf, *Seventh-Day Adventism* (Eerdmans); N.F. Douty, *Another Look at Seventh-Day Adventism* (Baker, 1962); J.H. Gerstner, *The Theology of the Major Sects* (Baker, 1960); W.R. Martin, *Kingdom of the Cults* (Bethany House Publishers, 1985), and *The Truth about Seventh-Day Adventism* (Zondervan, 1960).

Sheol ■ The abode of the dead (Gen. 37:35; 42:38; 1 Sam. 2:6; 1 Kings 2:6; Job 17:13, 16). Though Sheol has various meanings in the OT, it seems to refer to an intermediate state in which souls are dealt with according to their lives on earth. Van Gemeren lists six ways Sheol is used: "a place from which no one can save himself" (Ps. 89:48); "a place where all people go upon death" (Gen. 37:35), "a place where the wicked go upon death" (Job 21:13); "a place from which the righteous are saved" (Ps. 49:15); "a place over which God has absolute sovereignty" (Prov. 15:11); "as a metaphor or image for greed" (Prov. 27:20); (See Elwell's *Evangelical Dictionary of Theology*).

Sheol is not the same as hell, which is a place of eternal punishment. In the NT the word "Hades" has roughly the same meaning as Sheol in the OT. In some places it refers to the grave (Acts 2:31; 1 Cor. 15:55), though in others it refers to the place of eternal punishment (Matt. 11:23, 24; 16:18; Luke 16:23). See also: **Gehenna, Hades, Hell.**

Shintoism ▪ The indigenous religion of Japan. It consists chiefly of cultic devotion to deities of natural forces and worship of the Emperor as a descendant of the sun-goddess.

Sin ▪ A falling away from or missing the mark. The NT describes sin as actions contrary to God's expressed will (James 4:12, 17). Sin exchanges God for self as the absolute lawgiver (2 Tim. 3:1, 2; 2 Thess. 2:3, 4). The Greek NT has a dozen or more terms for sin. The word used most often in the NT, *hamartia*, means to transgress, to do wrong, to sin against God. It requires forgiving (Mark 2:5) and cleansing (Heb. 1:3). Paul speaks of *hamartia* almost in personal terms (Rom. 5:12, 21). Hebrews 3:13 warns that *hamartia* is deceptive. The concept of sin presupposes an absolute law, given by an absolute lawgiver: God. Therefore, many who do not believe God exists do not believe such a thing as sin exists. See also: Matthew 23:23; Romans 3:20; 4:7; 6:1–11.

See also: Terry L. Miethe, "The Christian and Sin," *The New Christian's Guide to Following Jesus* (Bethany House Publishers, 1984), pp. 123–126.

Sin Against the Holy Spirit ▪ This sin, blasphemy against the Holy Spirit, is unpardonable (Matt. 12:31, 32; Mark 3:28, 29; Luke 12:10). It is the willful rejection of God's activity in Jesus, and the belief that He was of Satan. Some of the Pharisees committed this sin, for they saw Christ's miracles but denied He was God and instead proclaimed that He was Beelzebub, the prince of Demons (Matt. 10:25). A person is guilty of this sin, therefore, when he knows Jesus is God but denies it, saying that God is the devil. See: Hebrews 6 (especially vv. 4–6) and 10.

Sin, Original ▪ The effect of Adam's sin on the lives of his descendants. Although Scripture does not use the term "original sin," it is inferred from biblical statements that all are in sin because of Adam's sin (Rom. 5:12, 19; 1 Cor. 15:21, 22) and that sin is universal (Matt. 7:11; 15:19; Rom. 3:9). All theologians generally agree to these points; what they debate is the connection between Adam's sin and the moral condition of his descendants.

Calvinists state that Adam's sin was immediately imputed to the entire human race, with the result that each individual is morally totally depraved and guilty of Adam's sin. In this view, when Adam sinned, all people sinned. Arminians argue that mankind inherited a predisposition to sin, but that people are not guilty for Adam's sin—each individual is accountable only for his own sins. Hence, the human race has not inherited Adam's sin, just its consequences.

Both sides agree that it is clear from the Bible that because of Adam's sin humanity inherits a fallen world, and because of Adam's sin death was passed on to all (Gen. 2:17; 1 Cor. 15:21–26; Rom. 5:12–17; 6:23). See also: **Calvinism; Arminianism; Depravity, Total.**

See also: Herbert Haag, *Is Original Sin in Scripture?* (Sheed and Ward, 1969); Clark H. Pinnock, ed., *Grace Unlimited* (Bethany House Publishers, 1975); Clark H. Pinnock, ed., *The Grace of God/The Will of Man* (Zondervan, 1989); Alan P.F. Sell, *The Great Debate: Calvinism, Arminianism, and Salvation* (Baker, 1983).

Sins, Mortal and Venial ■ Roman Catholic theology classifies sin into two types, mortal and venial. Mortal sins are deliberate sins done with full knowledge of their sinfulness; venial sin is committed despite an inner desire to the contrary. There is a conflict of purpose between the action and the person. Mortal sins extinguish God's supernatural, gracious, sanctifying life within an individual soul, causing spiritual death; and as deliberate acts of rebellion against God's infinite majesty mortal sins deserve eternal punishment. Venial sins, in contrast, weaken but do not destroy that life. Venial sins are usually done from ignorance, passion, temper, instinct. In the Roman Catholic Church, penance and purgatory atone for venial sin. See: Galatians 5:19–21; Ephesians 5:5; James 3:2; 1 John 1:8. See: **Penance, Purgatory.**

Sins, Seven Deadly ■ The seven sins Roman Catholic theology sees as root sins of all others: pride, covetousness, lust, envy, gluttony, anger and sloth. The word "deadly" highlights the severity of the sins. These are regarded as sinful tendencies rather than as mortal sins. See: **Anger; Covetousness; Envy; Gluttony; Lust; Pride; Sloth; Sins, Mortal and Venial.**

Situation Ethics ■ In philosophy, an ethical system which teaches that there are no absolutes, either good works or duties, except the absolute of love. Every ethical action is relative to what the individual considers to be the most loving act in a given situation. This dictates what is right or wrong in that situation. The most famous proponent of this view is Joseph Fletcher.

See: J. Fletcher *Ethics, Christian Situation Ethics: The New Morality* (Westminster, 1966); J. Fletcher and J.W. Montgomery, *Situation Ethics: True or False* (Bethany House, 1972); N.L. Geisler, *Ethics: Alternatives and Issues* (Zondervan, 1971), and *Options in Contemporary Christian Ethics* (Baker, 1981); E. Lutzer, *The Necessity of Ethical Absolutes* (Zondervan, 1981).

Slander ■ From the Hebrew and Greek words meaning "a false accusation" or "an evil report" (Num. 14:36; Ps. 31:13; Prov. 10:18). Gossip is often slanderous. See: 1 Timothy 3:11; 2 Timothy 3:3; Titus 2:3.

Slave ■ A state of involuntary servitude. The Bible mentions five ways of acquiring slaves: (1) by purchase from another slave owner (Gen. 17:12); (2) by reproduction, birth to slave parents (Gen. 17:12); (3) by capture, as during a war (Num. 31:9); (4) as payment of debt (Matt. 18:25); and (5) as a result of poverty, someone selling himself or a child (Ex. 21:2, 7).

In the NT slavery was not directly forbidden; slaves were told to obey their masters (Eph. 6:5–8; Col. 3:22–25). In God's eyes, the slave and master were equal (1 Cor. 7:21, 22), and masters therefore were to treat their slaves fairly (Eph. 6:9; Col. 4:1). When Paul wrote Philemon, however, he articulated principles that Christians later saw as incompatible with slavery. Paul asked Philemon to receive back Onesimus, Philemon's escaped slave, "no longer as a slave, but more than a slave, a beloved brother" (Philem. 16).

Sloth ■ In Roman Catholic theology, one of the Seven Deadly Sins. A common expression of sloth is the phrase: "It's too much trouble to be good." Catholics believe this to be directly contrary to the first of the commandments (Mark 12:30) and a mortal sin if it results in the breaking of a serious command. Physical laziness is also mortally sinful when it results in harm to others. See: **Sins, Seven Deadly; Sins, Mortal and Venial.**

Social Gospel ▪ An American movement of the early twentieth century that sought to conform society to Christ's teachings. Responding to the evils of rapid industrialization, advocates of the social gospel sought to relieve the plight of the urban poor, arguing that salvation had a social as well as a personal dimension. Washington Gladden and Walter Rauschenbusch were prominent leaders of this effort. Although the term "social gospel" applies primarily to this movement, some use it to refer to contemporary concern for social justice and social activism.

Christians must be concerned about the social conditions of the poor. James 1:27 says: "This is pure and undefiled religion in the sight of our God and Father, to visit orphans and widows in their distress, and to keep oneself unstained by the world." Personal salvation must never be minimized, but true faith impacts society as well.

See: Walter Rauschenbusch, *A Theology for the Social Gospel* (Abingdon, 1945).

Society of Jesus, The ▪ A religious order founded by Ignatius Loyola (1491–1556) in 1534. Often referred to as the Jesuits, the group was first known as the Company of Jesus. The first seven members, including Loyola, were theology students at the University of Paris. Today the Jesuits are the largest Roman Catholic religious order. They are led by a father general, or superior general, who answers directly to the pope.

Jesuit priests take a special vow to the pope; they are highly trained, normally for fifteen years. Primarily involved in education and missions, Jesuits are known for their scholarship and have founded many of the best Catholic colleges and universities, including Gregorian University (Rome), Saint Louis University, Marquette University, Loyola University of Chicago, Georgetown University, and Boston College, as well as many others.

See: T.J. Campbell, *The Jesuits: 1534–1921*, 2 vols. (The Encyclopedia Press, 1921).

Socinianism ▪ A movement birthed by the teachings of Faustus Socinus (1539–1604) of Siena, Italy. It emphasized morality and rejected predestination and original sin. More importantly, it denied Christ's deity: In Socinus' view, Jesus did not become God until after His resurrection, when the Father delegated some of His divine power to the risen Jesus. Socinus did accept Christ's miracles and virgin birth because he saw these as signs showing Jesus' unique role in becoming divine. Socinus also saw Christ's death as an example rather than as the price of sin paid to the Father. According to Socinus, repentance and good works are what gain forgiveness from God. This teaching grew into modern Unitarianism. See: **Unitarianism.**

Son of God ▪ The Messiah, Jesus Christ (Ps. 2:7; John 1:49). The term appears 45 times in the NT, 44 of which refer to Christ; the lone reference refers to Adam (Luke 3:38). Jesus is the only begotten Son of God (John 3:18). As the Son of God, He has the eternal, divine perfection of God (John 1:1–14; 10:30–38), and is equal to God (John 5:17–25). The word "son" is not meant in a physical sense; it rather signifies that He shares the same nature with God the Father. See: **Jesus, Lord.**

Son of Man ▪ In a general sense, all descendants of Adam are sons of man (Job 25:6; Isa. 51:12). In a specific sense, however, "Son of Man" refers to Christ. As a title it appears some 78 times in the Gospels. Christ called himself "Son of Man" not because He denied his deity, but to show His compassion and love for all mankind. Christ is both Son of Man and Son of God; the union of His two natures is called "hypostatic union." See: **Hypostatic Union.**

Soteriology ▪ From the Greek *soteria*, "safety," and *logos*, "the study of." Soteriology is the branch of theology that studies salvation. It examines the provisions of salvation through Jesus Christ and its application through the Holy Spirit, including topics such as the Fall and sin; God's revelation; and God's redemption of people by means of Christ's crucifixion, the atonement and grace. See: **Election, Grace, Justification, Perseverance, Regeneration, Salvation, Sanctification.**

Soul ▪ From the Greek *psyche*, "the breath of life." Although most theologians agree that the soul is the immaterial part of a human being, throughout Church history they have debated the relationship of soul to spirit. Dichotomists hold that the soul and spirit are two names for the same immaterial nature, while trichotomists think soul and spirit are two separate entities. Dichotomists believe the body consists only of matter and soul; trichotomists maintain the body consists of matter, soul, and spirit.

Either Christian view of the soul is different from that of Greek philosophy, which sees the soul as a preexistent entity imprisoned in the body at birth. At death the soul escapes its prison, the body, and for eternity remains a disembodied soul. Christians believe the spirit comes from God. It is infused into the body and a person becomes a living soul (Gen. 2:7). At death the spirit returns to God and the body to the dust of the ground. At the resurrection, spirit and body are again united and the individual again becomes a living soul, this time for eternity.

Soul Sleep ▪ See: Seventh-Day Adventism.

Soul, Traducianist view of the origin of the ▪ The view that both the soul and body are propagated by the parents. See: Traducianism.

Soul Winning ▪ A term conservative Christians use for evangelism. It is living in such a distinctive way that others can see the changes Christ has brought in your life. It is not just knocking on doors once a week and sharing the gospel. Soul winning has acquired a bad name because some equate it with "beating people over the head with the Bible." Real soul winning shows Christ's love to unbelievers, drawing them to seek salvation.

See: Terry L. Miethe, "Sharing Your Faith," in *The New Christian's Guide to Following Jesus* (Bethany House Publishers, 1984), pp. 111–116, and "Building the Faith in Our World," "Free to Win Souls to Christ," and "Free to Love the Unlovely," in *A Christian's Guide to Faith and Reason* (Bethany House Publishers, 1987); Joseph C. Aldrich, *Life-Style Evangelism: Crossing Traditional Boundaries to Reach the Unbelieving World* (Multnomah Press, 1981).

Sovereignty of God ▪ The doctrine that God is supreme in rule and authority over all things. Some assert that the primary difference between Calvinists and Arminians is that Calvinists

believe in God's sovereignty while Arminians do not, as in:

The doctrine of the sovereignty of God is emphasized especially in the Augustinian-Calvinistic tradition and is denied or compromised in the Pelagian, Arminian, and liberal traditions, which claim varying degrees of human autonomy.

This is clearly false. All Christians believe in God's sovereignty. See: Psalm 103:19; Daniel 4:17, 25, 34; 5:21; 7:14; 1 Chronicles 29:11; Matthew 6:13; Romans 1:16; Ephesians 1:11; 1 Timothy 6:11. See: **Arminianism, Calvinism, Election, Freedom of the Will, Predestination.**

See: J.I. Packer, *Evangelism and the Sovereignty of God* (InterVarsity Press, 1961).

Spirit ■ From the Greek *pneuma*, "wind," "breath." Like the wind the spirit is invisible and immaterial, but it can profoundly affect the material world. The term can refer to the individual spirit within a person (Luke 8:55; Acts 7:59; 1 Cor. 5:5; James 2:26), to unclean spirits or demons (Matt. 8:16; Luke 4:33; 1 Peter 3:19), to angels (Heb. 1:14), or to the Holy Spirit (Matt. 4:11; Luke 4:18). Man became a living being when God gave him a spirit (Gen. 2:7). See: **Soul, Holy Spirit.**

Sprinkling ■ A mode of baptism. Those who practice sprinkling say it portrays the sprinkling of the Christian with the blood of Christ or a washing away of sins (Heb. 9:10, 13, 14; 10:22). This mode developed because of water shortages and as a convenience for the elderly and infirm. Some who practice sprinkling contend that it began in the NT, based on the understanding that it would have been impossible to immerse the large numbers who came to Christ in mass conversions, such as in Acts 2. Christians who practice baptism by immersion assert that sprinkling is unbiblical because the verb "baptize" necessarily means "to immerse." Sprinklers respond that by NT times "baptism" had become a technical term and no longer denoted any particular form of washing.

Steward, Stewardship ■ From the Greek *oikonomos*, which refers to the manager of a household or estate. Stewardship is management of all God has entrusted.

God bestows many things, yet the most important gift a Christian must invest wisely is his own life—his abilities to think and to love: A Christian's body and mind are to be a "living sacrifice" dedicated to God (Rom. 12:1–2). A Christian should invest his time in study and service to God, seeking first His kingdom and His righteousness (Matt. 6:33). Once a Christian learns to be a good steward of mind and body then he will use all other gifts from God wisely. See: Luke 12:42; 16:1, 2, 8; 1 Corinthians 4:2; Galatians 4:2; Romans 16:23. See also: 1 Corinthians 4:1, of preachers of the Gospel and teachers of the Word of God; Titus 1:7, of elders in churches; 1 Peter 4:10, of believers generally.

See: Terry L. Miethe, "Christian Stewardship," in *The New Christian's Guide to Following Jesus* (Bethany House Publishers, 1984), pp. 97–102, and "Renewing the Mind: Key to Christian Living" in *A Christian's Guide to Faith and Reason* (Bethany House Publishers, 1987).

Sublapsarianism ■ The view of moderate Calvinists who try to avoid what some see as the dangerous implication of Supralapsarianism: that God is the author of sin. Rather than asserting that God *caused* Adam's sin, sublapsarians state that He only *foresaw* the Fall, including its consequence that those who were not elect would go to hell with no chance of entering heaven. Non-Calvinists contend that the outcome of sublapsarianism and supralapsarianism are identical: The non-elect have no chance to accept Christ or escape hell. See: **Infralapsarianism, Supralapsarianism.**

Subordinationism ■ From the Latin *sub*, "under," and *ordinare*, "to arrange." A view of the relationship of the Father and Son which subordinates the Son to the Father in essence and status and endangers the Son's divinity. Orthodoxy maintains that all three members of the Trinity—Father, Son, and Holy Spirit—are fully God, equal in power and glory. See: **Trinity.**

Summum Bonum ■ A Latin phrase meaning "the highest good." The reason for which human beings were created: To see and know God as He really is. Although this cannot be fully realized on earth, the Christian should daily know God better. The quest to know God will be fulfilled in the Beatific Vision when Christians are gathered in heaven. See: **Beatific Vision.**

Supralapsarianism ▪ The view that before the fall of Adam, God not only chose certain individuals to be saved and others to be reprobated to hell, but that He then caused Adam to sin. Non-Calvinists argue that the inevitable conclusion of this Calvinist view is that God is the author of sin, the cause of all evil. A modification of supralapsarianism, called sublapsarianism, attempts to correct this problem.

Synderesis Rule ▪ The first rule governing formal ethical reasoning: that good is to be done and that evil is to be avoided. It is a permanent or inborn disposition of the mind which enables the intellect to know the first principles of practical reasoning.

Aquinas felt there was a definite difference between conscience and synderesis. The synderesis rule is also found in the writings of Augustine (354–430). The real origin of the synderesis rule is probably the OT. Vernon J. Bourke says: "I have never read such a rule in writings outside the Judaeo-Christian tradition. There is nothing like it in the *Niocmachean Ethics* or in any of the ethical writings of pagan Greek and Romans that I have read." See: Psalm 34:14; 37:27; Ecclesiastes 7:1; Isaiah 1:16–17; 1 Peter 3:11. **Augustinianism, Natural Law, Thomism.**

See T.L. Miethe, "Natural Law, the Syderesis Rule, and St. Augustine," in *Augustinian Studies* 11 (1980), pp. 91–97.

Synergism ▪ From the Greek *synergos*, "to work together." A doctrine that asserts that conversion is the product of divine and human cooperation. Held by Erasmus (c. 1466–1536), James Arminius (1560–1609) and John Wesley (1703–1791), it attempts to reconcile the biblical teachings of God's sovereignty and human responsibility for making moral decisions. Synergism opposes Calvinistic views of conversion, which emphasize God's sovereignty at the expense of human freedom and responsibility. Such views of conversion were held by Augustine (354–430), John Calvin (1509–1564) and Martin Luther (1483–1546). See: **Semi-Pelagianism, Sublapsarianism, Supralapsarianism, Arminianism, Wesleyanism, Augustinianism, Calvinism, Lutheranism.**

Synoptic Problem ▪ The term for what some see as errors or discrepancies in the accounts of the life of Christ told in the Synoptic Gospels: Matthew, Mark, and Luke. Although they have different authors and distinctive purposes for being written, they all view the life of Christ in the same way. Because of the differences and similarities present in the Synpotic Gospels, the question has been raised as to what sources the Gospel writers used and why there are differences in some of their views of the same events. There are various opinions as to what the available sources were and how extensive they were.

What should be realized, though, is that the similarities and differences in the Gospel accounts can be solved by first realizing that the writers had extensive first-hand knowledge of the life of Christ; and second, that some of the stories about Christ had been written down before the Gospels were written (Luke 1:1–4). Whatever the sources might have been, it must be remembered that the Lord had promised that the Holy Spirit would teach them all things and would remind them of all that Jesus had said (John 14:26). Conservatives believe there are no contradictions present in the Gospels, although there are differences in perspective. For example, it has long been claimed that because in Mark 16:5 there is only one "young man . . . wearing a white robe" recorded in the tomb and in Luke 24:4 there are "two men in dazzling apparel" that there must be a contradiction in the Gospels.

This apparent contradiction can easily be explained by the differenct perspectives of the Gospel writers. It would be quite possible that one woman looked into the tomb from a certain angle and saw only one man while her companion looked from another angle and saw two men. It is also quite possible that one woman, in relating the story, mentioned only one man because only one spoke, but the other woman mentioned both men. It is absolutely fundamental to remember that one thing is not a logical contradiction of another unless the one denies what the other affirms in a direct way.

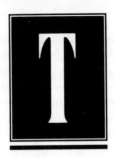

Teleological Argument ■ An argument for God's existence based on the premise that an undeniable relationship exists between the order and regularity of the universe and an intelligent Architect, a Designer of the world. One of the oldest attempts at demonstrating God's existence, the teleological argument is again gaining popularity among certain scientists, many of whom are relatively new Christians. In summary, it states that it is hard to deny that the universe seems intricately designed in ways necessary to support intelligent life. This purposeful order exists either by the intent of a designer or by a chance process, such as evolution. The universe, in other words, is either a plan or an accident. Since it cannot be an accident, it must be planned.

William Paley (1743–1805), archdeacon of Carlisle, framed the most popular form of the argument. He said that if he found a watch in an empty field, he would rightly conclude from its obvious design that there was a watchmaker. Similarly, when we look at the exceedingly more complex design of the world, we cannot help but conclude a great Designer is behind it. Philosophers generally consider this the weakest of all philosophical arguments for God's existence, though it was the favorite argument of Immanuel Kant (1724–1804). Kant, however, did not believe God could be proven rationally. Philosophers maintain that if the teleological argument proves anything, it is only a cause big enough to explain the physical universe, not an eternal, uncaused Cause of all that exists. See: **Cosmological Argument, Ontological Argument, Moral Argument.**

See: Norman L. Geisler, "Teleological and Moral Arguments," in *Philosophy of Religion* (Zondervan, 1974).

Teleology ■ From the Greek *telos*, "end," "purpose," and *logia*, "the study of." The study of evidences of design in nature, of apparent order or purpose in the universe.

Tempt, Temptation ▪ From the Hebrew and Greek words meaning "to test, try, or prove." The NT tells Christians to rejoice when exterior circumstances test their faith, for testing produces endurance (James 1:2–3; 1 Peter 1:6). Satan (1 Peter 5:8–9) and our sinful desires (James 1:14–15) tempt us. God does not tempt (James 1:13); and while He allows temptation, He is always in control, knowing how much temptation is unconquerable: "No temptation has overtaken you but such as is common to man; and God is faithful, who will not allow you to be tempted beyond what you are able; but with the temptation will provide the way of escape also, that you may be able to endure it" (1 Cor. 10:13). Although Christians should pray not to be tempted by Satan (Matt. 6:13), we must rely on God to help deliver us when temptation comes upon us (2 Peter 2:9).

Testament ▪ The Bible is divided into two "testaments," Old and New, though the Hebrew and Greek words translated "testament" are better translated as "covenant." The Old Covenant, given in the Ten Commandments, existed from Moses to Christ, whose death, burial, and resurrection brought about the New Testament or New Covenant. The Ten Commandments, which were written on stone, gave way to the teachings of Jesus in the Sermon on the Mount (Matt. 5—7) and the ministry of Christ, which were written in the Christian's mind or heart (2 Cor. 3:3). See: **Covenant, Sermon on the Mount.**

Thanksgiving ▪ A basic, vital element of successful Christian living. Christians should give thanks to God for all things (Eph. 5:20; Colossians 3:15, 17; 1 Thess. 5:18). Prayer and petition ought always be combined with thanksgiving (Phil. 4:6; Col. 2:7; 4:2; 1 Timothy 2:1). The mark of a Christian should be his thankful attitude toward God in the midst of all circumstances (Eph. 5:4).

Theism ▪ A philosophical term for belief in the existence of God, particularly belief in a personal God who created and rules the world. All Christians are theists, though not all theists are Christians. The Christian philosopher strives to defend the theistic world view from attack while showing the errors of conflicting

world views. See: **Atheism, Deism, God, Henotheism, Monotheism, Panentheism, Pantheism, Polytheism.**

See: S. Harris, *The Philosophical Basis of Theism* (Scribners, 1883); S.C.
Hackett, *The Resurrection of Theism: Prolegomena to Christian Apology*, 2nd
ed. (Baker, 1982); R. Swinburne, *The Coherence of Theism* (Oxford University Press, 1977).

Theocracy ▪ From the Greek *theokratia*, from *theos*, "God," and
kratein, "to rule, to govern." The view that God (or God's will as
understood by those who rule) is the head of an earthly government. OT Jews considered Israel a theocracy (Ex. 19:4–9; Deut.
33:4–5).

Theodicy ▪ Attempts to explain why evil exists in the world
when God is all-loving, all-powerful and Justice itself. Many who
do not believe in God cite the problem of evil as an argument
against God's existence, but the issue is crucial to Christian hope
as well as to evangelism. The Christian world view must adequately explain the purpose and origin of evil.

See: Terry Miethe, "The Problem of Evil," *The New Christian's Guide
to Following Jesus* (Bethany House Publishers, 1984); Norman L. Geisler,
"God and Evil," in *Philosophy of Religion* (Zondervan, 1974); Norman L.
Geisler, *The Roots of Evil* (Zondervan, 1978); C.S. Lewis, *The Problem of
Pain* (Macmillan, 1962).

Theology ▪ From the Greek *theologia*, "the study of God."
While this word does not occur in the Bible, the idea certainly
does. In general usage, theology is the study of religious truth.
As a technical discipline, theology is a systematic analysis of the
doctrine of God, including an analysis of His existence, knowability, person, attributes, names, works, decree and government. Also treated is the doctrine of the Trinity, an essential to
understanding His nature or person.

See: A. Campbell, *The Christian System* (Gospel Advocate Co., 1956);
R.T. France, *The Living God* (InterVarsity Press, 1970); R. Humbert, *A
Compendium of Alexander Campbell's Theology* (The Bethany Press, 1961).

Theology, Biblical ▪ The attempt to understand the teaching of the Bible as a whole. An organization of theological teachings by the portion of the Bible in which they occur, rather than

by topic. See: **Theology, Systematic.**
    See: W.L. Alexander, *A System of Biblical Theology*, 2 vols. (Edinburgh: T. and T. Clark, 1888).

Theology, Natural ■ See: **Natural Theology.**

Theology, Process ■ See: **Process Theology.**

Theology, Systematic ■ The discipline that attempts to present, interpret, arrange and justify in a consistent and meaningful way the teaching of Scripture. Systematic theology presents Scriptural truth in a coherent, understandable fashion to each age, relating Scripture to issues of practical Christian concern. It necessarily reflects the perspective of a particular organized system and that system's view of the Bible's teachings.
    See: M.J. Erickson, *Christian Theology*, 2 vols. (Baker, 1984); C.G. Finney, *Finney's Systematic Theology* (Bethany House Publishers, 1976); C.F.H. Henry, *God, Revelation and Authority*, 6 vols. (Word, 1976–1983); C. Hodge, *Systematic Theology*, 3 vols. (Eerdmans, 1960); A.H. Strong, *Systematic Theology* (Fleming H. Revell, 1954); H.C. Thiessen, *Lectures in Systematic Theology* (Eerdmans, 1979).

Theology, Revealed ■ See: **Revelation.**

Theonomy ■ The state of being ruled or governed by God. Though in this world people are governed by other people, this does not necessarily challenge God's sovereignty, for it was God who established human government (Rom. 13:1–7).

Theophany ■ A theological term for any visible or auditory manifestation of God. Some examples: the burning bush Moses saw (Ex. 3:2–6); the fire and smoke seen on top of Mount Sinai (Ex. 19:18–20); the voice heard after Jesus was baptized (Matt. 3:7); and the light and voice Paul heard on the road to Damascus (Acts 9:1–16). The ultimate theophany occurred in the life of Jesus Christ, who was God incarnate. See: **Incarnation.**

Theosophy ■ The belief that human beings are always evolving toward divinity through a series of reincarnations. This mystical philosophy teaches that human beings can save themselves and that knowledge comes either directly from the world of spirit or from the teachings of those more advanced in perfection. The modern theosophical movement originated in the United States in 1875 and follows Buddhist and Brahmanic theories of pantheistic evolution and reincarnation. See: **Buddhism, Brahmanism, Evolution, Pantheism, Reincarnation.**

Thomism ■ The philosophy and theology based on the thought of Thomas Aquinas (1224/5–1274). Thomism competed with Augustinianism as the dominant school of thought during the Middle Ages. By the sixteenth century, Thomism became prevalent in Catholic thought. Thomas taught that reason must support faith, and that both reason and revelation prove the existence and nature of God. For Thomas, God is the Prime Mover, First Cause, Necessary and Supreme Being, the only self-existent Being. He possesses no limitations, is changeless and unchangeable. Thomas also taught that human beings possess free will given by God.

Thomas built a system remarkable for its harmony and unity of thought. The fundamental principle of Thomism is the real distinction between an act and a potential act, expressed as: "That which is in the state of potency cannot pass from the state except by the intervention of something which is an act." By this principle is established the real distinction between essence and existence in created things, the truth of the principle of causality, etc.

Its advocates failed to adapt it to the findings of science, however, and by the end of the seventeenth century rationalism and empiricism surpassed it in popularity. Rediscovered in the early nineteenth century, Thomism again became a valid option for Catholic theology and philosophy with the publication of *Aeterni Patris* by Pope Leo XIII in 1879, resulting in a movement known as Neo-Thomism. In the last twenty years, Thomism has become popular in certain evangelical circles, in large part because of the work of Norman L. Geisler. See: **Augustinianism, Philosophy, Philosophy of Religion, Via Negativa.**

See also: V.J. Bourke, *Aquinas' Search for Wisdom* (Bruce Publishing Co., 1965), and *The Pocket Aquinas* (Washington Square Press, 1960); E.

Gilson, *The Philosophy of St. Thomas Aquinas* (Dorset Press, 1929); N.L. Geisler, "A New Look at the Relevance of Thomism for Evangelical Apologetics," in *Christian Scholar's Review*, 4 (1975), pp. 189–200; T.L. Miethe and V.J. Bourke, *Thomistic Bibliography, 1940–1978* (Greenwood Press, 1980)—lists 4,097 items written about Aquinas' thought.

Tithe ■ A "tenth" in the Hebrew. In the OT, tithing was commanded on the basis that "the earth is the Lord's and all it contains, the world, and those who dwell in it" (Ps. 24:1). The OT tithe thus acknowledged God's sovereignty and ownership of all the earth. A tithe not given was sometimes considered robbing from God (Mal. 3:8–10).

Given the importance of tithing in Jewish culture, it is interesting that Jesus never commanded His disciples to tithe. Nor do any of the New Testament writers record any commands concerning Christian tithing. What was practiced in the early Church was a freewill sharing of material goods (1 Cor. 16:1–2; Eph. 4:28). Christians were not commanded to give a tenth of what they earned but (1) to give themselves completely as a living sacrifice to God (Rom. 12:1–2), and (2) to give materially as the Lord leads (2 Cor. 8:1–5).

See: Terry L. Miethe, "Christian Stewardship," *The New Christian's Guide to Following Jesus* (Bethany House Publishers, 1984), pp. 97–102.

Tongues, Speaking in ■ Acts 2:4 states that all the Apostles "were filled with the Holy Spirit and began to speak in other tongues as the Spirit enabled them." Scholars debate whether "other tongues" refers to actual human languages foreign to Palestine or to another type of language bestowed by the Holy Spirit. While the context of Acts 2 indicates that the gift of tongues miraculously enabled the Apostles to communicate the gospel to foreigners in their native languages, 1 Corinthians 12–14 seem to indicate that the Spirit gave other, unintelligible languages for purposes other than evangelism, possibly either for prayer or for prophecy.

Four or five passages in the Bible refer directly to the miraculous gift of tongues: Acts 2; Acts 10:44–48; 11:13–18; Acts 19:1–7 and 1 Corinthians 12–14. Speaking in tongues is mentioned in Mark 16:9–20, though there are serious textual problems with this passage. It is not present in the oldest and best Greek manuscripts, and Eusebius (c. 260–c. 340) and Jerome (c. 340–420), the best authorities of the early Church, both rejected Mark 16:9–20 as unauthentic. See: **Glossolalia, Holy Spirit, Pentecostalism.**

See also: Larry Christenson, ed., *Welcome, Holy Spirit: A Study of Charismatic Renewal in the Church* (Augsburg, 1987); Michael Green, *I Believe in the Holy Spirit* (Eerdmans, 1975); Anthony A. Hoekema, *What About Tongue-Speaking?* (Eerdmans, 1966); Terry L. Miethe, "The Holy Spirit and Knowledge," in *A Christian's Guide to Faith and Reason* (Bethany House Publishers, 1987), pp. 78–84.

Torah ■ The Hebrew word *tora*, "law." The word refers to the Pentateuch, the first five books of the OT. See: **Pentateuch.**

Traducianism ■ A theory of the origin of individual souls that attributes production of the soul—as well as the body—to the parents. Tertullian (c. 155–220) described traducianism as a material generation, and for a period, Augustine (354–430) seems to have thought it was a spiritual generation. The two other attempts to explain the origin of an individual soul are (1) preexistence of the soul before conception, and (2) creation of the new soul by God at conception. The Bible does not directly address this topic, but traducianists find support in Genesis 2:7 and 5:3. Roman Catholics believe creation is the true doctrine. See: **Soul.**

Transcendence ■ Above and independent of the material universe. God is transcendent in Being, different from everything in Creation, "wholly other." While human beings and the rest of creation are finite and caused by God, He is infinite in character and is uncaused. While people can experience God's love or faithfulness, for example, God's love in its fullness far exceeds our ability to comprehend it. Because God is transcendent, nothing can transcend Him: No person or thing could be more omnipotent than God, the absolute standard by which all can be judged. He is ultimate value, and therefore worthy of praise and worship. See: **Attributes of God.**

Transfiguration ■ The event in which Jesus was transformed in such a way that ". . . His face shone like the sun, and His garments became as white as light." Moses and Elijah appeared at the transfiguration, talking to Jesus. Matthew 17:1–9; Mark 9:2–10; and Luke 9:28–36 record the event; it is here that the Father said of Jesus, "This is My beloved Son, with whom I am well pleased; hear Him!" Romans 12:2 and 2 Corinthians 3:18 apply the Greek word translated "transfiguration," *metamorphoo*, to Christians, but in these passages the word is usually rendered "transformation."

Transubstantiation ■ The Roman Catholic belief that Jesus' statements at the Lord's supper—"This is My body" and "This is My blood"—should be interpreted literally (Mark 14:22, 24). Those holding to this view assert that the wine and the bread taken during Mass actually become the Lord's physical body and blood. The term is defined by the Council of Trent (1545–1563— the official Catholic response to the Lutheran Reformation) as "the wonderful and singular conversion of the whole substance of the bread into the Body of Christ and of the whole substance of the wine into the Blood, the species of bread and wine alone remaining" (sess. xiii, can. 2).

Most Protestants believe neither Scripture nor history provide evidence for this belief. They see it as a dangerous basis for the view that the Mass is a repetition of Christ's sacrifice and that Christ's death was insufficient to atone for all sin, warping the reason for Jesus' life, death, and resurrection. See: **Communion, Eucharist, Lord's Supper.**

See: B.J. Kidd, *The Later Medieval Doctrine of the Eucharistic Sacrifice* (London: SPCK, 1958).

Trent, Council of ■ A major council—counted as the nineteenth ecumenical council—convened by the Roman Catholic Church from 1545–1563. The official Catholic response to the Lutheran Reformation, it met under Popes Paul III, Julius II and Pius IV. It instituted reforms within the Catholic church and stated its doctrines in clear opposition to those of the Reformers.

Tribulation ■ Scripture employs this word with both general and specific meanings. In the general sense it refers to the suffering that believers face living in a fallen world. These may include imprisonment (Acts 16:22–24), poverty (Phil. 4:11–13), sickness (Rev. 2:22), and persecution (1 Thess. 1:6). God allows believers to experience tribulations; it may be the primary way believers grow in their walk (Rom. 5:3–5).

In the specific sense, the term refers to the time of the second coming and the great tribulation described in Matthew 24, a time of suffering never before seen on earth. There are three views of this period: (1) Pretribulationism: Christ will come for the saints and remove, or rapture, them from the world before the seven years of tribulation. The saints will return at the end of the tribulation. (2) Posttribulationism: The Church will be preserved, yet remain on earth and go through the tribulation. (3) Midtribulationism. As it sounds, the Church will go through the first three and a half years and then be removed before the wrath of God, the great tribulation.

Trinity ■ The word "Trinity" never appears in the Bible, though the doctrine clearly does. The Bible states that there is but one God (Deut. 6:4; Mark 12:29); there are no others (Zech. 14:9). The unity of God is undeniable. Yet this teaching is not inconsistent with the doctrine of the Trinity, which states that there is indeed one essence, yet three persons of the Trinity share this divine essence: God the Father, the First Person of the Trinity; God the Son (Jesus), the Second Person; and God the Holy Spirit, the Third Person of the Trinity. The three Persons of the Trinity are equal, having only a functional subordination, that is, Jesus was subordinate—in function—to the Father while on earth.

The Nicene Creed (325) teaches all three members of the Trinity share in the divine essence, making them God. See: Matthew 3:16; 28:19; John 10:30; 14:16; 1 Corinthians 12:4–6; 2 Corinthians 5:19; Ephesians 1:3–14; Philippians 2:6. Any teaching that denies the Trinity, such as Tritheism (belief in three separate gods) or Unitarianism (belief in God as one person alone), is heretical. See: **Arianism; Nicea, Council of; Nicene Creed; Unitarianism.**

See: E.H. Blickersteth, *The Trinity* (Kregel, 1965); H.F. Stevenson, *Titles of the Triune God* (London: Marshall, Morgan and Scott, 1965).

Tritheism ■ The belief that Christianity worships not one God but three. Tritheism denies the unity in nature and substance of the three Persons of the Trinity. This view contradicts scriptural teaching (Deut. 6:4; John 10:30; 1 Corinthians 8:4; Ephesians 4:6; and James 2:19). See: **Trinity.**

Truth ■ Many in every age ask, "What is Truth?" Augustine (A.D. 354–430) was the first Christian theologian to systematically examine the importance of truth for the Christian. He argued that the human mind can know truth, especially truth about God, making theology and ethics possible. The Christian view of truth is therefore far from skepticism, which contends that certainty of truth is impossible. Christians assert that knowledge of God is possible by observing the world (Ps. 19:1; Rom. 1:20), though saving knowledge of Christ is possible only through the Gospel (Rom. 5:18).

If we acknowledge that truth is knowable, the value of apologetics—rational defense of the Christian religion—becomes obvious. Scripture was given in a historical context, and historical events can be authenticated, including Christ's resurrection. The heart of Christianity is not a fable but a historically verifiable fact (1 Cor. 15:12–34). See: **Apologetics, Resurrection of Jesus.**

TULIP ■ A mnemonic of the traditional five points of Calvinism: *T*otal depravity, *U*nconditional election, *L*imited atonement, *I*rresistible grace, and *P*erseverance of the saints. These five points were adopted by the Synod of Dort in 1618. See: **Calvinism; Calvinism, Five Points of; Dort, Synod of.**

Type, Typology ■ A scheme of thought that sees events and persons of the past as "types" or symbols of subsequently greater events and persons. Typology plays a large role in the Christian interpretation of the OT. For example, 1 Peter 3:21 says that the Flood of Noah symbolizes the practice of water baptism of the Church. In 1 Corinthians 10:11, Paul compares the exodus of the Jews and their wandering in the wilderness to the life of Christians in the Church. Studying the OT people and events which Scripture labels "types" of NT people and events often helps clarify understanding of a passage.

See: Patrick Fairbairn, *The Typology of Scripture*, 5th ed. (Zondervan, 1963).

Ubiquity ■ An attribute of God; omnipresence. Since God is not material, but purely spiritual, He is not limited by time and space. He is everywhere at every moment. This is not to be confused with Pantheism, which asserts that God *is* the world, for Christianity teaches that God is beyond and separate from the world. Yet He actively participates in the material world, which He himself created (Acts 17:24–25). Lutheran theology also uses the term to explain how Christ's body can be present in the Lord's Supper while He is in heaven. See: **Omnipresence, Pantheism.**

Unction, Extreme ■ From the Latin *unctus*, the anointing of the sick with oil; a sacrament of the Catholic and Orthodox churches. Unction was practiced by some during NT times (Mark 6:13), and in James 5:14–15 Roman Catholics see warrant for their belief that extreme unction is a sacrament of grace bestowing strength and spiritual and physical healing. During the Reformation, however, most churches rejected unction as a sacrament, because nowhere does Scripture speak of it being instituted by Christ. See: **Anoint, Anointing; Sacrament, The Seven.**

Unitarianism ■ The heretical belief that God exists in one person rather than in the Trinity. Modern Unitarianism finds its roots in the Italian Faustus Socinus (1539–1604), in the Racovian Catechism of 1605, and in Michael Servetus (1509–1553), a Spanish theologian burned at the stake in Geneva in 1553 for his unitarian teaching.

Unitarians came to America in the 1700s from England. Early Unitarianism did not believe Jesus was God but a perfect human being and perfect model to follow in life. Ralph Waldo Emerson (1803–1882) and Theodore Parker (1810–1860), prominent Unitarian leaders, rejected all supernatural aspects of Christianity. The American Unitarian Association (1825) merged in 1961 with the Universalist Church of America and became the Unitarian-Universalist Association. Modern Unitarians emphasize individual freedom of belief, the free use of reason in religion, a united world community and liberal social action. See: **Trinity.**

United Church of Christ ■ A denomination that resulted from a merger of the Congregational Christian Church and the Evangelical and Reformed Church in 1957. Though both were originally Calvinistic in theology, the groups shared little else. The Congregationalists traced their beginnings to the Mayflower and the English Puritans and insisted on local church autonomy. The Evangelical and Reformed, grandchildren of eighteenth and nineteenth century German immigrants to Pennsylvania and the Midwest, had adopted Calvin's presbyterian church government.

The United Church of Christ (UCC) is composed of local churches, Associations, Conferences, and a General Synod. A local church can still pick its own methods of organization, worship and education; choose its minister; adopt its constitution and confession of faith and control its own funds. UCC churches originally affiliated with the Congregational Christian tradition choose deacons to lead a local congregation. Churches originally from the Evangelical and Reformed elect both deacons and elders. Both men and women can be ordained to the ministry, and the UCC, in fact, has one of the highest percentages of women ministers of any denomination. The UCC is theologically liberal and places a strong emphasis on social action. See: **Liberal Protestantism.**

See: H. Douglas, *The United Church of Christ* (Thomas Nelson, 1962); M.L. Starkey, *The Congregational Way* (Doubleday, 1966).

Universalism ■ The belief that ultimately all will be saved. Universalists argue that an all-loving, all-powerful God would not allow any to go to hell. Universalism flatly contradicts Scripture at several points. First, it denies biblical teaching concerning hell as the eternal abode of those who refuse to accept Christ as

Savior (Matt. 25:41–46). Second, although God indeed wills for all to be saved, the Bible recognizes that some will accept salvation and some will not. Third, universalism removes all moral responsibility. If everyone goes to heaven, sin has no eternal consequence. Finally, witnessing becomes irrelevant. Why would Christ have commanded Christians to share the Gospel when everyone is already destined for heaven?

See: E. Cassara, *Universalism in America* (Beacon Press, 1971).

Unleavened Bread ■ A type of bread that does not rise because it is baked without yeast; also an annual Jewish feast. Jews celebrated the Feast of Unleavened Bread each spring at the first sign of the sprouting of the plants, abstaining for a week from using leaven in their bread. Unleavened bread, a sign of purity (Ex. 12:15–17), is also eaten in the Passover meal.

See: T.H. Gaster, *Festivals of the Jewish Year* (Sloane Publishers, 1952).

Utilitarianism ■ A theory of ethics that evaluates acts by their consequences. It is based on the "Principle of Utility"—that one should act according to what will bring about the greatest good for the greatest number of people. Its classical form was developed by Jeremy Bentham (1748–1832) and John Stuart Mill (1806–1873). In America utilitarianism is chiefly associated with the pragmatic ethics of William James (1842–1910) and John Dewey (1859–1952).

See: D. Baumgardt, *Bentham and the Ethics of Today* (Princeton University Press, 1952); J. Bentham, *The Works of Jeremy Bentham*, ed. J. Bowring, 11 vols. (Edinburgh, 1838–1843); J. Dewey, *Human Nature and Conduct* (Henry Holt and Company, 1922); W. James, *Pragmatism: A New Name for Some Old Ways of Thinking* (1907); J.S. Mill, *Utilitarianism* (Bobbs-Merrill, 1957).

Vanity ■ From the Greek meaning "emptiness" or "something void of results." Futility or worthlessness. The Bible teaches that unbelievers live in vanity. Separated from God, they cannot accomplish anything lasting (Eph. 4:17–19). False teachers speak vain words to appeal to lustful human desires (2 Peter 2:18). Christians are commanded not to live or talk in a vain way, because the emptiness of life has been filled with purpose: to bring glory to God (1 Cor. 10:31). Gathering treasure on earth is vanity; Christians are to store up treasure in heaven (Matt. 6:19–21).

Vatican, The ■ A sovereign state within the boundaries of Rome. Also known as Vatican City, it has been recognized since 1929. It includes the Church of St. Peter (also known as St. Peter's Basilica, the church is built on a site that has been occupied by a church since A.D. 320 to 350), the Sistine Chapel, the Pauline Chapel, the pope's palace, five museums of antiquities, libraries, the archives of the Roman Church and two art galleries. This area is regarded as the burial place of the Apostles Peter and Paul.

See: F. Roncalli, *Vatican City* (Gestione Vendita Pubblicazioni Musei Vaticani, 1981).

Vatican, Councils ■ There have been two Vatican Councils held by the Roman Catholic Church. The First Vatican Council gathered at St. Peter's Basilica in 1869–1870. Attended by more than 800 Roman Catholic priests from around the world, it formulated the doctrine of the supremacy and infallibility of the pope. Convened by Pope Pius IX, the Council resumed a century later as the Second Vatican Council.

The Second Vatican Council was called by Pope John XXIII and gathered in four separate sessions from late 1962 to late 1965. It was attended by more than 2,500 priests as well as by observers invited from all major Christian churches. After the death of Pope John XXIII, the council continued under Pope Paul VI. It addressed issues such as the Catholic attitude toward non-Catholic and non-Christian churches, revision of canon law, a reemphasis upon divine revelation, the education of priests, the missionary role of the Catholic church, and Mary as the Blessed Mediatrix and Mother of the church.

See: G.C. Berkouwer, *The Second Vatican Council and the New Catholicism* (Eerdmans, 1965).

Veneration of the Saints ■ See: Saints, Veneration of the.

Verbal Inspiration ■ The doctrine of revelation and inspiration which teaches that the Holy Spirit guided the writers of Scripture in a way that their choice of words conformed to God's intention. Though God inspired each word and the relationships between words, Scripture did not result from dictation. The personality of each writer is still obvious in the writing of Scripture. See: **Fundamentalism; Inerrancy; Infallibility; Inspiration; Inspiration, Dictation Theory.**

See: Benjamin Breckenridge Warfield, *The Inspiration and Authority of the Bible* (Presbyterian and Reformed, 1958); Carl F.H. Henry, *Revelation and the Bible* (Baker Book House, 1958); James Orr, *Revelation and Inspiration* (Eerdmans, 1952).

Via Negativa ■ In Latin, *via negationis*, "the negative way." The method of reasoning found in Thomas Aquinas' theology which shows what God is by first examining what God is not. What God is not is made clear from negative human characteristics, and by ascribing the opposite to God—in perfection—one can see what God must be. For example, human beings are finite, limited or contingent in every way they exist. God, then, must be infinite, unlimited or absolute in every way that He exists: He must be incorporeal, immutable, invisible and so on. See: **Thomism.**

Vicarious Atonement ■ The Christian doctrine that Christ died in our place to pay the penalty for our sins. See: **Atonement, Propitiation, Sin.**

Virgin Birth of Jesus ■ Two NT Scriptures refer to the virgin birth of Jesus (Matt. 1:18, 20–25; Luke 1:26–38), the teaching that Christ was miraculously conceived through the Holy Spirit. Paul also uses language that supports the uniqueness of Christ's birth; in his writings he uses the Greek word meaning "come to be" for Jesus' birth, instead of the Greek word meaning "to be born or begotten." Thus in Galatians 4:4, 23, Paul says Jesus "came to be" through woman, while Isaac and Ishmael were born to woman in the natural way.

The belief that Jesus was born of a virgin is an essential teaching of the faith as old as Christianity itself. The early Church fathers believed Jesus was born of a virgin: Ignatius (Smyr. 1:1), *The Apology of Aristides*, and Justin in *Dialogue with Trypho* (es. 43). It is impossible to argue that the virgin birth is a myth manufactured later in Church history.

See: J. Orr, *The Virgin Birth of Christ* (Scribners, 1927); J.G. Machen, *Virgin Birth of Christ* (Baker, 1967).

Virgin Conception ■ A better term for the Virgin Birth. Christ's conception, not his birth, was unique, because in it the power of the Holy Spirit was responsible, not human seed. Some use the term "virgin conception" to draw a distinction between the fact of Mary's virginity at the point of Jesus' conception and the Roman Catholic doctrine of Mary's perpetual virginity. That doctrine states that at birth Jesus simply passed through the wall of Mary's uterus rather than through the birth canal, so that Mary's hymen was unruptured and Mary remained a virgin her entire life.

Virtue ■ The Greek word *areta*, "virtue," was originally used in the Jewish court of law. It referred to someone whose behavior was unreproachable. One is considered virtuous if he is blameless, that is, morally pure. All believers ought to be virtuous. But it is Christ's sacrifice for our sins that makes the Christian virtuous before God (Col. 1:22). Christ is the archetype of virtue, with His sinless life (Heb. 7:26). He is the Lamb without blemish (1 Peter 1:19). Christ set the example for which all Christians must strive.

Virtues, Cardinal ▪ The highest virtues on which all others depend. Greek philosophy listed four basic or cardinal virtues: Wisdom (prudence), courage (fortitude), justice (righteousness), and moderation (temperance). Christian teaching adds theological virtues—faith, hope, and love, as in 1 Corinthians 13:13— and together these form the seven cardinal virtues. The NT gives several lists of virtuous qualities: 1 Corinthians 13; Galatians 5:22–23; Philippians 4:8; Colossians 3:12–16. See also: 1 Thessalonians 1:3; Galatians 5:5–6; Colossians 1:4–5; 2 Peter 1:3–5; Ephesians 2:8–10. See: **Cardinal Virtues, the Seven.**

Vocation ▪ From the Latin word meaning "I call." God's universal call to mankind to accept salvation. Although many today speak of being "called" by God into a specific profession or occupation, this is not implied by the NT use of the word. His "call" invites all to salvation and to growth toward the example of moral and spiritual purity shown in Christ's sinless life (1 Peter 1:16; 1 Cor. 3:18; 1 John 2:2–3). See: **Call, Calling; Ministry; Priesthood of All Believers; Will of God.**

See: Terry L. Miethe, "Ministry and the Christian" and "God and the Day's Work," in *The New Christian's Guide to Following Jesus* (Bethany House Publishers, 1981), pp. 103–110, 117–121; Paul E. Little, *Affirming the Will of God* (InterVarsity Press, 1971); Garry Friesen, *Decision Making and the Will of God* (Multnomah Press, 1980).

Vulgate, Latin ▪ The translation of the Bible by Jerome (342–430) from Greek and Hebrew originals into the common Latin of the day. Jerome worked on this translation in Bethlehem from 384–406, almost 25 years. All Roman Catholic Bibles are translated from the Latin Vulgate, the official text of that church. The Gutenberg Bible of 1456, the first book ever printed on a printing press, was a printing of the Vulgate.

See: *The Cambridge History of the Bible*, 3 vols. (Cambridge University Press, 1963–1970).

Wesleyanism ▪ John Wesley (1703–1791), founder of the Methodist Church, lived in England at a time when deism—the belief that God created the universe and then left it alone—prevailed. The emptiness of deism led him and a group of friends at the University of Oxford to seriously study Scripture. Their strict, organized study earned them the name "Methodists." Wesley stressed the importance of a personal relationship with God, making religious experience a high goal. He saw justification as the entry point to a life of sanctification. See: **Deism, Methodists.**

See: R.W. Burtner and R.E. Chiles, *A Compend of Wesley's Theology* (Abingdon Press, 1954); W.R. Cannon, *The Theology of John Wesley* (Abingdon, 1946); H.A. Snyder, *The Radical Wesley and Patterns for Church Renewal* (InterVarsity Press, 1980); J. Wesley, *The Works of John Wesley*, 3rd ed., 14 vols. (Baker, 1978); W. Williams, *John Wesley's Theology Today* (Abingdon Press, 1960).

Will of God ▪ God's sovereign plan for the universe, and, individually, for each Christian. Jesus died for our sins because it was the will of God (Gal. 1:4). Jesus yielded to the Father's will at Gethsemane as He said, "Abba, Father, everything is possible for you. Take this cup from Me. Yet not what I will, but what you will" (Mark 14:36, NIV). Christians are sons of God because of His perfect saving will (Eph. 1:5).

The Christian's goal should be continually to learn more of God's will and to act on that knowledge. In Romans 2:17–24, Paul discusses the importance of attempting to live out God's will by bringing our will into line with His. Paul says the Jews are hypocrites: They teach God's will to others, they do not live it themselves. Christians must be free from this, careful to put into practice what they study and learn about God's will from

Scripture: "But prove yourselves doers of the word, and not merely hearers who delude themselves" (James 1:22).

Christians often expect God to supply them with a blueprint detailing every aspect of their lives. Not so! Yet there are two points of God's will for everyone: (1) His general will is that a person be saved, that is, live in relationship to Him, and (2) His specific will is that each person offer his talents and abilities to God, freely choosing the way to serve Him that will be most fruitful, given the needs of the time and the individual's abilities.
See: **Abba; Call, Calling; Ministry; Vocation.**

See: T.L. Miethe, "Ministry and the Christian" and "God and the Day's Work," in *The New Christian's Guide to Following Jesus* (Bethany House Publishers, 1981), pp. 103–110, 117–122; P.E. Little, *Affirming the Will of God* (InterVarsity Press, 1971); G. Friesen, *Decision Making and the Will of God* (Multnomah Press, 1980); L.D. Weatherhead, *The Will of God* (Abingdon, 1944).

Wisdom ■ Scripture says: "How much better it is to get wisdom than gold! And to get understanding is to be chosen above silver" (Prov. 16:16; 2:6; 4:7). Wisdom is used in several contexts in Scripture. In Jewish culture, one was considered wise if he knew Scripture, and in the Gospels "wisdom" is a synonym of knowledge of the Law. Thus when people heard Jesus' teaching in the synagogue, they considered Him wise because of His vast knowledge and understanding of the Law (Matt. 13:54; Mark 6:2). Wisdom can also be worldly, as 1 Corinthians 1—3 points out. The wisdom of the world rejects the Gospel (1 Cor. 1:18–25). It is empty because it does not involve Christ, denying any need for Him (1 Cor. 1:18). Christ is the key to wisdom (Col. 2:3), though this is not to say that wisdom does not involve natural knowledge. Wisdom is a gift from God (Eph. 1:8, 17), and must translate into practical acts of goodness (James 3:13–15).

Witness, Witnessing ■ In the NT, witness refers to personal testimony regarding the truth of something. Jesus was a witness to the Father (John 5:36; 8:14, 26), and the Apostles were witnesses to Christ (John 21:24–25; Acts 1:8; 2:32). Evidence is vital to true witness. Jesus performed miracles to authenticate His witness of God (John 5:31–40). Gifts of the Spirit authenticated the Apostles' witness (Acts 2:43), as did the fact that they were eyewitnesses of Jesus' resurrection, a truth that could be examined by those hearing their testimony (1 Cor. 15:1–11).

Today, witnessing is important for all believers. The witness of Christians is authenticated by Scripture, the historical resurrection of Jesus, and the character of Jesus lived out in their lives. Witnessing should involve a verbal element—telling people about Jesus—but it must also involve the living the life of Christ before nonbelievers. See: **Evangelism, Priesthood of All Believers, Ministry, Soul Winning.**

See: T.L. Miethe, "Sharing Your Faith," in *The New Christian's Guide to Following Jesus* (Bethany House Publishers, 1984), pp. 111–116, and "Building the Faith in Our World," "Free to Win Souls to Christ," and "Free to Love the Unlovely," in *The Christian's Guide to Faith and Reason* (Bethany House Publishers, 1987), pp. 54–59, 60–69, 70–77; J.C. Aldrich, *Life-Style Evangelism: Crossing Traditional Boundaries to Reach the Unbelieving World* (Multnomah Press, 1981).

Word of God ▪ A phrase used to refer to the Bible as direct revelation from God to mankind. The Bible—OT and NT—is the Word of God. Jesus and the NT refer to the OT as the Word of God (John 10:35). The term is also used to refer to Christ's deity. Jesus is the living Word of God (John 1:1–11). See: **Bible, Inerrancy and Infallibility of the; Logos; Revelation.**

Works ▪ The relationship between faith and works is a crucial issue for the Christian. Salvation comes about through faith (Rom. 4:1–25; Gal. 3:6–14). Good works, however, are an important by-product of salvation (Matt. 7:15–23; 1 Tim. 5:10, 25), and James goes so far as to say that faith without works is dead (James 2:17). Salvation is not based upon works—it is a free gift from God—yet with the gift of salvation come certain responsibilities that must be taken seriously. Good works should result from the changed purpose for living that salvation brings (1 Cor. 3). See: **Faith.**

World View ▪ From the German *Weltanschauung*. A perspective of reality itself. A world view is a view of life, a comprehensive conception or apprehension of the world from a specific standpoint. A world view can be a formal philosophy that in a consistent or non-contradictory manner explains all the facts of experience. In a less structured way, however, every culture and

every individual has a world view, a perspective that both inter-
prets and guides life. In this sense a world view consciously or
unconsciously answers four questions, as Walsh and Middleton
note: Who am I? (What is the nature of human beings?); Where
am I? (What is the nature of the world?); What is wrong? (What
is the nature of evil?); What is the solution? (What is the nature
of good and salvation?).

See: Brian J. Walsh and J. Richard Middleton, *The Transforming Vision:
Shaping a Christian World View* (InterVarsity, 1984).

Worship ■ Several Greek words used in the NT are translated
"worship." They involve acknowledgement, praise, thanksgiving and service. Only God is worthy of worship (Matt. 4:10). He
is to be worshiped in spirit and truth, for He is Spirit and Truth
(John 4:23–24). The essence of worship consists not of practices
and rituals, but of giving one's life in attitude and action as a
"living sacrifice" (Rom. 12:1–2). Worship is not just being in
church on Sunday, but doing all things to God's glory (1 Cor.
10:31).

See: P. Brunner, *Worship in the Name of Jesus* (Concordia Publishing
House, 1968); T.L. Miethe, "The Meaning of Worship," "The Nature of
Worship," "The Purpose of Worship," and "The Attitude of Worship,"
in *The New Christian's Guide to Following Jesus* (Bethany House Publishers, 1984), pp. 67–84.

Yahweh ▪ The name of God revealed to Moses at the burning bush (Ex. 3:13–15). The Jews considered the name so holy that they never pronounced it, to prevent taking God's name in vain. After centuries no one knew how the name was actually pronounced. Much later, when vowel points were added to the Hebrew language, it came to be pronounced "Jehovah." But this determination was reached by taking the original Hebrew word "YHWH" and adding the vowel points from another word, the Hebrew for "Lord" (*adonai*). "Jehovah" is thus a mispronunciation of the word. Scholars believe the original pronunciation was probably "Yahweh." See: **God.**

Young Men's Christian Association ▪ An organization founded by George Williams in London in 1844 with the mission of winning young men to saving faith in Christ. Today the Y.M.C.A. is mostly a social and educational organization.

Young Women's Christian Association ▪ Originally founded in England in 1855 by Emma Roberts and Lady Kinnaird as two separate groups, the Y.W.C.A. was formed when these two groups came together in 1877. Today, the Y.W.C.A. has followed the Y.M.C.A. in becoming a social and educational organization.

Zealot ■ In modern usage, a zealous or fanatical person. In biblical times, a member of the party of the Zealots, an anti-Roman group that believed Israel should return to a theocratic form of government. Zealots followed the Law strictly, much like the Pharisees. Simon the Zealot was one of the twelve disciples of Christ (Luke 6:15; Acts 1:13), but since many of Christ's teachings—loving one's enemies, paying taxes to Rome—rejected those of the Zealots, it is doubtful Simon was an active member of the party or a member at all. He may have been dubbed "zealot" because of his zealous temperament. Paul called himself a religious zealot (Acts 22:3; Gal. 1:14). See: **Theocracy.**

Zionism ■ A movement dedicated to restoring the Jewish people to the land of Israel. It originated in A.D. 135, and after hundreds of years and the Nazi Holocaust, it found fulfillment on May 14, 1948, when British rule ended and the United Nations formally recognized the State of Israel. Today the "Christian Zionism" movement, motivated by a premillennial eschatology, actively supports the State of Israel. See: **Premillennialism.**

Zoroastrianism ■ A religion of Persia (modern Iran) based on the teaching of the prophet Zoroaster (Zarathustra), a polytheist. The religion, which dates from about the sixth century B.C., teaches that the world is locked in a struggle between the wise Lord (Ahura Mazda), often translated "lord of light," and the spirit of evil (Angra Mainyu). People should fight on the side of the wise Lord to bring about "good thoughts, good works, good deeds." Zoroastrianism has a messiah figure, Saoshyant, who will bring ultimate victory after a six-thousand year struggle. Three thousand years had already passed before the time of Zoroaster. See: **Dualism, Polytheism.**
See: G.W. Carter, *Zoroastrianism and Judaism* (AMS Press, 1970).